BOASTING IN THE LORD

BOASTING IN THE LORD

The Phenomenon of Prayer in Saint Paul

by

David M. Stanley, S.J.

PAULIST PRESS
New York / Paramus / Toronto

IMPRIMI POTEST
Terence G. Walsh, S.J.
Provincial, Province of Upper Canada

NIHIL OBSTAT
Fidelis Buck, S.J.
Censor Deputatus

IMPRIMATUR
✠ Philip F. Pocock
Archbishop of Toronto

April 10, 1973

The Nihil Obstat and Imprimatur are official declarations that a book or pamphlet is free of doctrinal or moral error. No implication is contained therein that those who have granted the Nihil Obstat and Imprimatur agree with the contents, opinions or statements expressed.

Library of Congress
Catalog Card Number: 73-84361

ISBN 0-8091-1793-2

Published by Paulist Press
Editorial Office: 1865 Broadway, N.Y., N.Y. 10023
Business Office: Paramus, N.J. 07652

Printed and bound in the
United States of America

Contents

INTRODUCTION 1

  Aim and Methodology 2
  The Terminology of Prayer in Paul . . . 5
  The Pauline Letters 9

1. THE INITIAL CONFRONTATION
   WITH THE RISEN LORD 11

  Some Contemporary Views of Paul's Conversion . . 12
  The Influence on Paul's Personal Life . . . 15
  The Last of the Post-Resurrection Appearances . . 21
  The Experience of the Twelve 25
  Paul's Conversion as a New Creation . . . 31
  The Revelation of God's Son 33
  An Interpretation by One of Paul's Contemporaries . 40

2. EXPERIENCES RELATED TO PAUL'S VIEW OF PRAYER . 43

  "Visions and Revelations by the Lord" . . . 44
  A Rare Glimpse of Paul's Personal Prayer . . 52
  Incident at Antioch 60
  "Tribulation in Asia" 69

3. PRAYERS IN THE PAULINE LETTERS . . . 73

  Doxologies 74
  Spontaneous Acts of Thanksgiving . . . 78
  Prayer as Wish 80
  Introductory and Final Wishes 87
  Prayer as Confession 93

4. PAUL'S OBSERVATIONS CONCERNING PRAYER . . . 99

Joy, Prayer, Thanksgiving 100
"In the Name of Our Lord Jesus Christ" 107
Prayer as Struggle: A Misunderstanding 110
Prayer and the "Building Up" of the Church . . . 113
Prayer as Awareness of Adoptive Sonship . . . 115
The Pauline Conception of Discernment . . . 130

5. THE SHAPE OF PAUL'S PRAYER 134

Paul's Creativity in the Thanksgiving 135
The Thanksgiving, Reflection of Paul's Prayer . . 136
Epistolary Function of the Thanksgiving 138
Thanksgiving in Philippians 140
Determining the Length of Other Thanksgivings . . 144
A Synopsis of the Thanksgiving in 1 Thessalonians . 148
Thanksgiving in Colossians 153

6. PAULINE PRAYER AND PAULINE THEOLOGY . . 165

The Dynamics and Structure of Pauline Theology . 166
Prayer Transposed into Theological Discourse . . 174
Theology of Apostleship and Apostolic Prayer . . 175
Prolegomenon to Paul's Self-Oblation to Divine Love 177
The Phenomenon of Pauline Prayer 179

INDEX OF AUTHORS 184

INDEX OF PAULINE PASSAGES EXPLAINED . . . 186

TOPICAL INDEX 188

FOR SISTER HENRIETTA

In Acknowledgment and Part-Payment
of an Unpayable Debt

Introduction

Prayer in Saint Paul is a topic which, surprisingly enough, has not in recent years received the attention its significance in his own life would appear to warrant from those professionally engaged in Pauline studies. The monumental and in many senses, classical work of Père Fernand Prat, S.J. on the theology of Saint Paul contains very few pages devoted to this subject.[1] The much more recent study by Msgr. Lucien Cerfaux of the Pauline view of Christian existence, the last of the late Louvain scholar's estimable trilogy on Paul's thought, says nothing in any organized manner about the place of prayer in Paul's life, nor in that of the Christian.[2] A most comprehensive set of texts dealing with prayer in the Pauline letters has been assembled by Father John R. Sheets, S.J. in a study of the phenomenon of prayer in the New Testament, where however the texts are largely left to speak for themselves.[3]

On the mysticism of Saint Paul, the beautiful monograph by Père Joseph Huby, S.J., now some twenty-five years old, remains a valuable source of insight into Paul's prayer-life, although progress in Pauline studies since the book appeared have made a new approach to the subject imperative.[4] This has been competently done in a brief but most perceptive work by Sister Sylvia Mary, C.S.M.V.[5] The astute critical investi-

[1] F. Prat, *La Théologie de Saint Paul* (Paris, 1920, 1922) in two volumes; see vol. II, pp. 142-147, 413 of the sixth French edition. The last cited page contains an apology for the brevity with which the topic is treated. "If we do not insist further, it is because there is nothing very special about it; for the practice of frequent prayer was a habit contracted by Saint Paul within Pharisaism."

[2] L. Cerfaux, *Le Chrétien dans la théologie paulinienne* (Paris, 1962).

[3] John R. Sheets, S.J., *The Spirit Speaks in Us: Personal Prayer in the New Testament* (Wilkes-Barre, 1968).

[4] Joseph Huby, S.J., *Mystiques paulinienne et johannique* (Paris, 1946).

[5] Sister Sylvia Mary, C.S.M.V., *Pauline and Johannine Mysticism* (London, 1964).

1

gation of the mystical element in Paul's prayer by Father Alfred Wikenhauser, now almost twenty years old, remains a solid source of information on this intriguing and difficult topic.[6]

More recently two compendious books on biblical prayer devote a certain amount of attention to that of Saint Paul, one in French by Père A. Hamman, O.F.M.,[7] the other in Spanish by Father Ángel González.[8]

But for books exclusively consecrated to prayer in Paul— apart from some not especially helpful, "devotional" treatments —one must go back almost forty years or more.[9] Meanwhile, of course, there have been a number of informative articles, of which two merit special mention: that by C. W. F. Smith, and especially that of Father Jerome D. Quinn, notable for its sensitivity and insight, as well as its scholarly competence.[10]

I

AIM AND METHODOLOGY

The modest purpose of the present project is to investigate the nature of prayer in the life of Saint Paul and to ascertain, through an examination of what his letters have to say on the

---

[6] Alfred Wikenhauser, *Pauline Mysticism: Christ in the Mystical Teaching of St. Paul* (New York, 1960).

[7] A. Hamman, O.F.M., *La Prière I: Le Nouveau Testament* (Paris: Tournai: New York: Rome, 1959). See Chapter III, "Saint Paul et la prière," pp. 245-334.

[8] Ángel González, *La Oración en la Biblia*, (Madrid, 1968). See also his article, "Prière," in the *Supplément, Dictionnaire de la Bible,* vol. VII (1969), cols. 556-606.

[9] Günther Harder, *Paulus und das Gebet* (Gütersloh, 1936); Ernst Orphal, *Das Paulusgebet* (Gotha, 1933); J. Eschlimann, *La prière dans S. Paul* (Lyon, 1924); Alfred Juncker, *Das Gebet bei Paulus* (Berlin, 1905).

[10] C. W. F. Smith, "Prayer", *Interpreter's Bible Dictionary,* vol. III, pp. 857-867. Jerome D. Quinn, "Apostolic Ministry and Apostolic Prayer," *Catholic Biblical Quarterly* 33 (1971), 479-491. Other articles that may be helpful: Ludwig Koch, "Das Gebet des Apostels Paulus," *Stimmen der Zeit* 111 (1926), 321-336; Peter Ketter, "Vom Gebetsleben des Apostels Paulus", *Theologisch-praktische Quartalschrift* 91 (1938), 23-40. Two in *Recueil Lucien Cerfaux,* II (Gembloux, 1954), "L'Antinomie paulinienne de la vie apostolique", pp. 455-467, and "L'Apôtre en présence de Dieu", pp. 469-481.

theme, the place Paul believed prayer must hold in the life of the Christian. The result, it is hoped, will be an informative and readable discussion of a fascinating, if at times baffling subject for anyone who is interested in learning how Paul prayed himself, and how he instructed others in this important Christian art.

It may not be inappropriate to recall from the outset the necessity of guarding against the assumption that we already know what Paul meant by the word prayer before we begin, for that would be to compromise the success of the inquiry by arguing in a circle. It is then of no little consequence to convince ourselves from the start that the answer to the question we are raising is veritably an unknown. And this, despite the fact that Paul recommends prayer and speaks about prayer frequently in his letters, that he has punctuated them with passages commonly (if not altogether accurately) regarded as prayers, that he leaves his reader in no doubt concerning his own convictions about the primacy of prayer in Christian existence.

It might be objected that to attempt to rid oneself of all presuppositions, where the topic of Paul's prayer is concerned, is unrealistic. Every Christian knows from experience what prayer is, or ought to be. Friedrich Heiler was undoubtedly right when he observed that "to be a Christian means to be one who prays".[11] To be authentically Christian, prayer must display a certain recognizable kinship with the prayer of others who share the same faith—notably those men and women of prayer, the saints, among whom Paul is to be ranked preeminently. Ultimately, of course, the prayer of Paul or of John must contain genuine echoes of the prayer of Jesus, who taught us all to pray, "Our Father . . .".

While admitting the truth of the contention to some degree, we must urge, again with Heiler, that prayer is "the most spontaneous and the most personal expression of religion".[12] The prayer of Francis of Assisi is distinguishable, and to be distinguished, from that of Francis de Sales. The spirituality of

[11] Friedrich Heiler, *Prayer: History and Psychology,* translated and edited by Samuel McComb (New York, 1958), p. 119.
[12] *Ibid.,* p. 119.

Teresa of Avila is not to be confused with that of Gertrude or Catherine of Siena. The response to the gospel by an Ignatius Loyola is not that of a Benedict, a Dominic, or a John of the Cross. One has only to recall the forcefulness and color of Paul's "supernatural personality", that has left an indelible stamp of individuality on his writings, to suspect that prayer for such a one must have connoted a distinctive, original, highly personal approach to God. To discover something of the meaning he attached to the word prayer, we must be ready to put ourselves to school to Paul by a painstaking scrutiny of anything he has left in writing that may provide a clue to its significance for him. This means that in the course of our inquiry we must be constantly willing to revise our notions, as new data present themselves to challenge our presuppositions. Two reasons among others indicate the necessity of such a procedure.

The first and most basic lies in the nature of prayer itself. It is necessarily enveloped, in the last analysis, by the impenetrable mystery of God's commerce with man through Jesus Christ. We are in quest of a reality that is never capable of being adequately articulated in any form of human speech. That Paul was vividly conscious of the mysterious silence in which Christian prayer remains wrapped is (as will become evident later) the only adequate explanation for what, I suggest, is the most baffling and tantalizing facet of his many-sided personality—his extraordinary reticence in speaking about his own prayer.

This is in fact the second reason for proceeding as we have suggested. Paul will be found never to relax his guard in the matter of carefully concealing his own prayer life. He urges the need of prayer tirelessly; he asks for the prayers of others continually; he appears indeed always to be talking about prayer, and about his own prayer. Yet the difficulty lies precisely in his talking *about* his prayer: he tells us only what he wishes, is never (or at any rate, almost never) betrayed into saying more than he intends concerning this closely guarded secret.

Actually, part of the problem arises from the very nature of Paul's literary remains: they are letters. He has not left any collection of prayers, such as is exemplified in the Old Testament by the Psalter. He wrote real letters to real people with real questions and difficulties, people with whom he was moreover personally acquainted for the most part. Because they had lived with him, they probably knew more about Paul's notion of prayer, about his personal practice of prayer than he could ever have communicated to them by letter. Besides, no one was so keenly aware as Paul that when he wrote, he was addressing himself to his communities, not to God. Thus even when, as he occasionally does, Paul bursts out spontaneously into what we recognize as truly prayer, he knows that he is communicating this to his fellow human beings as well as to God. The letter as a form of self-expression is a far cry from the diary.

How then do we propose to proceed in our inquiry into the nature of Paul's prayer and the esteem in which he held it for the living of the Christian life? We shall begin with those experiences alluded to in his letters, which may be thought to have influenced his own prayer-life. And here attention will be directed principally to the construction he himself puts upon these events: his conversion near Damascus in the first place, and thereafter, other experiences that may be considered relevant to his prayer. We shall then collect from his correspondence whatever may be judged to be genuine prayers: the doxologies, brief expressions of gratitude to God, wishes, and "confessions". The next significant material consists in the instructions concerning prayer, scattered through his letters. Lastly, we shall examine the "formal thanksgivings", with which his letters habitually begin, giving particular attention to their character as accounts of Paul's prayer, rather than actual prayers. We shall conclude by attempting to discern whatever parallels may be perceptible between Paul's prayer and his theology, specifically, his soteriological and Christological reflection, which has imbued his thought with its distinctive cachet.

II
THE TERMINOLOGY OF PRAYER IN PAUL

We must now examine briefly the vocabulary which Paul uses in his letters to designate the Christian's commerce with

God in prayer. It should be observed that most of these terms
exhibit a meaning of a general nature, and thus will prove to
be not especially informative about the specific quality of
Paul's own prayer. Moreover not a few of them appear in other
New Testament documents with more or less similar meaning.

Still we must present some idea, inadequate though it be for
the moment, of the rich variety of words for prayer that Paul
employs. We wish also to assess their relative frequency in
Paul and in other New Testament writers, and to mention by
contrast expressions not found in his letters. In this way we
shall assemble a set of categories, however broad in scope or
pale in meaning, which we may hope to fill with deeper
significance, as they are set back into the context of Paul's
correspondence.

The verb "to pray" (*proseuchesthai*) and its cognate sub-
stantive "prayer" (*proseuchē*) occur not infrequently, but they
are generic terms, indicating little of the nature or content of
the specific address to God. It is undoubtedly for this reason
that the verb is the most common means of referring to Jesus'
prayer in the Gospels. These two Christian terms differ from
the classical, and hence the pagan, Greek terms for prayer
(*euchesthai, euchē*), which connote fundamentally a wish. The
verb has this original sense once in Paul (Rom 9:3), and he
twice (2 Cor 13:7, 9) employs it for "pray".

Paul denotes prayer as expressly petitionary at times by his
use of the verb "to ask, beg" (*deisthai*) (1 Thes 3:10; Rom
1:10), and even more often through the corresponding noun
"petition" (*deēsis*) (Phil 1:4, 19; 4:6; 2 Cor 1:11; 9:14;
Rom 10:1; Eph 6:18 *bis*). Underlying these terms is the sense
of the felt need out of which the request has arisen. We also
find, somewhat rarely, the verb "to demand, request" (*aiteisthai*) with its cognate noun "request, petition" (*aitēma*),
which occurs once (Phil 4:6). In an account of what will
prove to be one of his most significant prayer-experiences (2
Cor 12:8) Paul utilizes the verb "to exhort, implore" (*parakalein*), which elsewhere in his letters retains its customary
parenetic meaning. The instance where the word describes an
urgent, persevering petition of Paul himself will be examined

later,[13] since it has a significant bearing on whether Paul may be said to have prayed immediately to Christ, or only to God the Father. The Johannine term *erōtān,* which, when used in the sense of "to pray", is reserved almost exclusively (cf. Jn 16:23) for the prayer of Jesus, since it presumes great familiarity with God, does not appear in Paul.

The verb "to intercede" (*entynchanein, hyperentynchanein*) describes the activity of the Holy Spirit in Christian prayer (Rom 8:27, 26), or denotes the celestial intercession of the exalted Christ (Rom 8:32; cf. Heb 7:25). Once Paul applies it to the intercession of Elijah (Rom 11:3), in an allusion to the celebrated experience of that prophet at Horeb, or Sinai (1 Kgs 19:10, 14). The very general word "to invoke" (*epikaleisthai*), never found in the Johannine writings, but frequent in Acts, occurs in two passages (1 Cor 1:2; Rom 10:12-14).

The prayer of praise is indicated by the term "to confess" (*exhomologeisthai*) in the hymn (Phil 2:11), which Paul cites from a familiar liturgy, but which he did not himself compose. Other words for prayer as praise, commonly employed elsewhere in the New Testament, are also present in Paul.[14] To be noted here is his use of the noun "praise" (*doxa*), to designate the Christian liturgy (2 Cor 1:20). Two magnificent examples of the prayer of praise as "confession" (2 Cor 1:3-11; Eph 1:3-14), introduced by the Old Testament phrase "blessed be God" (*bārûk Yahweh = eulogētos ho Theos*), actually constitute the longest prayers of Paul in his letters and are important as an indication of his indebtedness to the prayer of Israel.

The most frequently employed prayer-term in the Pauline letters, occurring some twenty-three times, is a Hellenistic Greek word "to give thanks" (*eucharistein*), only rarely found in the Septuagint, the Alexandrian Jewish version in Greek of the Hebrew Scriptures. The characteristically Christian sense

---

[13] See pp. 53, 56.
[14] *Doxazein:* 2 Thes 3:1; 1 Cor 6:20; 2 Cor 9:13; Gal 1:24; Rom 1:21; 15:6, 9; *doxa:* Phil 1:11; 2:11; 4:20; 1 Cor 10:31; 2 Cor 1:20; 4:15; 8:19; Gal 1:5; Rom 3:7; 4:20; 11:36; 15:7; 16:27; Eph 1:6, 12, 14; 3:21; *eulogein:* 1 Cor 10:16; 14:16; *epainos:* Phil 1:11; Eph 1:6, 14; *endoxazesthai:* 2 Thes 1:12.

of this relatively new Greek term, transmitted to Paul from the early Hellenistic Christian communities, derived from its use as a designation for Jesus' great act of thanksgiving at the Last Supper. Actually this new usage provides an insight into the difference between the Israelite and the Christian approach to God in prayer. The Hebrew word, frequent in the Psalter and often rendered "to thank" in English versions, basically means "to sing, or praise". Through Paul's influence, what came to color all Christian prayer most deeply was the returning of thanks to the Father for his gracious gift in Christ of man's salvation.

It should be noted that the noun (*eucharistia*), derived from the verb "to give thanks", appears in Paul's letters in two senses. It can mean "gratitude" (Phil 4:6; 2 Cor 4:15; 9:11; Col 2:7), or "an act of thanksgiving" (1 Thes 3:9; 1 Cor 14:16; 2 Cor 9:12; Col 4:2; Eph 5:4). In both senses however it is related to God. In fact the Christian semantic development of the verb "to give thanks" receives striking attestation in Paul, who only once employs it of an expression of gratitude to human beings (Rom 16:4). At the same time it may be observed that the use of the noun *eucharistia* to denote the central act of Christian worship, the Eucharist, is not found anywhere in Paul or indeed in the New Testament.

This rapid survey of the terminology Paul employs to describe his own prayer or to urge upon others this Christian duty, provides no more than a first approach to the subject. The very general words frequently used, "to pray" (sixteen times) and "prayer" (eleven times), leave intact the mystery surrounding his own prayer and that of others. The variety of terms for petitionary prayer indicate its importance in Paul's eyes for Christian living, as one might expect, from the great value which Jesus himself appears, from the evidence in the Gospels, to have attached to it. It may be significant that the verb connoting a petition made from a conscious need (*deisthai*) is only found, apart from Paul, in the Lucan writings (an exception is Mt 9:38), where it is frequent.[15] The preferred Pauline

---

[15] Lk 5:12; 8:28, 38; 9:38, 40; 10:2; 21:36; 22:32; Acts 4:31; 8:22, 24; 10:2.

word for "petition" (*deēsis*) recurs in the writings influenced by Paul (1 Tm 2:1; 5:5; 2 Tm 1:3; Heb 5:7; 1 Pt 3:12). Apart from these instances it appears only in Lk 1:13; 2:37; 5:33 and Jas 5:16. The verb "to give thanks" occurs outside Paul's letters, with three exceptions (Lk 17:16; 18:11; Apoc 11:17) for the entire New Testament, only in the prayer of Jesus himself [16] at the Last Supper, in the narrative of the feeding of the crowds, and one other occasion (Jn 11:41). Acts predicates it twice of Paul (Acts 27:35; 28:15). Thus we shall be led to expect that petition and thanksgiving will be found dominant in Paul's prayer-life. On the other hand, the accepted New Testament terminology for the prayer of praise is almost never used by Paul to designate his own prayer. Instead, as we shall have occasion to point out,[17] his favorite symbol for it is to be seen in the image of "boasting", an almost exclusively Pauline figure (cf. Heb 3:6; Jas 1:9; 4:16).

III
THE PAULINE LETTERS

It may be helpful to list the letters, ten in number, which are here considered authentically Pauline for the purposes of this study, and to give some indication of their probable date and place of origin. It is generally agreed that 1 Thessalonians is the first of Paul's extant correspondence. It may be dated from Corinth towards the end of 51 A.D. or the beginning of 52. 2 Thessalonians, whose genuineness is disputed by some critics, was probably composed a short time after the first letter.

The next period of Paul's literary activity of which we have some examples can be dated from his two or three years' residence in Ephesus (Acts 19:20; 20:31) between 55 and 58. Philippians and 1 Corinthians are from this period, while 2 Corinthians and Galatians were probably despatched during Paul's journey to Corinth through Macedonia early in 58. The assigning of Philippians to an Ephesian captivity, rather than

---

[16] Last Supper: Mt 26:27; Mk 14:23; Lk 22:17, 19; feeding of the crowd: Mt 15:36; Mk 8:6; Jn 6:11, 23.

[17] See pp. 46-49.

to the Roman imprisonment, has gained adherents in the last two or three decades. The most cogent reason for postulating an Ephesian captivity as the place of origin of this letter is the remark of Paul that, since he was in Thessalonica on his second missionary excursion, he has received no help from Philippi (Phil 4:16), as that community had lacked any opportunity (Phil 4:10). By the time of his Roman captivity Paul had twice visited the Philippian church (Acts 20:2; 20:6). To interpret Phil 4:10 as sarcasm or irony does not suit the general tone of this letter.

From the general similarity of theme evinced by Galatians and Romans, it is plausible to place their composition at approximately the same period. Romans may reasonably be supposed to have been written from Corinth during Paul's three months' stay there in the spring of 58 A.D. Philemon, Colossians, and Ephesians may be assigned to the Roman captivity sometime in the early sixties. The Pauline authenticity of Ephesians is more controverted than any of the other letters we have mentioned. Without entering into this dispute, which has not been definitively settled, we have included a few citations from this magnificent document, chiefly because it confirms certain tendencies, perceptible in Paul's prayer through his earlier letters, which are significant for certain aspects of it, notably its Trinitarian orientation.

I cannot conclude without expressing my great indebtedness to my colleague, Father Brian Peckham, S.J., for the many fruitful suggestions and the continual encouragement which he gave me in the preparation of this book. My grateful thanks are also gladly acknowledged to Mrs. T. Wilson, who generously typed the manuscript.

It has given me great satisfaction to be permitted to dedicate this study in Pauline spirituality to a religious and an educator of considerable distinction, who was a major influence in my early academic formation. Sister M. Henrietta is a member of the Sisters of Saint Joseph of Toronto.

March 19, 1973   Regis College,
Feast of Saint Joseph   Willowdale, Ontario

Chapter 1
The Initial Confrontation
with the Risen Lord

The event which inaugurated Saint Paul's life as a Christian, his meeting with the risen Christ on the road to Damascus, came to hold a place of first-rate importance in Christianity. Before that however, it played a crucial part in Paul's own formation, surpassing in significance all other experiences in a career that bears the imprint of momentous happenings of a kaleidoscopic variety, as well as being graced with extraordinary divine favors. This initial confrontation with the Lord Jesus not only altered the entire course of Paul's career, as it obviously did; it also continued to mold his most intimate religious attitudes, to stimulate his profound theological reflection, that would be of such moment for the development of Christian thought, and to inspire his unquenchable ardor in tirelessly carrying out the God-given mandate confided to him through Jesus Christ. To the end of his life Paul thought of himself as "one to whom the Lord has shown mercy" (1 Cor 7:25; 2 Cor 4:1), a recipient of "the graciousness of God" (1 Cor 15:10). "For if I preach the gospel, that gives me no cause for boasting: I am constrained by necessity. It would be misery for me were I not to preach the gospel. Hence, if I do it willingly, I have pay enough; if I do it apart from my own choice, [it is because] I have been entrusted with a stewardship" (1 Cor 9:16-17). "It is thus men must think of us—as servants of Christ and stewards of

11

the mysteries of God. In the last analysis what is looked for in a steward is that such a one be worthy of trust" (1 Cor 4:1-2).

I

SOME CONTEMPORARY VIEWS OF PAUL'S CONVERSION

That the primary experience in Paul's Christian existence still holds a fascination for modern scholarship is demonstrated by the wealth and variety of opinion its manifold character continues to elicit. At the present time studies of Paul's experience are chiefly concerned with the relation of this event to his theological thought. The day of psychological investigation into this unique conversion to Christianity of a zealous Pharisee appears to be over. The attempts to rationalize it in terms of Paul's mental or physical health, his dissatisfaction with Judaism based upon the implausible surmise of his having known Jesus (2 Cor 5:16), or his disillusionment in his own ability to observe the Law (Rom 7:7-25), or by some pre-disposition towards the "mystical", have been abandoned in turn as fanciful conjecture.

Philippe-Henri Menoud [1] has categorized the turning-point in Paul's life as a "theological" rather than a "spiritual" or "moral" conversion. Thus it explains Paul's new attitudes to revelation and tradition, the foundations of a Christian theology. The revelation granted to Paul at Damascus gave rise to three theological theorems which are cardinal in his thought. God's dealings with man in the new covenant are consistent with his action under the old covenant, and hence there is continuity between them. There is redemptive value in the cross, which thus reveals divine wisdom (1 Cor 1:18-25). Man's salvation is disclosed as being realized in two stages: Jesus' coming in weakness and suffering, and his coming in glory at the parousia. Paul's keen sense of the value of apostolic tradition, handed on to him by his predecessors in the faith, shows that he never regarded himself as the founder of Christianity. This respect for tradition is manifested by his care

---

[1] Philippe-Henri Menoud, "Révélation et Tradition: l'influence de la conversion de Paul sur sa théologie," *Verbum Caro* 7 (1953), 2-10; for the English version see *Interpretation* 7 (1953) 131-141.

to keep in communication with the other apostles, his constant acknowledgment of his reliance upon the transmission of what Jesus had said and done from earlier witnesses, and his concern to preserve the unity of the Church.

For Professor Joachim Jeremias "the key to Pauline theology" [2] is not found in the influence of Hellenistic religion or Hellenistic thought, nor in any schooling in rabbinic Judaism. It was Paul's meeting with the risen Christ on the Damascus road which gave a totally new meaning to the characteristically Pauline title "Lord", and enabled him to create his distinctive theology of the cross. Through this experience Paul was impressed with the omnipotence of God's grace, the graciousness of the divine choice of himself, a deep sense of sin, a certain anti-legalism. He was moreover given the grounds for a theology of hope. He was commissioned as an apostle, filled with zeal for the conversion of others, and provided with the basis of his theology of the Church.

Josef Blank [3] finds that Paul's call by God to be a Christian represents a totally new beginning, inexplicable in terms of anything that preceded it. The experience created his personal relationship to the risen Christ, his apostolic commission, and his theology. These did not derive from any prior, pre-Christian influences or experience, and can only be correctly explained in the light of Paul's own witness regarding them contained in his letters.

Professor Günther Bornkamm [4] inveighs against the "subjectivist" interpretation of the Pauline texts which deal with the Damascus event. This misconception that Paul made the appearance of the risen Lord to himself the sole source of his gospel, with complete disregard for the traditions of Jesus' earthly life preserved by the primitive Church, "adversely affects our picture of Paul: a question mark is set against him, and he is stigmatized as an enthusiast and individualist." [5] His

---

[2] J. Jeremias, "The Key to Pauline Theology," *Expository Times* 76 (1964-65), 27-30.

[3] Josef Blank, *Paulus und Jesus: Eine theologische Grundlegung* (München, 1965), p. 184.

[4] Günther Bornkamm, *Paul* (New York: Evanston, 1969), translated by D. M. G. Stalker, pp. 13-25.

[5] *Ibid.*, p. 22.

conversion moreover was not that "of a man without faith finding the way to God, but of one zealous for God, more in earnest than anyone else about his demands and promises . . . a devout man whose way God blocked through the Christ who had died a shameful death on the cross, and on whom he made the light shine" (2 Cor 4:6).[6]

Dom Jacques Dupont [7] interprets the Damascus incident as a personal experience of the concrete realization of salvation in the person of the risen Christ, who revealed himself to Paul as endowed, through his resurrection, with the power to make the believer share one day in his glory. Paul aligned these data of experience with the faith of the primitive Church in the redemptive character of Jesus' death "for our sins" (1 Cor 15:3). Also, in consequence of this confrontation with the Lord Jesus, Paul came to reject his former Pharisaic view of salvation through the observance of the Law in favour of the originality of Christian soteriology, that salvation can come only through and in Christ to those committed to him by faith.

Dom Jacques comes close to the interpretation of H. G. Wood [8] who states his position by saying that "Paul was converted to Christ rather than to Christianity." By this I take him to mean that the personal element, Paul's falling in love with Christ, must be given precedence over the doctrinal consequences which flowed from his new relationship of faith to the risen Lord: "thereafter" as Dr. Wood explains, "Paul had to readjust his whole thinking." "The vision of the Damascus road meant first and foremost the conviction, or one might say, the revelation, that Jesus has been raised from the dead and is seated at the right hand of power. Henceforth, for Paul, Jesus is Christ and Lord." [9]

These last two studies, with their emphasis on the primacy of the new interpersonal relationship between Christ and Paul,

---

[6] *Ibid.*, p. 23.

[7] Jacques Dupont, "La conversion de Paul et son influence sur sa conception du salut par la foi," *Analecta Biblica* 42 (1970), 67-88.

[8] H. G. Wood, "The Conversion of St. Paul: Its Nature, Antecedents, and Consequences," *New Testament Studies* 1 (1954-55), 279.

[9] Ibid., p. 281.—An excellent discussion of the various twentieth-century views by scholars of Paul's conversion may be found in Béda Rigaux, *Saint Paul et ses Lettres* (Paris: Bruges, 1962), pp. 63-97.

come closer to our own interest in Paul's conversion, which is concerned not directly with its repercussions on Pauline theology or Christology, but on its value for his prayer-life and the high regard in which he held prayer. An investigation of this aspect of Paul's experience, which as far as I can ascertain has not been conducted hitherto, gives rise to the following questions. How much did the meeting on the Damascus road affect Paul's religious attitude to God and to the risen Christ? How far did it change his comprehension of God's way of justifying the non-believer, and impart a new conception of the presence of God and of his will? What repercussions did it have on his view of the earthly life of Jesus? To what extent did it influence the formulation of Paul's gospel, or his attitude towards his own call to be apostle of the Gentiles?

We shall review in the first place the passages in Paul's letters where he gives his own interpretation of this encounter with Christ (Phil 3:7-15; 1 Cor 15:8-10; 9:1; 2 Cor 4:6; Gal 1:15-16, 12). Then we must examine the manner in which it was understood by one of Paul's contemporaries and associates, Luke the author of Acts (Acts 9:1-19; 22:3-16; 26:12-18). For although Luke's understanding of Paul's experience will be found to diverge from that of Paul himself, it will provide certain valid and valuable insights into its meaning for the early Church through the eyes of one of its distinguished members.

It is of paramount importance for our evaluation of the Pauline texts we are to examine, to bear in mind that they were all written almost two decades and more after the incident with which Paul's Christian life began. Thus the various constructions which he puts upon his conversion spring from many years of living as a Christian and an apostle, when Paul had become adept in the art of Christian prayer and had acquired a fully developed prayer-life. It is for this reason that these passages will prove of great assistance to our investigation.

II
THE INFLUENCE ON PAUL'S PERSONAL LIFE (PHIL 3:7-15)

The passage we have first to consider is set in the context of controversy, where Paul's adversaries not implausibly were

Jewish Christian missionaries, who insisted on circumcision and the perfect practice of the Mosaic Law. Dr. Helmut Koester [10] maintains that "the basic factor of this attitude was the belief that a complete fulfilment of the Law was possible . . . and brought about the possession of the eschatological promises in full, that is, the Spirit and spiritual experiences of such heavenly gifts as resurrection and freedom from suffering and death."

To correct the errors in this heterodox view Paul gives a definition of Christian existence. "We are the [true] circumcision, who worship God by his Spirit and found our boast in Christ Jesus, putting no confidence in the flesh" (Phil 3:3). The triadic orientation to God, the Spirit, and Christ is to be noted. Any authentic cult of God, in which for Paul, as will be seen presently, prayer is given a high priority with the liturgy, or public worship, is animated by the Holy Spirit and is expressed through union with the risen Christ as praise and thanksgiving. We shall shortly have occasion to discuss the meaning of "boasting" for Paul,[11] one of his characteristic turns of phrase. In his critique of his opponent's false position Paul enumerates the privileges which were once his own boast as a member of Israel, and then recalls the event which transformed his religious existence. He first contrasts his former ideals as a Pharisee with his new life in union with Christ by means of metaphors borrowed from book-keeping, profit and loss.

7 "But whatever I counted as assets I have come, because of Christ, to reckon as loss. 8 Indeed, more than that, I count it all as loss because of the supreme asset, the knowledge of Christ Jesus my Lord. It was through him that I suffered the loss of all these things. I assess them as so much rubbish in order that I may gain Christ as asset, 9 and find myself united to him. I mean, that I may possess, not any justification of my own making, that comes from law, but that justification through faith in Christ—the justification given by God through faith. 10 [My aim is] to know him, that is, the power of his resur-

---

[10] Helmut Koester, "The Purpose of the Polemic of a Pauline Fragment (Philippians iii)," *New Testament Studies* 8 (1961-62), p. 331.
[11] See pp. 46-49.

rection and the sharing of his sufferings, thus being molded together with him to his death, 11 that somehow I may attain to the resurrection from the dead."

The peculiar interest of this passage (as of the verses which follow) for our inquiry is that Paul discusses his conversion solely in function of its effect upon himself and on his life as a Christian. He passes over its relation to his career as an apostle. The radical transformation of his existence has been effected "through Christ" (v.7), yet it is to the initiative of God the Father that Paul ascribes the grace of "justification by faith." His use of the language of accounting provides an easy transition to the forensic terminology of "justification," which here makes its first appearance in Paul's letters. It is thanks to this justifying action of God that Paul can henceforth "find myself united to" Christ. Indeed, this experience was the beginning of a quest which was to engage Paul's heart and mind for the rest of his life, the continuing search for an answer to the question, "Who is Christ?" For "the knowledge of Christ Jesus my Lord" is not mere theological or speculative knowledge. It should not be imagined that the turning-point in Paul's life on the Damascus road was simply a shift in viewpoint. It was the start of an experiential learning of who Christ truly is. There is nothing of the gnostic in Paul; he invariably uses "knowing" in the biblical sense, particularly of experiencing God in Christ. That Paul, as a result of his conversion, found himself united to Christ means that the risen Lord became and remained for him the embodiment of God's dynamic presence, the "supreme asset" (v.8). This is shown by Paul's description of what "knowing him" means: to experience in his life "the power of his resurrection and the sharing in his sufferings" (v.10). By his reception of baptism (Rom 6:4-5) Paul was first "molded together with him to his death," and this process was to constitute the dialectic of his entire existence in this world. This transformation initiated long ago near Damascus will only reach its term and climax in the future when he will "attain to the resurrection from the dead" (v.11). Only then will Christ become his "saviour" in the fullest sense. Meantime, like the citizen of a Greek city-state living in one of the colonies, his

citizenship is registered in heaven, where alone one day he
will be granted full possession of its privileges. "For our city-
state remains in heaven, whence we await also as Saviour the
Lord Jesus Christ, who will transform this humble body of ours,
remolding it in the likeness of his own glorious body through
the dynamic power, by which he is able also to subject all
things to himself" (Phil 3:20-21).

At this point in his development Paul presses into service
another image, borrowed here as elsewhere only indirectly [12]
from the foot-race in the Greek games. In order to grasp Paul's
meaning correctly it is important to recognize, as several translations do not, that his symbolism is now drawn from the
racecourse. To speak of Paul as "seized" by Christ, thus perhaps mistaking the imagery for that drawn from wrestling, can
give the false impression that the beginning of his Christian
life was of a violent nature.[13] It also appears to suggest, again
wrongly, that Paul's call to the faith came only from Christ
and not initially from God the Father. Paul wishes to clarify the
issue between himself and the judaizers, the meaning of Christian perfection.

12 "Not that I have already won [the prize]. I have not
yet attained perfection. On the contrary, I keep running hard
to reach the goal, by virtue of my having been overtaken by
Christ Jesus. 13 No, brothers! I do not judge myself to have
reached the goal. One thing only I bear in mind. Forgetting
what lies behind, 14 I press on eagerly to what lies ahead: I
run hard towards the goal for the prize of the call heavenwards
by God in Christ Jesus. 15 Therefore, this is the attitude of
those of us who are perfect. Hence if you have a different attitude, God will also reveal this to you."

It will be recalled that Paul has earlier in this letter made
use of a general athletic metaphor, in combination with one
drawn from the civic sphere, in urging the Philippians to de-

---

[12] Victor C. Pfitzner, *Paul and the Agon Motif: traditional athletic
imagery in the Pauline literature* (Leiden, 1967), pp. 76-81, 139-153.

[13] Lucien Cerfaux, "L'Apôtre en présence de Dieu: essai sur la vie
d'oraison de saint Paul," *Recueil Lucien Cerfaux*, vol. II, pp. 471-473.

velop what we would call nowadays a "sense of community." "Only act as citizens in a manner worthy of the gospel of Christ, in order that whether I come to see you, or whether I am absent, I may hear it reported of you that you stand firm in one spirit, taking part in the contest together (*synathlountes*) with one heart by faith in the gospel" (Phil 1:27). A few verses later he will describe the church as "engaged in the same contest (*agōna*) as you have observed in myself as you now hear about me" (v.30). This "contest" is one of Paul's favourite ways of describing the advance in the Christian life, and this pursuit of a common ideal should produce a deeper bond of union among the members of the Philippian community.

The figure of the foot-race appears elsewhere in Paul's letters. "Surely," he writes to the Corinthians, "You are aware that runners in the stadium all take part in the race. Yet only one wins the prize. You must run in such a way as to reach the goal" (1 Cor 9:24). The "prize" of which there is question is the same as that indicated here to the Philippians, the "imperishable crown" (v.25) of eternal life. Paul reverts to the same metaphor in speaking of the conversion of the Gentiles in Rom 9:30. "Gentiles, who did not run hard for justification, have reached the goal—justification, that justification that comes from faith."

Paul's use of the foot-race to symbolize justification by faith throws light on the connection between vv.12-14 of our passage in Philippians and his earlier reference to the Damascus experience (vv.7-10) in terms of profit and loss. He states that he has not "won the prize" as yet, but continues to "run hard to reach the goal" (v.12). In view of his rejection of any justification "of my own making" (v.9), it becomes clear that the illustration of the foot-race does not express hectic striving, as if his reaching the goal depended upon his own determination.[14] Nor does the image suggest anxiety as the motive for his "running hard". As has already been said, there is nothing that implies Paul's conversion was of a violent character. He ascribes

[14] Joachim Gnilka, *Der Philipperbrief* (Freiburg: Basel: Wien, 1968), p. 198.

his ability to "run hard" to his being overtaken by Christ the runner in the race—he who first made him experience "the power of his resurrection" (v.10).

At the same time Paul does not forget that his Christian vocation was a summons by God, calling him "heavenwards" where the goal of the race lies (v.14). Still his call remains a "call in Christ Jesus." The glorified Lord, with whom Paul was united by faith at their first encounter, has truly become through his own resurrection the concrete realization of "the call heavenwards by God." There is no suggestion here that Paul beheld the risen Lord resplendent with the light of glory, as will be mentioned elsewhere (2 Cor 4:6). However the picture of the celestial Christ in v.21, which is of considerable consequence for Paul's refutation of his adversaries, is an indication of its origin in the Damascus experience. Then Paul had beheld Christ's "own glorious body" and had learned, in consequence, that through his power Christ would one day be agent of the resurrection of the faithful.

What may be gathered from this interpretation of his conversion, written over twenty years after the event, that is relevant to Paul's life of prayer? It testifies to the position of eminence held in it by Christ. The continuing quest for a deeper "knowledge of Christ Jesus my Lord" (v.8) governed Paul's entire approach to God. It was essential to Paul's religion as a "worshipper of God by his Spirit" to "found his boast in Christ Jesus" (v.3). In his race for the goal he never forgets that it is a "call heavenwards by God in Christ Jesus" (v.14), that the dynamism graciously imparted to him by God, that keeps him "running hard to reach the goal," was communicated by his "having been overtaken by Christ Jesus" (v.12). As a result of this meeting, the risen Lord became for Paul the incarnation of the nearness of God, an element that is a *sine qua non* for the possibility of Christian prayer.

In such prayer faith is a basic ingredient in "the attitude of those of us who are perfect" (v.15), for this attitude is a free gift of God's graciousness which he is willing to give to all. Paul's first confrontation with the risen Christ had given him this priceless divine gift. It had also given to Paul's prayer its fundamentally eschatological orientation, since it disclosed Christ in "his glorious body" as the future "Saviour" who would one day bring Paul to share in the final resurrection (vv.20-21). Thus this initial encounter explains the prominence of hope in Paul's prayer-life, for the Lord Jesus had been revealed to him as the embodiment of Christian hope. Although Paul does not here expressly mention his love for Christ, the whole passage is redolent with it. "To know him" (v.10) which Paul reckoned "the supreme asset" (v.8) cannot be rightly comprehended except in terms of the deepest love. It is only "in Christ Jesus" and "boasting in Christ Jesus" (v.3) that Paul can address in prayer the God who near Damascus had given him "the call heavenwards in Christ Jesus" (v.14). Paul has summed up this attitude earlier in this same letter: "For me to live is Christ, and to die is an asset" (Phil 1:21).

III
THE LAST OF THE POST-RESURRECTION APPEARANCES
(1 COR 15:8)

A noteworthy construction is put on his first meeting with the risen Lord in Paul's first letter to the Corinthian community. It shows that he came to look on this episode as being on a par with the experiences of the earliest of Jesus' disciples after his resurrection. In fact, there is evidence that he regarded his confrontation with the glorified Christ as the final occurrence of these privileged encounters.

In his recital of a very early credal formula (1 Cor 15:3 ff.) Paul enumerates several of these incidents as they were included in this primitive creed. "He appeared to Cephas, then to the Twelve; next he appeared to more than five hundred of the brothers at one time. . . . then he appeared to James, and later to all the apostles" (vv.5-7). It is probably this last word which makes Paul add: 8 "Last of all he appeared also to me as to an 'abortion'. 9 For I am the least of the apostles: I am not worthy of the call as an apostle, because I persecuted the Church of God. 10 But by God's graciousness I am what I

am! Indeed, his graciousness towards me has not been ineffectual. In fact, I have labored far harder than any of them! Of
course, I do not mean that I [did it] of myself. Rather it was
God's act of graciousness towards me. 11 So whether they, or
I—what matter! This is how we preach and this is how you
came to the faith."

Paul's use of the precisely identical formula to express his
own experience on the Damascus road as that employed in the
credo of the early Church, manifests his conviction that he had
actually seen the risen Christ, who presented himself to him in
his glorified body, not less truly than he had manifested himself
to Peter, James, the Twelve, and others. The meeting was not
in Paul's eyes to be classed with those other "visions and
revelations of the Lord" (2 Cor 12:1) he was to behold in
ecstasy later in life, about which he always displayed the greatest reticence. The Damascus event deserved, it would appear
from Paul's juxtaposition of it alongside the other disclosures
of himself by the risen Christ, to be proclaimed in the Christian
creed and the kerygma quite as much as the privileged encounters granted to Peter and the Twelve after the resurrection.

Certainly it was upon this claim alone that Paul founded his
claim to be an apostle. "Am I not free? am I not an apostle?
have I not seen Jesus our Lord?" (1 Cor 9:1). This reference
to the Damascus meeting as the origin of his vocation to be an
apostle is an aspect of its interpretation that did not appear
in Phil 3:7-14. As Paul reflected upon his conversion through
many years, he came to see it also as imparting to his Christian
life its specific form: his apostleship. He will describe himself
in writing to the Roman church as "Paul called [to the Christian faith] as an apostle" (Rom 1:1). It is this view of his
apostolic commission as a modality of his personal Christian
existence which is responsible for the essentially apostolic character of Paul's prayer. We shall see later how he habitually
brings into the presence of God all his concerns for the communities he has founded. It is before God that he conducts
his theological reflection upon the truths of the faith which will
bear a rich harvest in his theology expressed through his letters.

Paul also considered his conversion "an abnormal birth" in

the faith: why? It is possible that he employed a sobriquet for himself with which his enemies had dubbed him as a derogatory epithet, because he had become a Christian after the Church had replaced the synagogue. He was then born to Christ after his "mother" was dead. Dr. Josef Blank [15] has discerningly observed that Paul was "last" in his own eyes in a *qualitative* sense, without reference to the other apostles. He himself asserts that "I am the least of the apostles: I am not worthy of the call as an apostle, because I persecuted the Church of God" (v.9). He had no qualifications for his apostolic vocation, since he had not been schooled, as had the Twelve, by any experience of Jesus' earthly life. He had not even been predisposed to it by disillusionment with his old religious way of life. Moreover, what had made his election by God to apostleship even more unthinkable was his activity, immediately preceding his call, in persecuting the followers of Jesus of Nazareth.

It is often asserted that nowhere does Paul in his writings display the virtue of repentance. This is scarcely true, at least in the light of his constant, sorrowful recollection of his attacks upon the Jewish Christians (cf. Phil 3:4,6; Gal 1:13, 22-24; 2:17; Eph 3:8). It is this complete unpreparedness and unsuitability, naturally speaking, for the apostolic commission which constitute the grounds for his applying to himself the nickname, "abortion," given him by his opponents.

Thus, Paul insists that it was simply and solely the graciousness of God that created him an apostle out of nothing. He expresses this in existential language: everything he now is, all he continues to be and to accomplish, he owes to the divine graciousness. And the proof of that is the effectiveness and magnitude of his work as apostle. "I have labored far harder than any of them!" is not idle boasting, but rather the proof of the dynamism of God's graciousness, the authentication of the validity of his vocation. Paul does not for a moment credit his achievements to himself, but to "God's act of graciousness towards me". No natural endowments can qualify a man to be an apostle. "Circumcision is nothing; lack of circumcision is

---

[15] Josef Blank, *op. cit.*, p. 190.

nothing: [what counts is] a new creation" (Gal 6:15). When he writes to the Corinthians, "If a man be in union with Christ, he is a new creation," he thinks of himself as well as of others. It is a truth of which he had personal experience in being called to apostleship.

Paul frequently recalls with gratitude that his apostolic vocation and his apostolic achievements constitute a demonstration of God's graciousness.[16] It was this that made him founder of the Corinthian community. "By virtue of the graciousness of God imparted to me I laid a foundation like a skilled architect . . . no man can lay any other foundation than that already laid, which is Christ Jesus" (1 Cor 3:10-11). It was the recognition by James, Cephas, and John "regarded as the pillars" of the mother-church of Jerusalem, of that graciousness "imparted to me" which led to their acknowledgment of Paul's specific vocation as apostle of the Gentiles (Gal 2:9). The strongest recommendation of himself Paul can make to the Roman community, with which he is as yet unacquainted, is God's graciousness in calling him to be an apostle. At the outset of his letter he draws attention to the fact that it is "Jesus Christ our Lord, through whom we received the grace of apostleship" (Rom 1:5) from God his Father. As he begins his admonitions to the Roman Christians, he reminds them that he does so "by virtue of the graciousness imparted to me" (Rom 12:3). And as he concludes his entire communication to Rome he adds by way of apology: "I have written somewhat boldly to you to refresh your memories in virtue of the graciousness imparted to me by God, by making me a minister of Christ Jesus to the Gentiles, exercising my priestly office [by preaching] the gospel of God" (Rom 15:15-16). A passage in Ephesians echoes the thought Paul has already expressed in 1 Cor 15:8-9. "I became a minister [of the gospel] by virtue of the gift of God's graciousness imparted to me according to his dynamic power. To me *the least of all saints* this grace has been given, to

---

[16] Paul consequently is rightly regarded as the theologian of grace. This term, from the Latin *gratia*, directs attention to the free or wholly undeserved quality of the divine gift, while the Greek word (*charis*) points to the divine good pleasure, the source of the gift. Hence, we have most frequently translated it, "graciousness."

gospel to the Gentiles the unfathomable riches of Christ" (Eph 3:7-8).

Paul's continual recollection of the *graciousness* of God, manifested to him through the confrontation with Christ on the Damascus road, and his profoundly sensitive attention to the recurring manifestations of this same graciousness throughout his apostolic career, provided as will be seen somewhat later,[17] the principal reason for his untiring practice of prayer of thanksgiving and his insistence upon the value and necessity of thanksgiving in his instructions on prayer to those to whom he wrote his letters.

But the most significant consequence for our inquiry into Paul's prayer-life of this passage (1 Cor 15:8) is his conviction that his experience near Damascus was to be considered a post-resurrection appearance of the risen Lord like those granted to the Twelve. For it enables us to comprehend Paul's attitude to Jesus' earthly history, and to assess the contrast between his approach to Christ and that of the earlier disciples. For this reason it may not be unhelpful to review briefly the way in which the Twelve were formed for their future vocation as apostles. We shall then be in a better position to appreciate his view of Jesus "in the days of his flesh" (Heb 5:7).

IV
THE EXPERIENCE OF THE TWELVE

Paul was certainly not unaware, nor did his opponents allow him to forget, that he had had no part in those events which constituted the public ministry of Jesus, and which in consequence occupy a preponderant part of our Gospels. "Even if we had known Christ according to the flesh, we now no longer know him thus" (2 Cor 5:16). It is not improbable that this statement is of a polemical character, aimed at those who sought to discredit Paul in the eyes of the communities he had founded. It will be recalled that it is this very lacuna in the experience of Paul, so clearly his hero in Acts, that prevented

[17] See pp. 77-78, 83, 88, 105, 164.

Luke from classing him as an apostle of equal status with the Twelve (cf. Acts 1:21-22).[18]

Indeed, students of Paul have been puzzled by his almost complete silence regarding the episodes of Jesus' earthly ministry in his letters. In fact Paul relates only one of these, the institution of the Eucharist at the Last Supper (1 Cor 11:23-26), where the terse, stylized form of the narrative would appear to suggest that it is the citation of a liturgical formula. Paul, it must be granted, does occasionally quote a saying of Jesus (1 Thes 4:2,9,15; 1 Cor 7:10; 9:14 [cf. v.4]; Rom 14:14).[19] What is noteworthy about these Pauline references to the sayings of Jesus is the fact that Paul invariably ascribes them, not to the historical Jesus (as is the modern practice), but *to the risen Lord.* Their value in Paul's eyes, it would appear, derives not simply from their historicity, but from that divine authority conferred upon Jesus (cf. Mt 28:18) at his glorification. "You know what instructions we gave you through the Lord Jesus" (1 Thes 4:2). "We tell you this based on a saying of the Lord" (1 Thes 4:15). "I know and am convinced by [a saying of] the Lord Jesus: nothing is unclean of itself" (Rom 14:14). "In this way moreover did the Lord ordain that those who proclaim the gospel should live by the gospel" (1 Cor 9:14). "I command those who have been married—indeed, it is not my command but the Lord's . . ." (1 Cor 7:10). These examples, together with a number of allusions in his letters to Jesus' parables, surely indicate that Paul was familiar with the evangelical traditions that were still being passed on by word of mouth in his day. He asserts categorically to the Galatians that "there is no other gospel" than the one he preached (Gal 1:7-9). With the Corinthian community he insists that no kerygma can be orthodox if it announces "a different Jesus, whom we have not proclaimed . . . or a different gospel which you did not receive" (2 Cor 11:4).

What then was the specific value of the paschal experience

---

[18] Ernst Haenchen, *The Acts of the Apostles* (Philadelphia, 1971), p. 114.
[19] D. M. Stanley, "Pauline Allusions to the Sayings of Jesus," *Catholic Biblical Quarterly* 23 (1961), 26-39.

of meeting the risen Jesus for those who had known him during his public life?

The experience of the Twelve occurred at two distinct chronological moments and at two very disparate levels of faith. The first of these comprised the disciples' immediate involvement as "the original eyewitnesses" (Lk 1:2) in the events of Jesus' public ministry, his sufferings and death on the cross. They saw what he did, heard what he taught in Galilee and Jerusalem. They had been attracted to follow Jesus at first, as the Gospel record attests (cf. Jn 1:38-39) by some mysterious, winning quality. They were soon impressed by the original and independent traits of mind and heart that made themselves perspicuous in his manner of teaching (Mk 1:27), quite unmatched by that of other scribes and rabbis. As they lived with him, absorbed his doctrine, witnessed those mighty "acts of power" (Mt 13:54) or "signs" (Jn 9:16), they were led to regard him as a prophet (Lk 7:16) like those of old (Mk 8:28; Lk 9:8). At one privileged moment during the public ministry, which the Synoptic tradition has in part linked with Caesarea Philippi (Mk 8:27-28; Mt 16:13-20), the Twelve began to see in Jesus the historical verification of the ancient messianic hope of Israel. He was in fact "the Messiah", the Lord's anointed. This was the peak point of the disciples' grasp of the mystery surrounding Jesus prior to his resurrection.

This devotion and loyalty to Jesus, only gradually acquired by the disciples in the course of their life with him, was not merely human. It was interpreted by the light of faith—the traditional faith of Israel. Such faith, which they possessed as devout Jews, was not however sufficient to sustain the disciples' commitment to Jesus through the traumatic disillusionment of his Passion. Actually Jesus himself had predicted this tragic dénouement: "All of you will lose faith in me" (Mk 14:27). This eclipse of his followers' expectations is confessed by two disciples as they journey with the yet unrecognized risen Jesus towards Emmaus. "We had been hoping that he was the one who is to redeem Israel" (Lk 24:21). The Fourth Gospel in a masterly manner underscores the ineffectual char-

acter of this pre-resurrection faith in the Master whom these
disciples, despite their relatively long schooling by him, knew
only superficially (cf. Jn 14:8-10).

We are now in a position to gauge the transcendent value,
for the first disciples, of their meetings with the risen Lord.
It was actually these experiences that made them Christians.
The Gospel narratives of these supremely significant encounters are intended chiefly to describe the genesis of Christian
faith in the hearts of the Twelve and of the faithful women.
In addition, where the risen Christ's appearances to the Twelve
are recorded, it is the evangelists' intention to relate also the
Lord's commission to "preach the gospel to all nations" (cf.
Mt 28:16-20; Lk 24:35-52; Jn 20:19-29; 21:1-25). These
encounters with the glorified Master also made them apostles.

The post-resurrection appearances revealed to the Twelve
the heart of the mystery that had remained veiled during
Jesus' mortal life: that he is the Son of God, who as a consequence of his exaltation sends the Holy Spirit (Lk 24:49; Acts
1:4-5; 2:2-4). It was the risen Christ, as Luke in particular
insists, who imparted to the disciples the Christian understanding of the Old Testament (Lk 24:25-27, 45-47). The fourth
evangelist, for his part, dwells upon the totally new understanding given to the disciples of what Jesus had said and done
during his earthly ministry. The Holy Spirit "will teach you
everything and cause you to remember all that I have said to
you" (Jn 14:26), since it was precisely the role of the Holy
Spirit "to lead you into the whole range of truth" (Jn 16:13).
This divine illumination through the gift of Christian faith was
specially directed towards Jesus' words and actions which the
Twelve had personally witnessed. For this reason Jesus promised that "everything he makes known to you, he will draw
from what is mine" (Jn 16:24).

It is crucial, for a proper appreciation of the true authority
of the Gospels, to understand that the paschal experiences of
the Twelve were essentially experiences of Christian faith.
None of the evangelists whose books form part of the New
Testament canon (as modern critical scholarship has demonstrated) had actually enjoyed that immediate, personal experi-

ence which had been accorded to "the original eyewitnesses" as a group. From this point of view, it should be noted, the authors of our Gospels were in the same position as Paul. They were the recipients of the evangelical traditions created by one or other of the Twelve. Without any personal contact with "Christ according to the flesh", these inspired writers were given a specially privileged experience in the Spirit of what Jesus had said and done. And it is this Spirit-filled experience that they have intended to record for us in their Gospels. Paul makes a claim to have had this kind of experience himself, when he declares "we possess the mind of Christ" (1 Cor 2:16); "I believe that I also possess the Spirit of God" (1 Cor 7:40). This explains his unwavering confidence that "what I write to you is a commandment of the Lord" (1 Cor 14:37).

St. Thomas Aquinas had expressed the fundamental character of the post-resurrection experiences of the Twelve with his usual admirable clarity. "After his resurrection the apostles saw the living Christ, whom they knew to have died, with the eyes of faith (*oculata fide*)." [20] This greatest of medieval theologians perceived that the appearances of the risen Christ to his own were in a most profound sense an experience of Christian faith. His statement however in no way implies that these were subjective phenomena induced by group hysteria, or that the glorified Lord was not bodily present on these occasions. Nor does St. Thomas' observation detract from the unique quality of these experiences by the apostles, since they unquestionably founded the faith of all subsequent Christian believers. St. Thomas' assertion does however remind us that—as Paul himself was always aware—the Apostle of the Gentiles was not at any disadvantage vis-a-vis the Twelve in urging his claim to equal status with them in what concerned his apostleship. He had had the same paschal experience as the Twelve, and he had, as they, been commissioned in the same moment "to preach the gospel among the heathen" (Gal 1:16).

What then was Paul's attitude towards the traditions regarding the earthly life of Jesus? In the first place, he insists repeatedly upon the value of these traditions. He never tires of

[20] *Summa Theologica,* tertia pars, quaestio 55, art. 2 ad 1.

asserting that he himself *had received* them (he employs Greek terms which correspond to the technical Hebrew terminology, "receive from", "hand on", in use among the rabbis). "I myself received from the Lord" (1 Cor 11:23, 15:3, Gal 1:12) is a statement Paul evidently considered of the highest moment. This repeated assertion by Paul reveals his conviction that the authority behind the gospel tradition is none other than that of the risen Lord Jesus. The Pauline narrative of the institution of the Eucharist speaks of "how *the Lord Jesus* on the night he was handed over took bread . . ." (1 Cor 11:23). Paul's consciousness that, while he was not an eyewitness of what Jesus had said and done, he had been granted an experience of these things in the Spirit, explains his puzzling remark to the Galatian communities. "I remind you, brothers, that the gospel preached by me is not any human thing. I neither received it from any man, nor was I taught it, but [I received it] *through a revelation of Jesus Christ*" (Gal 1:11-12). There is no contradiction between this strong asseveration and Paul's habit of acknowledging himself to have been a recipient of the gospel tradition. The "revelation of Jesus Christ" is of course his encounter on the Damascus road, which imparted to him his Christian faith and his apostolic commission. Paul's consequent reflection of faith upon the data of the tradition which "he himself *received*," gave him an experience *in the Spirit* of what Jesus had said and done during his earthly life. It was this precious experience, the fruit of the activity of the risen Lord through his Spirit in Paul, which was truly "a revelation of Jesus Christ." Without this, the mere knowledge of "Christ according to the flesh" (2 Cor 5:16), or of "the historical Jesus" in modern terminology, would be simply a barrier to his personal relationship of faith. So it had in fact been proven to be for Paul before Damascus. Paul does indeed clearly recognize the significance of the earthly life of Jesus by his repeated insistence that he had "received" the earlier traditions regarding it. The fact remains that "the historical Jesus" was never for Paul the *adequate* object of Christian faith, any more than for those writers who composed the accounts of Jesus' earthly life in the Gospels.

V
PAUL'S CONVERSION AS A NEW CREATION

We must return, after a long if very necessary digression, to the consideration of Paul's interpretations of his confrontation with the risen Lord on the Damascus road. There is an important allusion to this event in Paul's lengthy exposition of his understanding of his own apostleship in his second letter to Corinth (2 Cor 2:14–6:13). The development is governed by two polarities: Paul's total unpreparedness, unworthiness, weakness, and God's absolute, infinite, creative power. On the one hand, no man is equal (Paul least of all) to such a divine calling (2:16); the necessary qualifications can only come from the favour of God (3:4-6); Paul's commission is in fact an act of the divine mercy (4:1), for he is like a fragile earthenware vessel that carries such a treasure (4:7). All he can hope to do is to avoid giving offence in any way (6:3), to recommend himself by steadfast endurance (6:4) and a host of other virtues (all gifts of the Holy Spirit [6:6-7]), displayed amid the vicissitudes and perils of life (6:8-10).

There is however another aspect of Paul's apostleship: it bears the divinely indelible mark of God's graciousness (2:14). Through his union with Christ the apostle shares in God's triumphal procession (2:14); he is the "sweet fragrance" offered to God by Christ (2:15), a divinely qualified minister of the new covenant (3:6), whose glory eclipses the splendor of the old economy reflected on the face of Moses (3:7-11). Through his union with Christ the apostle has indeed become nothing less than "a new creation", since "all this comes from God" (5:18). He is an ambassador for Christ, through whom God himself exhorts his hearers (5:20). Such is the lofty concept of God's *graciousness* that is Paul's, a graciousness totally unwarranted, particularly in his own case, which he first experienced through his meeting with the risen Christ on the Damascus road. For this reason, in the midst of this whole development on the significance of his apostleship, Paul compares

that confrontation with Christ to God's creation of light, recorded on the first page of the Bible (Gen 1:3).

"The God who said, 'Light shine out of darkness,' is [the
same] who shone in our hearts [to effect] the illumination of
the knowledge of God's glory upon the face of Christ" (2
Cor 4:6). In the beginning of this fourth chapter we find a
reference to the historical moment on the Damascus road when
Paul was given his apostolic commission, which he acknowledges to have been the effect of the divine mercy: "holding
this commission, which we owe to an act of the mercy of God"
(4:1). At that moment, "we renounced the things men hide
for very shame" (cf. Rom 6:21). As a consequence Paul is
always conscious, when preaching "the word of God", that
he stands "in God's presence" (v.3), since it is God himself
who is the source of "the illumination of the gospel of the
glory of Christ, who is the image of God" (v.4). This divine
act of illumination comes through the gift of Christian faith
enabling him to accept the gospel. Paul speaks of "the gospel
of the glory of Christ" since it is "the proclamation of Jesus
Christ as Lord" (v.5). It is as "the last Adam" (1 Cor 15:45)
that the glorified Jesus has become "the image of God" (2 Cor
4:4). Because he presents the gospel, which he was commissioned to preach by an act of God's mercy at the beginning of
his Christian life, as the illuminating action of God himself,
Paul is led to compare the moment when the risen Christ first
appeared to himself with the divine creative activity, whereby
God brought light into being by his word. It was the same God
who declared, "Let there be light" (Gen 1:3) who caused the
illumination of faith in Paul's innermost being, when he received "the knowledge of God's glory" which he beheld "upon
the face of Christ", who met him on the Damascus road.

Paul is the first New Testament thinker to employ the
imagery of creation, especially that found in the opening
chapters of Genesis, in his exposition of the Christian mystery of
the redemption.[21] In the passage under consideration the commissioning of an apostle is compared to the creation of light,

[21] D. M. Stanley, "Paul's Interest in the Early Chapters of Genesis,"
Analecta Biblica 17 (1963), 241-252.

because the apostle's primary task is to preach the gospel (1 Cor 1:17), and because, on the occasion of its proclamation, God himself remains always the author of that "illumination" of faith making possible the reception of the message by the believer.

There is still another reason for Paul's comparison. On the Damascus road he himself received the divine illumination through his confrontation with the risen Christ upon whose face he then beheld "the glory of God". This experience strikes Paul as a creative act of God because he is always intensely aware that there was nothing in himself or in his previous life as a Pharisee that could adequately account for this signal favour. It was totally an act of the *graciousness* of God the Father, springing from his entirely free love of predilection by which he chose and called Paul as apostle of the Gentiles. The Twelve had been prepared for the gift of paschal faith after Jesus' resurrection by their association with him during his public ministry. Paul considered that in his own case nothing in his former way of life prepared him for the grace of Christian faith: all his old religious practices, sincere and zealous as they had truly been, were simply "loss with respect to Christ" (Phil 3:7). Thus his coming to the Christian faith was of its very nature in Paul's eyes, because of his deep awareness of his total unpreparedness in contrast with the Twelve, a preparation for his ministry to the Gentiles whose chief characteristic was their lack of knowledge even of the true God of Israel and of his Son, Jesus Christ.

VI
THE REVELATION OF GOD'S SON

There is a final passage in Paul's letters which gives an interpretation of the momentous meeting near Damascus, that is of superlative value in providing an insight into Paul's prayer. It occurs in the highly polemical section of the most angry letter of his that has survived, that to the churches he had founded in Galatia. Paul is concerned to defend the uniquely

divine origin of his call as an apostle and his conviction that
he had been entrusted with his gospel "through a revelation by
Jesus Christ" (Gal 1:12). He was attacked by certain judaizing
Christian missionaries for not conceding to the Mosaic Law a
necessary role in the acquisition of salvation. And indeed Paul
reaffirms this position unambiguously in Galatians.

However, as Günther Bornkamm has recently pointed out
most perceptively,[22] Paul's adversaries surely did not accuse
him of a too great dependence upon the apostles in Jerusalem.
Such an idea would have seemed preposterous to them. Paul's
insistence upon the rarity of his communications with Jerusalem
did not spring from any disregard for the traditions concerning
Jesus' earthly life of which "the pillars" (Gal 2:9) were the
responsible guardians. It is more plausible to assume that Paul
wished to avoid a clash with the Jewish Christians in the
mother church, who had not yet perceived the inconsistency
(and the eventual incompatibility) between continuing to ad-
here to the Mosaic institutions and the exercise of true freedom
in Christ. What is crucial for a correct understanding of Paul
and of particular relevance for our investigation into his prayer
is to see clearly that he never depreciated in any way the value
of the traditions regarding Jesus' earthly life, transmitted by the
primitive community of Jerusalem to himself and others. To
imagine that Paul's gospel diverged from that created by the
Twelve, because Paul restricted himself to what he had learned
of Christ at his conversion or through other visions, is to make
Paul a crank and an "enthusiast". What is worse, it is to con-
tradict his own most emphatic asseveration that "there is no
other gospel" (Gal 1:6-9).

What in fact does Paul assert about that conversion in his
apologia pro vita sua in his letter to the Galatians? "When it
pleased him, who set me apart from my mother's womb and
called me through his graciousness, to reveal his Son in me,
in order that I might gospel him among the Gentiles . . ."
(Gal 1:15-16). Paul remained very much aware that the
revelation that Jesus Christ was the Son of God involved a
totally new disclosure concerning the God he had worshipped

[22] Günther Bornkamm, *op. cit.*, p. 18.

and served as a Jew. "The God" (as Paul often calls him), the God of Israel, the God of the patriarchs, was revealed to him as "the Father of our Lord Jesus Christ" (2 Cor 1:3; 11:31; Rom 15:6; Col 1:3; Eph 1:3). Once, in fact, Paul calls him "the God of our Lord Jesus Christ" (Eph 1:17).

It is highly important for a correct assessment of Paul's relationship to God the Father to appreciate how radically his conception of the God of Israel was transformed by his meeting with the glorified Son of God.[23] This is not to say that Paul rejected the God of the Old Testament. Paul never evinced the attitude to "the Scriptures", which was later displayed by the heretic Marcion. His conviction as a Christian that God's way of dealing with man was fundamentally the same under the new as under the old covenant is manifested continually in his repeated citations of Israel's sacred books. Still, the fact that Paul was the one who coined the phrase "the Old Testament" (2 Cor 3:14) exemplifies how profoundly altered was his view of God after he became a Christian.

There is no title for God in Paul's letters that he employs with such frequency as "Father". Not only is God "the Father of our Lord Jesus Christ", he is "our Father" (thirteen times), as he is simply "Father" (twenty-one times). Nor is Jesus Christ alone called "the Son of God" (eighteen times); Christians are "sons of God" (Gal 3:26; 4:7; Rom 8:14, 19; 9:26), "sons and daughters" of God (2 Cor 6:18), "God's children" (Phil 2:15; Rom 8:21; 9:8, 36). For Paul, he is "our God" (1 Thes 2:2; 3:9; 1 Cor 6:11; Eph 5:20), "my God" (Phil 1:3; 4:19; 2 Cor 12:21; Rom 1:8).

The feeling of loving intimacy with and confidence in God, which this usage reveals, demonstrates how profoundly Paul recognized his relationship with the God of his fathers to have

---

[23] Thus it is difficult to accept without certain distinctions the view expressed by Msgr. L. Cerfaux, "Paul is and he remains a Hebrew and a Jew, by race and by religion," *Le Chrétien dans la théologie paulinienne* (Paris, 1962), p. 70. The remark of Eduard Freiherr von der Goltz, *Das Gebet in der ältesten Christenheit* (Leipzig, 1901), p. 106, deserves to be cited: "Paul does not pray to the 'God of Abraham, Isaac, and Jacob,' but to the 'Father of our Lord Jesus Christ.' He does not recall God's saving acts for Israel, but the redemption in Christ Jesus."

been altered. In contemporary Judaism God was rarely invoked in prayer as Father. It is true that in the Hebrew Scriptures the covenant-relationship of God with his people was described as one of a father to his son. "Israel is my first-born son" (Ex 4:22); "Out of Egypt I called my son" (Hos 11:1); "I have become a father to Israel, and Ephraim is my eldest son" (Jer 31:9). God's relationship to Solomon is described as that of father (2 Sam 7:14; 1 Chr 17:13; 22:10; 28:6; cf. Ps 2:7). It is indicative however of the change in attitude in late Judaism, motivated by reverence for God, that the Greek translators of the Scriptures in the centuries immediately preceding the Christian era found such expressions too bold. Accordingly they rendered 2 Sam 7:14 as "I shall be *like* a father to him, and he will be *like* a son to me". This same minimizing expression is read in the translation of Jeremiah 31:9 and the texts of 1 Chronicles already referred to above, while the text of Hosea 11:1 is profoundly modified: "Out of Egypt have I summoned his children". Only in the Greek version of the third Isaiah has a straightforward assertion of God's fatherhood of Israel been allowed to stand: "You are our Father" (Is 63:16; 64:7).

In the psalms the image of father is applied only rarely to God: "Father of the fatherless" (Ps 68:6); "As a father has pity on his children, so the Lord takes pity on all who fear him" (Ps 103:13). David is pictured as declaring to God, "You are my father", while God in turn promises, "I will call him my first-born son" (Ps 89:26-37). Ps 2:7 represents God as announcing to the newly anointed Israelite king, "You are my son: this day have I begotten you".

It has been claimed, and with good reason, that Paul's prayer was influenced by the Psalter.[24] The piety of Judaism was nourished by this collection of hymns and prayers. As a fervent Pharisee (Phil 3:5; Gal 1:14), Paul would undoubtedly have made constant use of the psalms in his devotional life. The characteristically Pauline expression, "My God"

---

[24] Carl Schneider has written perceptively on Paul's prayer against the background of contemporary Judaism and Hellenistic religion in an article, "Zwei Paulusstudien" *Angelos* 4 (1932), 11-47.

(Phil 1:3; 4:19; 2 Cor 12:21; Rom 1:8), rarely found elsewhere in the New Testament, occurs relatively often (some fifty-six times) in the Psalter. Paul describes God in phrases reminiscent of the psalms. He is "the God of compassion" (2 Cor 1:3; Rom 12:1; cf. Phil 3:1), "the God of peace" (1 Thes 5:23; Phil 4:9; 1 Cor 14:33; 2 Cor 13:11; Rom 15:33; 16:20), "the God of consolation" (2 Cor 1:3; Rom 15:1); he is "faithful" (1 Cor 1:9; 10:13; 2 Cor 1:18; Rom 3:3). Paul's God is "the God of mercy" (Phil 2:27; Rom 9:15, 16, 18; Eph 2:4), for Paul, like the psalmists, thinks of himself as a specially favoured recipient of divine mercy (1 Cor 7:25; 2 Cor 4:1).

However, the divine titles most characteristic of the Psalter are notably absent from the Pauline letters: "king", "rock", "the highest", "the holy". "Lord", in constant use in the Greek Psalter as a surrogate for the unpronounceable divine name, is transferred by Paul to the risen Christ. The divine name "Saviour" is used but once by Paul, who applies it to the parousiac Christ (Phil 3:21). Rarely does he speak of God as the one who judges (1 Cor 5:13; Rom 2:16; 3:6).

What distinguishes Paul's approach to God from that of the psalmists, however, is the dominance of the image of God as Father. God remains for him above all "our Father and the Father of our Lord Jesus Christ". This conception, which would have struck Paul's Jewish contemporaries as bordering on irreverence for the divine majesty and transcendence, was an integral part of the revelation communicated to the Apostle through his first meeting with the risen Son of God. This realization, that God is above all *Father,* transformed Paul's prayer. It would moreover govern his later theological reflection on the redemption, as we shall presently have occasion to see.

Gal 1:15-16 makes it abundantly clear that if it was the risen Christ who confronted Paul near Damascus, he was convinced that this meeting and the far-reaching consequences it held for him were the effect of the initiative taken by God the Father. It was the Father who—solely from his own good pleasure—had set Paul apart from the very beginning of his existence, who now called him "by his graciousness" to the

Christian faith and appointed him apostle to the heathen. Paul did not see the Father either on this occasion or subsequently during his life. Yet this experience was revealed to him as the result, primarily, of the Father's choice and his dynamic action upon himself. Still, if Paul customarily attributes his vocation to the Christian faith, his mission as apostle of the pagans to the Father, he is also aware of the active part played by the glorified Christ. He consistently calls himself "apostle of Jesus Christ" (1 Cor 1:1; 2 Cor 1:1; Col 1:1; Eph 1:1). In fact, he considers his appointment to have come from them both: he is "apostle . . . through Jesus Christ and God the Father, who raised him from death" (Gal 1:1). He can assert that "Christ sent me to preach the gospel, not to baptize" (1 Cor 1:17). He speaks of his own powers as apostle as "the authority which the Lord gave me" (2 Cor 13:10). He insists that the gospel which he proclaims he had received "through a revelation by Jesus Christ" (Gal 1:12). Thus while Paul recognizes that in all this the initiative belonged to God the Father, the Son was also actively engaged in making him what he was.

One arresting phrase in Gal 1:15-16 is particularly worthy of attention. Paul states that God was pleased "to reveal his Son *in* me". "In me" conveys that sense of personal intimacy with Christ which is reflected elsewhere in Paul's letters by the very frequent expression "in Christ", "in Christ Jesus". It also highlights Paul's consciousness of the abiding character of Christ's presence. Subsequently in this same letter (Gal 2:20), Paul describes with great feeling his appreciation of the new life imparted to him by the Damascus experience. "It is no longer I that live—Christ lives in me!" It is nothing less than this that "my life of faith in my present bodily existence" means for the Apostle. It is, as he well knows, the most highly prized benefit God has conferred on him: "*the* charism of God is eternal life in Christ Jesus our Lord" (Rom 6:23). In the passage under consideration, Paul adds, "I will not repudiate the graciousness of God" (Gal 2:21). The inauguration and the continuance of his Christian life are to be ascribed, in Paul's view, to the initiative of the Father and the activity of the risen Lord. It would not be inaccurate to say that he considers that the presence within him of the living Christ *is* the powerful, dynamic presence of the Father in his Christian life. To live "in Christ Jesus" is in fact "living for God" (Rom 6:11).

Paul's more customary manner of expressing this union with the risen Son of God, as we have said, is to be found in his characteristic phrase "in Christ". It is this vital, intense awareness of his relationship with the Christ he had met on the Damascus road which keeps him continually aware of the presence of God while engaged in his apostolic ministry. "It is as coming from God that we, in Christ, proclaim (the word) in the presence of God" (2 Cor 2:17). "In God's presence we speak in Christ" (2 Cor 12:19). For the ancient Israelite the presence of God was concretized in the sanctuary and the cultus, the locus of those theophanies so often commemorated in the psalms (Ps 48:12-14; 24:7-9; 29:9-10; 114:4-8). For Paul the presence of God was experienced as a powerful reality in the initial manifestation of himself by the exalted Lord Jesus, which inaugurated his apostolic career by leading him to the Christian faith.

The dimensions of the experience which brought Paul the Christian faith, expressed in this last reference to it in his letters (Gal 1:15-16), had a profound impact upon Paul's prayer. That God has revealed himself as the Father of Jesus by raising him from death, that he is also revealed as "our Father" through the interpersonal union of faith between the risen Lord and the believer (Gal 3:26), that Jesus Christ has been disclosed as Son of God by his redemptive death and resurrection, are all aspects of Christian belief which are accorded a prominent part in Paul's prayer. That prayer in fact, orientated to the Father through the Son by the dynamism of "the Spirit of his Son" (Gal 4:6), had as its principal function to create a deeper and deeper experience of what it means to be a "son" or "child" of God. This filial attitude expressed itself tirelessly in acts of faith and love. It was moreover sustained by hope that the Father would bring to its fulfilment that "adoptive filiation" (a uniquely Pauline word) imparted through baptism by the future "redemption of our body" (Rom 8:23). The eschatological element so characteristic of Paul's prayer is dominated by this specific hope.

VII

An Interpretation by One of Paul's Contemporaries

We cannot leave our discussion of the meaning for Paul's prayer of his conversion-experience without mentioning the impression which the traditions regarding it made upon Paul's contemporaries. We have a precious record of this in Luke's book of Acts. This interpretation of what happened near Damascus is a highly personal one and Luke has chosen to present it three times in his book through the medium of a literary form, already familiar from its use in the Old Testament, as Dr. Gerhard Lohfink has recently shown in a brilliant monograph.[25]

Our own interests at present compel us to content ourselves with pointing out two themes, dominant in Luke's presentation of sacred history both in his Gospel and in Acts, which are operative in his interpretation of Paul's conversion. Luke is celebrated for the interest he displays in prayer; he is no less celebrated for his interest in the Church. The salient feature of the construction he has put upon Paul's meeting with the risen Lord near Damascus is its ecclesial character. This may be seen by the scrap of dialogue between Paul and Christ which is the one element common to all three Lucan narratives (Acts 9:4-5; 22:7-8; 26:14-15). "Saul, Saul, why do you persecute me?"—"Who are you, Lord?"—"I am Jesus whom you are persecuting".

On this view the great revelation is the identity of this obviously divine being *in some mysterious way* with the followers of the rabbi Jesus whom Saul had wished to exterminate. It would be an exaggeration to conclude that Luke wished to in-

[25] Gerhard Lohfink, *Paulus vor Damaskus* (Stuttgarter Bibel-Studien 4) (Stuttgart, 1967), pp. 53-60.

sinuate that Paul realized here the great truth he would express years later, that the Christians are members of Christ's body (1 Cor 12:12-27). Luke does state that Paul was given to see that in attacking "the way" (Acts 9:2) he was attacking the "Lord". What should be noted is that, in Luke's eyes, this truth was communicated to Paul by means of another self-identification by Christ. This glorified divine being announced his identity with Jesus of Nazareth, an insight which was to have a marked effect upon Paul's approach to Jesus' earthly life. For, as we have seen Paul himself insist, the sayings and actions of Jesus remained always for Paul the sayings and actions of the risen Lord. Moreover, as will be seen, it was always through Christ and by reason of their common union with Christ that Paul would address his fellow-Christians in his letters, after having prayed on their behalf through Christ to the Father, whom he could call to witness "how I long for all of you in the heart of Christ Jesus!" (Phil 1:8).

There is an interesting detail in Luke's first narrative of Paul's conversion which may well reflect a personal reminiscence by the man who baptized Paul. Ananias is directed to approach the blinded Saul, who after his confrontation with Christ had been led into Damascus to the house of a certain Judas "in the street named Straight". Ananias is dispatched with the words, "Note, he is praying" (Acts 9:11). This for Luke was the means of recognizing Saul; his conversion had resulted, even before his baptism, in prayer. That Luke has recalled this relationship between Paul's experience and his prayer is significant. For Luke and for Paul's contemporaries he was above all a man of prayer. Throughout Acts Paul is represented as having recourse to prayer: in the jail at Philippi (Acts 16:25), at his leave-taking in Ephesus (Acts 20:36), on his return to Jerusalem (Acts 22:17), during the shipwreck at sea (Acts 27:29).

Luke's hint that Ananias identified Paul by the fact that he was praying as a result of his conversion to Christ suggests that the practice and love of prayer was the one personal treasure that Paul preserved from his religious past as a Jew. As a Pharisee he believed in the resurrection of the dead and shared the missionary zeal (Gal 1:14) which characterized that group. I suggest however that the most important link between his Christian life and Pharisaism was that devotion to prayer for which the Pharisees were rightly celebrated and held in esteem among their people. If one may conjecture about Paul's preparation for the overpowering event which changed his life, surely the chief element was prayer.

Chapter 2
Experiences Related to
Paul's View of Prayer

In the course of his letters Paul makes references to several experiences, in addition to his conversion, which will be seen to have affected his own life of prayer, or to explain the importance he attaches to prayer in the Christian life, or to account for the prominence of specific elements in his own practice and teaching regarding prayer, such as gratitude and petition. The special value of these episodes for our investigation lies in the interpretation which Paul himself puts upon them. Moreover, the fact that he is still reflecting upon them years after they happened, employing what he has thus learned to new situations, indicates the formative influence which they exercised on his attitudes to the Christian life and to prayer.

Despite the obscurities and uncertainties which attend any attempt to disentangle the chronology of Paul's life, the relative position of the incidents in which we are interested can be demonstrated with a fair degree of certainty. It will be observed that all of them, with the exception of the severe crisis which confronted him at Ephesus (2 Cor 1:8-10), had occurred well before Paul wrote any of his letters. The first of these, a mystical experience of the highest order, happened some fourteen years before the writing of the letter in which he records it (2 Cor 12:2), that is, about 42 A.D. The meaningful experience in prayer occasioned by "the thorn for the flesh" (2 Cor 12:7-10) would appear, from Paul's own indication, to belong approximately to the same period of his life. His clash with Peter at Antioch, which provides the occasion for his description of his gospel to the Galatians (Gal 2:15-21) many years later, may be plausibly assumed to have taken place about 49-50 A.D., if Paul's conversion be dated around 32-34. The grave threat of death which Paul faced at Ephesus, which, as will be shown, he still regarded as inevitably fatal to himself when he wrote 2 Corinthians, was caused by some death-dealing malady, which afflicted him around the years 56-57.

There were of course other significant influences which contributed to Paul's personal prayer and to his teaching on the subject. The most important of these undoubtedly lay in the traditions regarding the role of prayer in Jesus' earthly life and his instructions on prayer, now recorded in the Gospels, to his disciples. Paul's familiarity with the teaching of Jesus on prayer is perceptible in his esteem for petitionary prayer (Mt 11:24), his earnest exhortations to unceasing prayer (Lk 18:1-8), and the high value he places on prayer for others (Mk 9:29; Mt 5:44; Jn 17:9-12, 20-23). Public worship, particularly the Eucharistic liturgy, had also its part to play in Paul's prayer-life (1 Cor 11:28-34; 14:18-19), and its influence upon the priority which he spontaneously gave to thanksgiving will be examined in another chapter.[1] As a devout Pharisee Paul must have been inspired in his prayer by the Psalter, as we have seen from the occasional traces of its effect upon the articulation of his prayers.[2]

I
"Visions and Revelations by the Lord"
(2 Cor 12:1-6)

The principal problem which confronts the inquirer into Paul's prayer is the apostle's great reticence with respect to his own interior life. If this is true of the more normal forms of

---

[1] See Chapter Five, pp. 135-136.

[2] R. Travers Herford, *The Pharisees* (London, 1924), p. 161: "The essentials of prayer were known in the experience of Pharisees and Rabbis . . . two great witnesses can be called . . . The Book of Psalms and the Jewish Liturgy. The former was arranged and in part composed by Pharisees, and the latter is the creation of the Rabbis; both, therefore, the devotional expression of the Pharisaic mind."

prayer which Paul shared with other Christians of his own day, it should cause no surprise that he guarded the secret of those mystical graces with which he was favored with particular diligence. It is necessary however to discuss the sparse data which his letters provide regarding these extraordinary graces, in order to appreciate properly the figure of Paul as one of the greatest of Christian mystics. Père Joseph Bonsirven has rightly insisted on the importance, for an adequate understanding of Pauline theology, of being aware that Paul was actually more a mystic than a religious thinker. Since the term mysticism evinces a chameleon-like character in much modern writing, it is necessary to make clear from the outset the exact sense in which the word is being employed. Père Bonsirven has performed a service by giving an exact description of what he means by the mysticism of St. Paul. "The mystic in the proper sense is not necessarily one who has enjoyed ecstatic phenomena, received supernatural visions, or reacted docilely and passively to the divine action. He is rather a man who experiences habitually or sporadically an awareness of his own supernatural life, of his union with God. He is a man whose faith has become transparent through love. It is in just this sense that we class Paul among . . . the mystics of the first rank".[3]

We shall shortly have a chance to examine Paul's description of his union with God through Christ (Gal 2:19-21), which alone would qualify him as a mystic in the sense just defined. Is there however any indication from his letters of what one might call more dramatic mystical experiences? Certainly the initial confrontation with the risen Christ at his conversion can be classified as one of the great spiritual experiences in the history of Christian spiritually. Paul himself however, as is evident from the preceding chapter, considered it to belong to a different category. For him it was the last of the post-resurrection appearances of the risen Christ. Some commentators claim that Paul speaks of having experienced ecstasy by his remark at 2 Cor 5:13. "If we have been beside ourselves, it was in relation to God; if we are now in our right mind, it is

[3] Joseph Bonsirven, *L'Évangile de Paul* (Paris, 1948), p. 17.

for your good". The Greek word (*existēmi*), here rendered "be beside oneself", occurs nowhere else in Paul, and its precise meaning is obscure. From the context it would appear to be used here in the sense of "be insane", a charge doubtless made by Paul's adversaries.

There is a reference, unique in Paul's writings, to an extraordinary favor he had enjoyed, which must be considered a mystical grace of a high order (2 Cor 12:1-6). The chief interest which the narrative holds for us is the indication it provides that Paul was acquainted with the entire range of possibilities in Christian prayer. He was consequently keenly aware of the profound mystery which surrounds the reality of prayer. This no doubt explains why Paul almost never gives any direct hints about the nature of his own prayer. In describing the experience we are about to consider, he discloses actually very little of its precise character (2 Cor 12:5).

Before taking up Paul's narrative, it may be helpful to direct attention to a term which appears in it, that of "boasting", an expression characteristic of Paul as it is rare elsewhere in the New Testament (cf. Heb 3:6; Jas 1:9; 4:16). The metaphor is used by Paul to describe the religious life of the Christian, designated in the Fourth Gospel as the worship of God "in spirit and truth" (Jn 4:23-24). "We are the [true] circumcision, who worship God by his Spirit and found our boast in Christ Jesus, putting no confidence in the flesh" (Phil 3:3). The text indicates how central to Christianity, in Paul's eyes, is this practice of "boasting". It springs from the recognition by faith of God's activity in one's own life and in that of others. Thus Paul can frequently declare that he "boasts" of the communities under his care (1 Cor 15:31; 2 Cor 7:14; 8:23; 9:2-3). The fact that he looks forward to "boasting" of them before the supreme tribunal of Christ at the parousia reveals the eschatological character of this boasting (1 Thes 2:19; 2 Cor 1:14). God's gracious action in commissioning Paul as apostle provides grounds for the community's boast in himself (Phil 1:26). Accordingly, this boasting is closely related to those "confessions" of the mighty works of God which found a prominent place in the liturgy of the worshipping community of Israel (Ps 5:12; 149:5).

Rudolf Bultmann has drawn our attention to the element of thanksgiving in this Pauline boasting, thus providing an explanation for the prominence of this religious attitude in Paul's references to his own prayer. "A constituent element in all such glorying is that of confidence, joy, and thanksgiving, and the paradox is that the man who so glories looks away from himself, with the consequence that his glorying is a confession of God." [4] It would appear that "boasting" has replaced in Paul's writing the more common designations for the prayer of praise, found relatively rarely by name in his letters.[5]

One indicated source of this concept of "boasting in the Lord" is the text in Jer 9:22-23, alluded to twice by Paul (1 Cor 1:31; 2 Cor 10:17). "The wise man must not boast in his wisdom, nor the strong in his strength, nor the rich man in his wealth. Rather, it is in this that the one who boasts should boast: in understanding and knowing that I am the Lord, exercising mercy and judgment and justice on the earth, since in these things does my will consist."

One fairly extensive passage, which might be termed "Paul's boast" (2 Cor 10:7—12:10), abundantly illustrates the complexity and paradoxical nature of the Pauline notion. The issue with which Paul is concerned is the defence of his own apostolic authority, called into question by his opponents. Since he is intensely conscious that "the Lord has given" him the responsibility as well as the privilege of apostleship, Paul is prepared to run the risk of "boasting a little too much of my authority" (2 Cor 10:8). He remains faithful however to his principle of refusing to compare himself with others (cf. Gal 6:4), since his real aim is to praise and thank God, as well as to summon other men to the duty of praise and gratitude, for the divine graciousness towards himself, and through him,

[4] See the article, *kauchaomai*, etc. in *The Theological Dictionary of the New Testament*, G. Kittel, translated and edited by Geoffrey W. Bromiley, vol. III (Grand Rapids, 1965), p. 647.

[5] See p. 7.

towards the communities of which he has been given the charge (10:12-15). Thus it is seen, not as self-glorifying, but rather as "boasting about the Lord" (10:17).

At the same time Paul appears to sense a certain "folly" (11:1) in his boasting. "What I say is not according to the Lord; rather [it is asserted] through folly by this confidence in boasting" (v.17). Still, because he is forced by the Corinthians' criticism "to play the fool", as he will state somewhat later (12:17), Paul enumerates an impressive list of the many dangers and sufferings he has undergone (vv.23-27), to which are appended his more interior trials (vv.28-29). He instinctively feels, however, that "if it is necessary to boast, I shall boast of my weakness" (v.30). To illustrate his meaning he presents a lively picture of the somewhat ludicrous manner of his escape from Damascus under King Aretas (vv.32-33).

At this juncture in his development Paul appears to return to a more positive view of boasting. "It is necessary to boast! It yields no advantage, but I shall come to visions and revelations by the Lord" (12:1). The meaning of this verse is obscure, since the original text is probably impossible to restore. It is evident that Paul broaches these hitherto scrupulously guarded secrets with the greatest reluctance. In fact, before he is well launched on his disclosure, he suddenly breaks off abruptly. "However I omit mention [of such things], lest I be esteemed beyond what any man can actually see in me or hear from me" (v.6). Yet Paul does not interrupt his narrative before he has revealed to his readers the precious grace he was once given.

2 "I know a man in Christ, who was, some fourteen years ago, caught up to the third heaven—whether in the body or without the body I do not know, God knows! 3 Yet I do know that this man—whether in the body or without the body I do not know, God knows!—4 was caught up to paradise. And he heard things too sacred to utter, which are not permitted to human tongue to repeat" (vv.2-4). Paul tells what he does simply because he realizes that *"it is necessary to boast"*, (v.1), that is, it is God's will that he should publicly acknowledge with

deepest gratitude such signal favors as he has received, in order to defend his authority as an apostle. At the same time, he asserts that "it yields no advantage". This may be taken to mean that it produces no *spiritual* advantage to himself, the sense which the expression has elsewhere in Paul (1 Cor 6:12; 10:23; 12:7) and in the New Testament (Mt 19:10). Such mystical graces as Paul received are no necessary index of the personal holiness of the recipient; yet they are given in view of some task to be performed for the good of the Church (2 Cor 10:8). Paul is certainly not insensitive to the fact that "boasting" could indicate the sin of presumption (1 Cor 4:7), particularly in the religious sphere (Rom 2:17, 23).

Paul had announced his intention of speaking of "visions and revelations" accorded him by the risen Christ. Actually he relates nothing of what he saw, and seemingly he makes reference to but a single "revelation". The experience is described in the language of Jewish apocalyptic as a kind of "ascension". Yet the sobriety of the narrative contrasts sharply with the extravagant fantasy of the ascension of Henoch and other figures in inter-testamental literature.[6] Nor does Paul's account suggest any affinity with contemporary Hellenistic mysticism. As Alfred Wikenhauser has pointed out, "The experience has no connection with salvation." [7] Paul does not in fact suggest in any way that he was actually admitted to the vision of God. His remark, "Whether in the body or without the body I do not know", reflects simply the irrelevance of such a consideration so far as Paul is concerned. He is very much aware that ordinary sense perception is of no avail in an experience of this kind. The value of this rapture to "the third heaven", or to

[6] See "Book of Enoch", 16-16 in R. H. Charles, *The Apocrypha and Pseudepigrapha of the Old Testament in English* (Oxford, 1913), pp. 196-199. Also in the same volume there is the text of a Jewish work, revised by a Christian hand, "The Greek Apocalypse of Baruch, or III Baruch", (pp. 533-541), in which Baruch is translated to the fifth heaven.

[7] Alfred Wikenhauser, *Pauline Mysticism* (New York, 1960), p. 218; he adds, p. 222, "It must be borne in mind that Paul makes no mention of a revelation of God or of Christ; what he did experience were heavenly places and unutterable words . . .".

"paradise" can only be judged by Christian faith. It is to be noted, as Joseph Huby has pointed out,[8] that Paul employs auditory, not visual symbols for the terse description he gives of his experience. "He heard things too sacred to utter, which are not permitted to human tongue to repeat". Paul has elsewhere employed the image of hearing to describe the genesis of Christian faith (Rom 10:17).

There can be no doubt that Paul is here describing a singular mystical grace. He presents it as happening to "a man in Christ", whom he rhetorically distinguishes from himself. To interpret what is a literary conceit in psychological terms, as proof of a split personality, is to go beyond the evidence. Still, by speaking of himself as "a man in Christ" Paul clearly intends to assert considerably more than simply "a Christian". The phrase, "in Christ" carries a broad range of meaning for Paul.

It always designates the relationship of the believer to the risen Lord, which has been bestowed by faith and baptism (Gal 3:26-37); and thus frequently becomes the equivalent of "Christian" (1 Thes 2:14; Gal 1:22). It can also at times exhibit an ecclesial meaning (Phil 1:1; Gal 1:2), drawing attention to the unity of the Church (Gal 3:28). Occasionally, it manifests an eschatological dimension (Eph 2:6), although the future union of the believer with Christ in heaven is more regularly denoted by "with Christ" (1 Thes 4:14; 2 Cor 4:14). However Paul also employs "in Christ", or the equivalent "in him", (Phil 3:9) to underline a special awareness through faith of this union with Christ (1 Thes 4:18, Phil 2:5; 3:14; 2 Cor 2:17; 5:17; Rom 6:11; 8:39; 12:5).

This latter meaning, I suggest, is the one we are intended to take for the phrase "a man in Christ" in 2 Cor 12:2. Since it is question of the very unusual grace of "rapture", Paul is well aware that the favor bestowed on him is well beyond the normal Christian consciousness of union with the risen Lord. Moreover, it is this "ascension" *in Christ* which chiefly distinguishes

[8] Joseph Huby, *Mystiques paulinienne et johannique* (Paris, 1946), p. 120.

Paul's experience from anything remotely comparable in Jewish apocalyptic, or in the treatises on Hellenistic mysticism.

Thus it becomes possible to define, with some degree of verisimilitude, the character of this great mystical experience which Paul declares he enjoyed. Through his union with Christ he has been given an experiential knowledge of Jesus' glorification. Even if, as he admits, he is incapable of articulating the insight given him into this mystery of Jesus' exaltation, the experience undoubtedly had some influence upon his subsequent theological thought. It is probably no accident that he couples with this narrative the account of another divine favor (2 Cor 12:7-10), which we shall see exerted a formative influence on his attitude to Jesus' earthly life.

Paul's mystical experience of the "ascension", together with the understanding he was afterwards given of the significance of weakness in the life of the incarnate Son of God "in the days of his flesh" (Heb 5:7), formed the foundation of a characteristically Pauline conception, that of "the Mystery", which constantly recurs in his letters. His use of this term owes nothing to the Hellenistic mystery religions [9], but comes out of the privileged graces bestowed on him in prayer. "The mystery of God" centers in "Jesus Christ and him crucified" (1 Cor 2:1-2). The risen Christ has become for Paul the concrete embodiment and so the revealer of "the mystery enshrouded in silence for countless ages, but now manifested through the writings of the prophets, made known by the decree of the eternal God to all the pagans for the obedience of their faith" (Rom 16:25-26). Later Paul will describe it very graphically in writing to the former pagans of the Colossian community as "Christ in you, the hope of glory" (Col 1:27). The revelation of this redemptive relationship of Christ to the whole of humanity, Jews as well as Gentiles, does not remove its essential character as "mystery".

This explains why ultimately Paul's description of his experi-

[9] Raymond E. Brown, "The Semitic Background of the New Testament Mysterion", *Biblica* 39 (1958), 426-448; 40 (1959), 70-87; "The Pre-Christian Semitic Concept of 'Mystery'", *Catholic Biblical Quarterly* 20 (1958), 417-443.

ence of the mystery of the "ascension" remains so tantalizingly obscure. It was not simply the result of self-consciousness or innate modesty in disclosing the divine favor, since Paul could have deleted these lines from his letter. Nor was it merely a fear that his "boasting" might be misconstrued as arrogance, since he leaves his readers in no doubt as to the extraordinary quality of the grace God had bestowed. It was rather his deep sense of the impenetrability of the mystery with which all Christian prayer is inextricably involved: the mystery of God's graciousness in redeeming man from sin and offering him in Christ a share in his own divine life as an adoptive son. This discretion in guarding the secrets of his own prayer-life creates, as we have said before, the chief difficulty for any inquiry into the meaning of prayer for Paul. It will accordingly be only indirectly and by inference, for the most part, that we shall be able to arrive at some comprehension of the form and content of Paul's prayer.

II
A Rare Glimpse of Paul's Personal Prayer

Paul's letters are indeed filled with many instructions on prayer, with repeated warnings about the necessity of constant prayer in the Christian life. Yet many passages in his letters which have been called prayers turn out, upon examination, to be in fact *reports* of his prayers for various communities. And these of course tell us only what Paul wants known about how he actually prayed. It may well be that his constant and careful circumspection, despite an apparent abundance of examples of his manner of prayer, can account for the very puzzling and wide divergence of opinion about certain aspects of Paul's prayer, which one might think ought to be easily ascertainable.

In what light, for instance, did Paul regard his relationship to God the Father? It was the contention of the late Dr. Albert Schweitzer that Paul's was a "Christ-mysticism", not a "God-mysticism".[10] On the other hand, there is a fairly strong conviction on the part of a number of Pauline scholars that Paul

---

[10] A. Schweitzer, *Die Mystik des Apostels Paulus* (Tübingen, 1930).

prayed only to God, not to Jesus Christ. The late Msgr. Lucien Cerfaux maintained this view in a most forthright manner.[11]

There is actually but a single narrative in all his correspondence where for a brief moment Paul may be seen to lift the veil guarding his personal prayer: 2 Cor 12:7-10. The passage is of special interest to us for several reasons. It is in the first place the record of a request made, not to the Father, but to the risen Lord. Secondly, it was a petition made with the greatest urgency at a most critical period, probably early in Paul's career as an apostle, when his effectiveness in carrying out his apostolic calling seemed to hang in the balance. Thirdly, Paul tells us that his plea was answered by Christ beyond, and indeed in a sense contrary to, his furthest expectations. This point must be insisted upon, as in the opinion of a good number of commentators, Paul did not actually obtain his request. As will become evident, Paul himself did not share this view. Moreover, there can be little doubt but that this experience, the recollection of which he so jealously guarded in the privacy of his own heart, impressed Paul with the absolute necessity of persevering, petitionary prayer, as also with its infallible efficacy. Finally, it gave him the strong conviction, which he would express many years afterwards, that "we do not know how to pray as it is necessary" (Rom 8:26).

A more positive aspect of this lesson which Paul learned deserves attention also. Despite the ineptitude and unawareness of the divine will for himself, which so frequently characterizes the prayer of most Christians, that prayer is always answered, and *in addition* the suppliant is shown *by the way his prayer is answered* the true sense, at first only dimly perceived (if at all), of what he was unwittingly praying for.

Paul's narrative appears as a kind of appendage to the lengthy development which we have termed "Paul's boast" (2 Cor 10:7—12:10). "And so, because of the superlative grandeur of these revelations,—lest I become unduly elated— there was given to me a thorn for the flesh, a messenger of Satan to pommel me—lest I become unduly elated" (2 Cor

---

[11] L. Cerfaux, "L'Apôtre en présence de Dieu", *Recueil Lucien Cerfaux*, II, pp. 475-477.

12:7). The "revelations" to which he refers were illustrated by the rapture or "ascension" examined in the preceding section. It is a question here of an exquisitely painful difficulty to which Paul was subjected by God. He avoids naming God explicitly from reverence, as was customary in late Judaism, by employing the passive "was given". It was through his prayer to be delivered from this trying situation that Paul had come to see the real source and the true purpose of this "thorn for the flesh", which was to ground him in trust in God and free him from relying on his own competence and drive, by giving him a personal experience of the weakness endured by Jesus himself during his earthly life.

The specific nature of the trial Paul endured is not disclosed by the narrative. Paul is concerned to present its meaning for himself by means of two symbols, both suggesting its traumatic, persistent, and evil character. He describes it as a thorn piercing the flesh and causing increased suffering as the wound festers. The word he uses meant in classical Greek a "stake" such as was used for impaling criminals. The term was in fact sometimes employed in connection with crucifixion, as in Origen's citation from the heretic Celsus.[12] Most modern translators and commentators however regard the metaphor in this passage as denoting a thorn.

The second symbol, "messenger of Satan", implies that Paul looked on this affliction, although ultimately caused by God, as something maleficent and the work of the devil. The Old Testament represented Job as being tested by God through the instrumentality of Satan (Jb 1:8-12; 2:1-10). Habitually Paul saw the activity of Satan behind the opposition to his work as an apostle. Thus in this letter he views his adversaries, the "pseudo-apostles" (2 Cor 11:13-14), as tools of the evil one. Earlier he had informed his Corinthian addressees that he had forgiven the man who offended him, in his official capacity as "the representative of Christ", and he adds his reason: "For fear we be outwitted by Satan, since we are not unacquainted

---

[12] W. F. Arndt and F. W. Gingrich, *A Greek-English Lexicon of the New Testament and Other Early Christian Literature* (Cambridge: Chicago, 1957), p. 763.

with his wiles" (2:10-11). Some years previously he had written to the Thessalonian community, attributing his inability to return to them in their need to Satan's thwarting of his plans (1 Thes 2:18). Accordingly, when Paul now ascribes his painful, perhaps also humiliating, certainly enduring ordeal to Satan's "messenger", he provides a clue to its nature from the viewpoint of faith. Whatever concrete form it may have assumed, it was something which seriously inhibited his work as an apostle. Thus Paul turned to Christ, whose ambassador he was (2 Cor 5:20), with every confidence that he would be free from what he considered a grave obstacle to the successful exercise of his ministry. Jesus himself had indicated during his own public life that he was the "stronger man" who had come to loot Satan's possessions (Mk 3:27). If we are to appreciate the scope of the lesson Paul learned on this occasion, we must must bear in mind how convinced Paul must have been of the propriety of his request and how confident that he would be delivered by his Lord from this critical situation.

Once the significance Paul saw in this grievous affliction has been grasped, the mere historical question of the concrete nature of this "thorn for the flesh" becomes secondary, even irrelevant. The various conjectures prompted by the curiosity of commentators remain very hypothetical. Was it the unremitting antagonism of some enemy, or was it a disease—eye-trouble, epilepsy, fever, hysteria? The magnitude and number of Paul's achievements in the apostolate after this period in his life, the punishment, physical and psychological, so successfully sustained from the elements or from human agencies, above all, the fact that Paul never mentions expressly any illness of a chronic kind to which he was subject during the years of his greatest activity, all these argue for a sound bodily and mental constitution in a man who lived to be some sixty years of age— a lifespan considerably beyond the average life-expectancy in the ancient world.

Much more to the point for a proper assessment of Paul's prayer to be rid of this frustrating obstacle is his clear and unequivocal assertion that his prayer was indeed answered (v.9). That his request was not granted in the way he had anticipated reveals how much Paul learned through this incident about the nature of petitionary prayer.

"Concerning this [adversary] three times I besought the Lord that he might withdraw from me" (v.8). Paul's description of the manner in which he made his plea deserves some scrutiny. He testifies that he prayed with earnestness and urgency, as well as with perseverance. The use here of the term "besought", instead of one of his more customary words for prayer, indicates the importunate nature of his request. Nowhere else does he use "beseech" to designate his prayer. It sometimes has the sense of "console", particularly in relation to God's activity (2 Cor 1:4; 7:6). Most frequently it describes his own solemn act of exhorting his communities as an apostle to greater fidelity in the living out of the gospel. That Paul uses the word here suggests that it was in his character as an apostle of Christ that he begged to be relieved of this impediment to his missionary task. The phrase "three times" implies his perseverance despite the fact that in the first two instances he received no answer. In the view of most commentators this "three times" is to be taken at face value, not as a symbolic number. Whether it is plausible to see in it a reminiscence of Jesus' threefold prayer in Gethsemane is a question to be examined shortly (Mt 26:44).

The image of the "thorn" does not reappear in Paul's account of his petition, which is expressed only in terms of the withdrawal of the Satanic attack on his ministry. This recalls Luke's remark at the close of his narrative of Jesus' temptations: "The devil withdrew from him until the appointed time" (Lk 4:15). Paul gives no hint that he pleaded simply to be rid of some natural disability or malady, nor does he suggest that it was an appeal for liberation from persecution. This latter, he was well aware, was in fact a proof of the authenticity of his apostolic commission (2 Cor 4:7-12). He "besought the Lord" because he was convinced that his effectiveness as an apostle was being seriously hampered. It may be that Paul here intimates that he was actually asking for an increase of faith and strength to cope with what he could only regard as a crippling handicap in his work.

Another significant feature of Paul's narrative, which cannot be permitted to pass unnoticed, is his clearly expressed conviction that the risen Lord did in fact answer his petition. "And he has given me his response, 'My graciousness is all you need, since [my] power is being brought to its perfection by [your] weakness' " (v.9). The use of the Greek perfect tense ("he has given me his response") shows not only that Paul recognized his prayer had been heard, but also that the response continued to have its promised effect until the present moment. Paul knows that the "graciousness" of Christ is much more than a benign attitude towards himself: it is an exercise of divine power. What Paul learned through this experience about this power of Christ was that, to be deployed with full effectiveness, it must be allowed to operate through the weakness of his apostle. Any merely human strength, springing from natural endowments, or competence, or experience, could only prove to be a barrier to the dynamism unleashed by God in the risen Christ. Already in this letter Paul has described himself as no more than an "earthenware vessel" enveloping the "treasure" of his apostleship. The image tells us how aware Paul was that "the transcendent power belongs to God and does not come from us" (4:7). He has well learned the lesson illustrated by the Johannine parable of the grain of wheat, which must die in order to produce a rich harvest (Jn 12:24). "Hence death is at work in us, but life in you" (4:12). Christ has answered his prayer, Paul knows, by giving him a new and deep sense of the power of the risen Lord at work in his apostolic activity.

This reply to his prayer brings to Paul two further graces. In the first place, he has been given an unshakable confidence in the effectiveness of unremitting petitionary prayer. Secondly, he feels a deep spiritual joy, one of the most highly prized fruits of the Spirit (Gal 5:22). "Therefore, most gladly will I boast in my weaknesses, in order that Christ's power may spread its tent over me. This is why I take delight in manifestations of weakness, in [bearing] acts of insolence, in hardships, in persecutions and frustrations, when they are endured for Christ, since it is when I feel my own weakness that I am powerful" (vv.9-10). Here we are given the reason why Paul has twice asserted that he will boast only of his own weakness

(11:30; 12:5): it is to magnify the power of Christ that is best exercised through that weakness.

Paul borrows from the Old Testament a meaningful symbol to represent the protection and security afforded by the dynamic presence of the glorified Lord Jesus, which he has continually felt in all the struggles of his missionary career. He compares its sheltering support with "the tent of the presence" (Ex 40:1 ff.), in which God had dwelt with Israel during her wandering in the desert. The author of the Fourth Gospel will make use of the same comparison (Jn 1:14), in order to express his conception of the new covenant embodied in Jesus Christ, the Word of God become man. For Paul the dynamism exercised in his life as an apostle by the risen Christ enables him to remain aware of God's presence continually. It is upon this sense of the nearness of God through Christ, "constituted Son of God in power by resurrection from the dead" (Rom 1:4) that Paul has built his prayer-life. Paul can "take delight" in the various manifestations of his own weakness, because they bring him the assurance of his Lord's assistance; and this in turn means that God himself has drawn near him, that Paul becomes more deeply aware that he stands always in the presence of God as he carries out the duties of his ministry.

This unique glimpse into Paul's own personal prayer indicates that this experience in fact bore a certain resemblance to Jesus' prayer and struggle in the garden, as that incident came to be interpreted by the New Testament writers who narrate it. It must be admitted that Paul's account of his urgent plea to Christ yields little, if any evidence that he ever thought of comparing this crisis in his own life with that of Jesus. There is however some evidence that this incident in Paul's life gave him a real experience of that weakness to which Jesus exposed himself during his mortal life; and this was exhibited most dramatically in Gethsemane on the eve of his passion. It is deserving of attention that, shortly after his account of how he was brought to see the redemptive meaning of his own weakness, Paul describes Jesus' life before and after his glorification in terms of weakness and power. "Truly he was crucified out of weakness, but he is alive by the power of God. And we in our turn experience weakness in him, but we shall live with him by the power of God [displayed] towards you" (2 Cor 13:4). Thus through his own experience of weakness and by the judgment he was able to pass on it with Christian faith Paul learned what he would henceforth regard as the salient feature of the life of the Son of God become man. This was his "poverty" (2 Cor 8:9), the result of his "emptying himself" (Phil 2:7), the consequence of his coming "in the likeness of sinful flesh" (Rom 8:3), of his being "made into Sin" (2 Cor 5:21). These bold expressions prove how deep was Paul's insight into the mystery of the incarnation, whereby the Son of God entered the sinful solidarity of the fallen human race in a most real manner.

It is this same problem, which can be a "scandal" or stumbling block for Christian belief in the divinity of Jesus Christ, that five inspired writers wrestle with in quite personal and independent fashion, as they narrate Jesus' prayer and struggle when he faced the dénouement of his earthly career (Mk 14:27-42; Mt 26:31-46; Lk 22:39-46; Jn 12:20-32; Heb 5:7-10). That none of these authors attempt to gloss over this paradoxical episode in Jesus' life proves how greatly they valued that touchstone of orthodox faith that "Jesus Christ has come in the flesh" (1 Jn 4:2). The sacred writers moreover indicate by their narratives that they treasured this painful demonstration of Jesus' humanity for its relevance to the practice of Christian prayer. In fact, this mysterious incident may be rightly gauged to have been regarded in the primitive Church as *the school of prayer* for all devout believers. Hence it is not surprising that the interpretations of Jesus' experience by the five New Testament authors provide certain parallels with Paul's account of his petition to be delivered from the "thorn for the flesh".

It is the narratives by Mark and Matthew which offer the closest parallels to Paul's account. It is these two evangelists alone who speak of Jesus praying "three times". This relatively superficial similarity yields in importance to a much more striking resemblance. By prefixing Jesus' prophecy of the scattering of the little band of loyal disciples to their narratives (Mk 14:27, Mt 26:41), these writers appear to indicate the symbolism they have seen in "the cup" from which Jesus recoiled when it was presented to him by his Father. The constancy and devotion to himself of this small group of companions was all that Jesus had to show for the labors and struggles of his public ministry as he approached the end of his mission on earth. What God was demanding of him was nothing less than the complete destruction of that mission by accepting to drink the cup of the passion. Mark and Matthew are alone in depicting Jesus as returning three times to speak with Peter, James, and John. What reason did these evangelists have for this construction? Surely it was not simply to imply that Jesus now sought comfort from the company of these sleeping followers. I venture to suggest that it was rather to underline Jesus' deep concern for the safety of his disciples, to make sure that for the moment at least they had not been dispersed. We have seen that Paul, like Jesus, urgently demanded to be rescued from what he regarded as a dire threat to the mission confided to him by Christ. Like Jesus also, Paul is led by persevering petition to recognize and accept the divine answer to his prayer, although it was so very different from what he had envisaged it might be. Like Jesus, Paul came to accept the supreme paradox of the gospel, embodied in the cross, that only by losing oneself and the achievement which self demands for its own fulfilment can the life of self be in reality saved (Mk 8:35).

III
INCIDENT AT ANTIOCH (Gal 2:15-21)

Acts informs us that the founding of the Christian community at Antioch in Syria was the result of a novel departure by Hellenist missionaries in the first years of the Church's existence. These men preached the gospel to pagans as well as to Jews upon coming to this city, the third or fourth greatest in the Roman empire (Acts 11:20-21). The church which emerged from this unprecedented step was of a very different

complexion from the entirely Jewish-Christian community of
Jerusalem, and from its inception it faced a problem without
parallel in the experience of the mother church of Christen-
dom. It was found necessary to establish an authentic Christian
fellowship by the integration of former pagans with converts
from Judaism. To achieve this important goal, the age-old
prejudice of former Jews, who had been brought up to look upon
all Gentiles as unclean and consequently to eschew fraterniza-
tion with them, had to be overcome. For his part, the new
Christian of pagan provenance had to be willing to make certain
concessions to Jewish-Christian sensibilities, especially in the
matter of food, in order to show his openness towards his
newly acquired Jewish brothers in Christ. It is quite probable
that the dietary and disciplinary regulations set forth at the
meeting of the apostolic group in Jerusalem some years after
the founding of Christian Antioch (Acts 15:28-29) stemmed
chiefly from the initiatives taken at Antioch; and these rules
were drawn up with a view to similar mixed Christian
congregations.

That the delicate question of integration within the member-
ship of the community was successfully solved at Antioch may
be inferred from Luke's remark that it was here "for the first
time that the disciples came to be called Christians" (Acts
11:26). A unique quality in this happy fellowship between two
groups formerly antagonistic to each other made the identity
of the Antiochian disciples readily discernible not merely from
their pagan neighbors, but also from the Jews. It would appear
from the passage in Galatians which we are about to consider
that the principal symbol of this novel Christian fellowship was
simply "to eat together" (Gal 2:12). It is difficult today perhaps to appreciate the momentous significance of this simple
action, particularly as in our culture there has never been any
sense of the religious meaning attaching to the taking of a meal,
as was prevalent in the ancient Near East. Barnabas, it would
seem (Acts 11:22-23), a man noted for his wisdom as for his
courage, and a leader in the Antiochian church (Acts 13:1),
took the lead in promoting this unheard of experiment in Christian *koinōnia*.

From the evidence at hand it would seem that the celebration of this common meal was not necessarily connected with the Eucharistic liturgy. This may be inferred from Paul's silence about "the Lord's supper", which he mentions in a similar situation at Corinth (1 Cor 11:20). It may be gathered moreover from the nature of his complaint against Peter for his action in withdrawing from the common meal, thus refusing to eat with former pagans. Paul accuses Peter of "forcing the Gentiles to judaize" (Gal 2:14), whereas he does not imply that Peter was guilty of irreverence, much less sacrilege, towards the Lord's body. Indeed, this strong indictment provides proof of the success of this symbolism of a common meal in this integrated church.

Paul's story of how he confronted Peter and reprimanded him for his vacillation at Antioch contains a twofold interest for our investigation. In the first place it gives a clear indication that, at least by the time Galatians was composed about 58 A.D., Paul considered that his entry into the Christian Church was a change of religion: his was a conversion in the full sense of that word. This point is of some importance as a number of scripturists incline to deny it,[13] despite Paul's unequivocal language in contrasting his religious life as a Jew with his Christian existence (Phil 3:7-9). Secondly, the passage ends with a description by Paul of what his life in Christ had come to mean to him, and thus it provides background for our understanding of Paul's prayer.

It should be borne in mind that what Paul here represents as a speech is not to be taken as an account of what he actually said on this occasion, or even as necessarily his recollection of what he had said to Peter years before. The contemporary imbroglio in the Galatian churches was Paul's chief preoccupation, and it is to them primarily that his words are addressed. These communities were predominantly, if not entirely, composed of converts from paganism, descendants of those Celtic immigrants from north-west Europe who had settled in Asia Minor some three hundred years previously. The crisis which

---

[13] L. Cerfaux, *Le Chrétien dans la théologie paulinienne* (Paris, 1961), pp. 68-71.

occasioned Paul's fiery letter to these young churches had been precipitated by the teaching in their midst of certain Jewish-Christian missionaries bent on inducing these former Gentiles to adopt, *as necessary for salvation,* the practices and pre-scriptions of the Mosaic Law. Paul saw at once that this un-orthodox claim was tantamount to a denial of the universal efficacy of Jesus' redemptive death, and he bent every effort to disabuse these Celtic Christians of their erroneous tendencies.

The contamination of the purity of the gospel in this manner was not a new phenomenon. It had already been essayed a decade or two previously by Jewish-Christian visitors to the mixed community of Antioch (Acts 15:1). Paul was reminded of the harm that had been done then, and of Peter's shilly-shallying during the crisis. He recalled too his own vindi-cation of the very principles under attack at the moment in Galatia. Thus in writing to these churches he was led to retro-ject into the historical context of his altercation with Peter, the arguments by which he sought to offset the propaganda of those who were now trying to force his Galatian converts "to judaize" (Gal 2:14).

Since Paul addresses himself in his letter to the danger to faith which threatens the Galatians, he insists very strongly upon the doctrine of justification by faith in Christ, which needs no assistance from the "works of the Law". This is in-deed a capital point in Paul's gospel: it is not however the sole, or the principal point. To single out this theorem, as many students of Paul incline to do, as the chief criterion of Chris-tian orthodoxy is to give an unbalanced view of Pauline theolog-ical thought.[14] By the time Paul will come to compose his

---

[14] W. D. Davies, *Paul and Rabbinic Judaism,* 2d edition (London, 1955), pp. 222-223: "It is a simplification and even a falsification of the complexity of Paul's thought to pin down Justification by Faith as its quintessence . . . the centre of that thought is to be found . . . in his awareness that with the coming of Christ the Age to Come had become present fact, the proof of which was the advent of the Spirit: it lies in those conceptions of standing under the judgment and mercy of a New Torah, Christ, of dying and rising with that same Christ, of undergoing a New Exodus in Him and of so being incorporated into a New Israel, the community of the Spirit." See also D. E. H. Whiteley, *The Theology of St. Paul* (Philadelphia, 1966), p. 160.

letter to the Romans he has recovered from the heat of controversy, and will be able to set forth a more equilibrated exposition of his gospel.

Paul represents himself in the passage in which we are interested as speaking to Peter, but he is actually engaging his Jewish-Christian adversaries who are disrupting the peace of mind of the Galatian converts. 15 "We were Jews by birth, not sinners from paganism. 16 Yet because we knew that a man is not proven upright through the works of the Law, but through faith in Jesus Christ, we too put our faith in Christ Jesus, in order that we might be proven upright through faith in Christ, and not through the works of the Law, since through the works of the Law 'no human being can be proven upright' " (Gal 2:15-16).

A distinction, then, is to be made between the acceptance of the gospel by Jews and the submission to it on the part of pagans. The Jews possessed the faith of Israel in the one true God, and were custodians of divine revelation as given through Moses and the prophets. They regarded the Gentiles as "sinners", not merely because of their sinful lives, but chiefly because of their total ignorance of "the oracles of God" (Rom 3:2). To embrace Christianity meant something very different for the Jews from what it implied in the case of the pagan, who had to "turn to God from idols, to serve the living God, the only one worthy of the name" (1 Thes 1:9). The Jew's conversion focussed on the total surrender of himself to Jesus Christ, as the agent of the fulfilment of the divine promises of salvation announced by the prophets.

Paul here throws a strong light upon the interpersonal nature of this new relationship to Christ, which had in fact revolutionized his own idea of religion and of God, by calling it literally "faith *into* Christ Jesus" (v.16). Elsewhere he sums up the total novelty of his attachment to Christ as Son of God by the formula, "Jesus is Lord!" (1 Cor 8:5-6; 12:3; 2 Cor 4:5; Col 2:6). Henceforth his relation to God, revealed to him at Damascus as "the God and Father of our Lord Jesus Christ" (2 Cor 1:3) is transformed by the Christian's incorporation "into Christ Jesus", the Son of God and his Lord.

The strange newness of the situation of the converted Jew is illustrated by Paul, for the purpose of controversy with the judaizers in Galatia, in terms of a vote of no confidence in "the works of the Law". This characteristically Pauline turn of phrase is not to be found in the Old Testament. It has however been discovered among the Qumran documents. Paul is not inveighing against "good works" as such, that is, the living out of the Christian life according to the "imperatives" communicated by faith and baptism (cf. Rom 6:12-23). The Catholic doctrine concerning merit is in no way contradicted by the statements of Paul. What he constantly opposes is the excessively legalistic attitudes to the fulfilment of the demands of the Law, prevalent in late Judaism. In that point of view such "works" were regarded as guaranteeing salvation as something upon which a man had an absolute claim. God was thus, so to say, put in the debt of him who performed what the Law prescribed. God was obliged to give such a one eternal life, not as a grace, but as his just deserts. Such a view came close to idolatry by making what is nothing more than a created reality, dependent upon God's graciousness, a religious absolute.

The Christian hope of being "proven upright" by God's creative declaration, which makes a man just in the divine sight, lies solely, Paul insists, in "faith in Christ". For it is only by this faith that the Christian is granted to participate in the redemptive death of Christ. This principle, which must remain operative through the entire course of Christian existence, must exercise a profound influence upon the prayer of the Christian. Prayer is not to be thought of as a kind of magic formula, automatically proving the uprightness of the Christian. Its efficacy, deriving from the redemptive work of Jesus Christ, springs from a vital faith, of which true prayer is an authentic expression.

Paul has now to meet an objection, which he had frequently encountered in his evangelizing. "But if by seeking to be proven upright through Christ, we ourselves were also shown to be sinners, does that make Christ an abettor of sin? God forbid!" (v.17). The gospel summons the Jew no less than the pagan to acknowledge his state of sinfulness and utter helplessness apart from Christ and his saving death (cf. Rom 2:1 ff.). The Jew is called upon to give up his wrongly placed confidence in the absolute efficacy of "the works of the Law" and give himself wholly to Jesus Christ. This is in fact how Paul understood his own conversion to have involved a complete reversal of his former religious values. The objection proceeds from the hidden presupposition of the judaizers, that the Mosaic Law still retains its prerogatives as the necessary means of salvation.

Paul now gives two answers in refutation of this erroneous point of view. In the first, he retorts that it is not Christ but the judaizer, whose real aim is to subject the Christian to the entire Law, that is truly the "abettor of sin". "Because if I now attempt to rebuild the structure that I pulled down, I really do admit that I am a sinner" (v.18). Some interpreters understand the statement to mean that a return to the practice of the Law would be tantamount to an admission of sin in having abandoned it for Christ. It is more probable that Paul has in mind here the impossibility of keeping the Law (cf. Gal 3:19; Rom 7:7-11), with the result that anyone returning to its practice becomes inevitably a transgressor of its demands.

Of particular interest to us is Paul's awareness that he has rejected his former way of life and has no intention of returning to it. The reversal of his religious values caused by his meeting with the risen Lord on the Damascus road must then be considered as a conversion to a new religion, even though, in the case of a pagan, it would mean something vastly different than what it had meant for Paul.

The second reason Paul advances, despite a certain difficulty in Paul's expression which makes his meaning hard to grasp, is a more satisfactory reply to the objection that has been raised. To abandon Judaism for Christianity is not simply a question of choosing a new religion in place of the old. It means acceptance of "faith into Christ Jesus" (v.16), who had actually been put to death by the Law as one "cursed" by it. "Christ redeemed us from the curse of the Law by becoming on our behalf a curse" (Gal 3:13). Thus the acceptance of the gift of Christian faith from God means ultimately to experience crucifixion with Christ crucified (Rom 6:3-4). For Paul belief in Christianity went beyond the rejection of the Law of Moses: it was incorporation into Jesus' death. "Hence, my brothers, you also were put to death to the Law through the body of Christ so as to belong to another—to him who was raised from death, in order that we might produce a harvest for God" (Rom 7:4). Paul states this same view to the Galatians: "Because through the Law I died to the Law, in order that I might live for God, that is, I was crucified together with Christ" (v.19).

In this conclusion Paul sketches a lively and very moving picture of his own personal Christian life. "It is no longer that I live—Christ lives in me. With regard to my present bodily existence, I live my life by faith in the Son of God, who loved me and handed himself over for my sake. I will not make void the graciousness of God! If uprightness is to be obtained through the Law, then truly Christ died to no avail" (vv.20-21).

This beautiful confession of faith, it should be observed, is what "living for God" (v.19) has meant for Paul: that "Christ lives in me". It is through this very intimate union with the risen Lord that God himself has drawn near, enabling Paul to live totally for him. It is this indwelling of the glorified Christ, so infinitely precious in Paul's eyes, that has given him the possibility of existing in union with God. Paul's "Christ-mysticism" is in reality a "God-mysticism".

We have earlier taken cognizance of the meaning of the expression "in Christ", by which Paul frequently describes his relationship with the Son of God. In this passage, as elsewhere, he speaks of it as the existence of Christ within the believer. "Test yourselves to see if you are living the life of faith: practice discernment. Are you not yourselves aware that Christ Jesus is in you?" (2 Cor 13:5). The Christian practice of examining one's innermost reactions in prayer, to be discussed in a further chapter,[15] is advocated in Paul's letter to Thessalonica. "Do not quench the Spirit; do not belittle prophetic utterances—test everything about them: hold onto what is good, shun every appearance of evil [in them]" (1 Thes 5:19-22). We find much the same advice given by the author

[15] See pp. 130-133.

of 1 Jn 4:1. "Dear friends, do not trust every spirit, but discern the spirits to see if it is from God, since many false prophets have gone out into the world." Paul warns the Romans,
"If a man has not Christ's Spirit, he does not belong to his
party. But if Christ is within you, your body is dead so far as
sin is concerned and your spirit is alive with regard to uprightness" (Rom 8:9-10). In writing to the Colossians Paul
speaks of this presence of Christ as the great Christian mystery:
"the Mystery, concealed for ages and generations, but now
manifested to his saints, to whom God has determined to disclose the riches of the glory of this mystery among the pagans
—I mean, Christ in you, the hope of glory" (Col 1:26-27).

This magnificent disclosure of the secret of his interior life to
the Galatians by Paul points to the heart of his life of prayer.
Later theology will speak of it less concretely and less humanly
as "sanctifying grace". For Paul it is a divine person, become
man to "hand himself over for me" whom he encounters in
this shrine which is in his own heart. It is to Christ within him
that Paul continually turns in faith and love; he is "the hope of
glory". His whole preoccupation is to grow in the knowledge of
who Christ is by becoming increasingly aware of his unique
relationship to God. He does this by returning tirelessly in faith
and love to that historical event by which Christ has redeemed
him, reminding himself with joy and thanksgiving of the love
which "the Son of God" displayed for him personally in his
death and resurrection.

And here we discover the most fundamental reason why
Paul resolutely refuses to "build up" that former religious existence according to the Law, which he "has torn down". For
that would be to reject the greatest historical revelation of the
gracious mercy of God (v.21). He has stated this in the auto-
biographical section of his letter to the Philippians. 8 "I count
it all as loss because of the supreme asset, the knowledge of
Christ Jesus my Lord. It was through him that I suffered the loss
of all these other things. I assess them as so much rubbish, in
order that I may gain Christ as an asset 9 and find myself
united to him. I mean, that I may possess, not any justification
of my own making that comes from law, but that justification

through faith in Christ—the justification given by God through faith. 10 [My whole purpose is] to know him and the power of his resurrection and the sharing in his sufferings, thus being molded together with him to his death, 11 that somehow I may attain to the resurrection from the dead" (Phil 3:8-11).

We have devoted considerable space to this passage in Galatians, because it presents so simply and vividly Paul's life of prayer as the prayer of faith. It explains his insistence, which otherwise might appear exaggerated, upon the necessity of being "devoted to prayer" (Rom 12:12; Col 4:2), of praying "without ceasing" (1 Thes 5:17). We are thus made aware of the way in which Paul maintained his delicate sensitivity to the truth that the Christian can only "be proven upright by faith in Christ" (v.16). He is keenly conscious that the fidelity and attentiveness with which he activates his life of prayer is itself a marvellous gift of God's "graciousness" which he refuses to "make void" (v.21). And always, as we have said, Paul is driven by a consuming desire to "know Christ" more truly and intimately.

Perhaps no Christian writer on the subject of prayer has managed to retain such a lively sense of the poverty of his own knowledge of the risen Christ as has St. Paul. To continue living in this world has meaning for him only in function of pursuing this quest and deepening his union with the Lord. "For me indeed living *is* Christ, and death is an asset" (Phil 1:21). By the Damascus road Paul had embarked upon a voyage of discovery that was to carry him through his life, and beyond: "to be with Christ" (Phil 1:23).

IV

"TRIBULATION IN ASIA" (2 COR 1:8-11)

Hitherto we have reviewed certain happenings in Paul's career which occurred well before any of his extant letters were composed. We have now to reflect on an incident, the gravity of which for Paul's very existence cannot be enough stressed. It was not merely that death stared him in the face on this occasion, for he had probably already faced death several times before (cf. 2 Cor 11:23; 1 Cor 4:9; 15:32). Now the blow which afflicted him was a mortal one. Paul knew that there was no means of escape from what he himself calls "the sentence of death". God had, in his mercy, merely granted him a reprieve, and Paul seems assured that through his graciousness he would do so again. But from this point until the end of his life, it would appear, Paul knew he was doomed.

8 "I do not wish you to be ignorant, brothers, of the tribulation I experienced in Asia. I was crushed by an excessively heavy burden that was beyond my power to bear, so that I even despaired of living. 9 In fact, in my heart I have accepted the death-sentence. It was intended to teach me not to put my trust in myself, but in the God who raises the dead. 10 He it is who rescued me from such grave perils of death, and so it is he who will continue to rescue me. Upon him I have set my hope irrevocably: he will rescue me yet, 11 provided you too will join in helping on my behalf by prayer. Thus gratitude will radiate from many faces as thanks are offered to God on my behalf for his act of graciousness towards me" (2 Cor 1:8-11).

Paul displays his customary reticence regarding anything that is private and personal to himself. Actually he speaks of himself here in the first person plural, which (since it is so obviously an epistolary device) we have translated by the singular. We remain in ignorance as to the concrete nature of this "tribulation in Asia". The latter term designates the Roman province, *Asia,* of which Ephesus was the capital. Since it is manifestly a recent experience, which Paul still feels keenly, the affliction is probably not to be identified with the critical incident which had occurred a year or so earlier than this, before Paul wrote 1 Corinthians. In that letter he described it as a combat "with wild beasts" (1 Cor 15:32). Nor is there any reason to connect the present trial with the riot of the silversmiths in Ephesus (Acts 19:23-40) in which Paul was involved according to Luke.

Paul does however betray his belief that there was really no escaping this "death-sentence" that had been passed on him. Such is the force of the Greek perfect tense, "I have accepted".

The most plausible explanation is that Paul has come to realize that he was suffering from some incurable malady, which had at one point almost killed him. He has recovered from the first virulent attack, but he retains no illusions. "Death is at work in us" (2 Cor 4:12), he will presently affirm. Perhaps he echoes this same view at the end of this letter, when he writes, "For we indeed are weak in him, but we shall live with him by the power of God [displayed] towards you" (2 Cor 13:4).

The most striking sign of Paul's consciousness of the gravity of his condition is to be seen in his reference to the crisis he has undergone as "the tribulation". This term, with its cognate verb, is a favorite with Paul. More than half the instances of both words in New Testament usage are found in the Pauline letters. "Tribulation", while taking some historical form (physical danger, famine, persecution) points to a deeper underlying reality. For the Church, it is part of her inheritance to continue the unremitting sufferings of Israel. In Paul's eyes tribulation is a notable part of the Christian and especially the apostolic calling (1 Thes 3:3-4), and hence inseparable from Christian existence in this world (2 Cor 6:4).

What makes the experience of tribulation specifically Christian is seen in Paul's intuition that "the sufferings of Christ overflow onto us" (2 Cor 1:5). "Now I rejoice in my sufferings on your behalf: I am in fact filling up what is wanting of *the tribulations of Christ* in my own flesh on behalf of his body, which is the Church" (Col 1:24). This bold statement discloses the Christological and soteriological dimensions that Paul sees in his endurance of tribulation. They are judged by faith to be more Christ's sufferings than his own; and so they have a redemptive value for the community of which Paul is the apostle.

Moreover, Paul's use of the term tribulation attests a new Christian understanding of the ongoing process of history since the death and resurrection of Christ. The Christians are that people "on whom the end of the ages has burst" (1 Cor 10:11). This means that the afflictions of the end-time, announced by the prophets of Israel, are already breaking in upon the present era (1 Cor 7:28-29). This eschatological view of tribulation relates it to "the great tribulation" of which Jesus had himself spoken (Mt 24:21), that recognized by the seer of Patmos in the destiny of the martyrs (Apoc 7:14). Paul in his turn has perceived the activity of death in the tribulations of the Christian (Rom 8:36) of which he has had frequent personal experience (2 Cor 4:8; 7:5). It is this negative aspect of tribulation which brings into relief its character as "temptation", a trial or testing (1 Thes 3:3-5) that must be offset by Christian faith.

A more positive aspect is visible in its relation to hope, and it is this aspect which Paul emphasizes in the passage we are examining. In fact he asserts that the lesson he learned from "the death-sentence" he has accepted is the important lesson of hope. Paul, rightly regarded as the theologian of hope, locates the special activity of this virtue in the context of the Christian endurance of tribulation (cf. 2 Thes 1:4-5; Phil 1:17-20). "We boast in the hope of the glory of God. Not only that, but we also boast in tribulations, because we are aware that tribulation produces endurance; endurance, tried virtue; tried virtue, hope" (Rom 5:2-4).

Paul sees "the tribulation in Asia" as an invitation to place his hope securely "in the God who raises the dead" (v.9). Knowing as he well does the precariousness of his own hold upon life, produced by the fatal malady, he turns with increased appreciation to the help which the prayers of the Corinthian community can offer him. The turn of phrase he employs however ("provided you too will join in helping on my behalf by prayer") implies that he is himself praying with greater earnestness and confidence than ever before. The crisis through which he has passed thus far successfully has deepened his faith in the power of prayer. It has also given a new impetus to his hope. This virtue is Paul's eyes was not a form of escapism, but a sharpening of the Christian faculties of endurance in the face of the harsh realities of this life.

Chapter 3
Prayers in the
Pauline Letters

When we attempt to select passages that appear to be prayers in the letters of Saint Paul, we are confronted at once with a difficult problem. By the very fact that we regard these writings as genuine letters, we admit that Paul is communicating with the communities he is addressing, while prayer is by its very nature addressed to God. From this point of view it might be maintained that there are really no prayers in the strict sense in all Paul's correspondence. Indeed, there are passages which are to be considered more his reporting of his prayer than actual prayers. This is true of all the formal thanksgivings with which most of his letters begin (Phil 1:3-11; 1 Cor 1:4-9). We shall devote an entire chapter somewhat later to a discussion of these highly informative sections.[1]

There are however brief passages which may rightly be called prayers: the doxologies, the spontaneous acts of thanksgiving, as well as a series of wishes directed to God and to Christ. In addition, there are two lengthy passages which are to be taken as real prayers, both exhibiting the ancient biblical form of "benedictions" (2 Cor 1:3-11; Eph 1:3-14). It is with these prayers that the present chapter will deal.

It may be suggested at once that the presence in Paul's letters of these frequent moments, in which he turns to God or to Christ, reveal how deeply saturated with prayer all Paul's apostolic endeavors were, and how rightly his letters may be regarded as the fruit of his own prayer. This is all the more

[1] See Chapter Five, pp. 134-164.

striking, if it be recalled how careful Paul always was to safe-guard the secrets of his personal prayer. Our chief interest in examining these Pauline prayers is to discern, if possible, any indications they may provide of the character, or content, or orientation of Paul's conversation with God.

I
DOXOLOGIES

The doxology is an expression of the praise of God, often containing explicit references to the divine "glory", that power, majesty and splendor of God *as revealed* to man through the mighty works of creation and redemption. Examples of this type of prayer are scattered throughout the Old Testament, par-ticularly in the Psalter. The fivefold division of this collection of Israel's prayers is indicated by the insertion of concluding doxologies (Ps 41:14; 72:18-20; 89:53; 106:48), while the last psalm of the entire series is completely doxological. This arrangement would appear to indicate the distinctively liturgi-cal purpose of the Psalter, since the doxology was probably created for use at public worship. The role of the doxology as an articulation of praise and thanksgiving to God, intended as the prayerful termination of a sequence of thought, as the dis-position of the Psalter itself illustrates, must be kept in mind in our inquiry into the meaning of the Pauline doxologies.

Paul expresses this kind of prayer under two forms: by his use of the term "Blessed", and with the word "Glory". It is an open question whether these brief sentences, which have no verb as a general rule, are to be construed in the form of a wish ("Blessed be", "Be the glory"), or taken as an affirmation ("Is blessed", "Belongs the glory"). There is some evidence that when he employs the doxology of the first type Paul intends to make a statement. Moreover, man can add nothing to the divine "glory", which belongs inalienably to God alone. Man is assigned the duty of acknowledging that glory manifested to him through the revealed works of God. God is to be "blessed" by man, whose "confession" includes gratitude for what God

has done, and above all, for what God is. Thus the suitability
of the doxology for public worship becomes evident, and this
cultic character is confirmed by Paul's consistent addition of
the term "Amen", except for one instance (2 Cor 11:31).

Paul has given a specifically Christian meaning to the acclamation Amen, which was a borrowing from the liturgy of Judaism. In writing to Corinth a second time Paul states that God
himself is shown to stand behind the gospel he preaches as a
guarantor of its reliability and lack of tergiversation by the
fact that it proclaims Jesus Christ as the unequivocal fulfilment
of the divine promises of salvation. "God is the guarantor that
our word [announced] to you does not vacillate between Yes
and No. For the Son of God, Jesus Christ, the one preached
by us among you . . . was not found wavering between Yes
and No. The Yes has become a reality in him. He is in fact
the Yes to all God's promises. That is why too we utter the
Amen through him whenever we give glory to God" (2 Cor
1:18-20). Paul's use of the word Amen is an affirmation of
faith in the redemptive work of Christ, recognized as continuing in his mediation of all Christian prayer to God. It is a
reminder that our praise and thankfulness is supported by the
Son, who allows us to unite our prayer with his own. Consequently, while the Pauline doxologies are invariably addressed
to God the Father, they are meant also as an expression of
Paul's reverent and grateful attention to Christ.

An example of the first form of the doxology is found in
the discussion of the sin of the pagans, idolatry (Rom 1:18-
32). "They exchanged the truth about God for a lie, revering
and worshipping creation instead of its creator—he who is
blessed forever! Amen" (Rom 1:25). A detail in Paul's description of the sin of the pagans should not be overlooked,
because of the light it throws upon his understanding of the
doxology as primarily an act of thanksgiving. The pagans, he
says, stand condemned "because while they knew God, they
did not glorify him as God, *or give thanks*" (v.21). To "give
thanks" is for Paul the essential purpose of the doxology. There
is a clear indication in this doxology that this kind of prayer
is understood as an affirmation by Paul, since he inserts the

word "is" into the formula here. We may infer then that the other two instances of this type in Paul's letters should be taken in the same way.

"The God and Father of the Lord Jesus knows—he who is blessed forever—that I am not lying" (2 Cor 11:31). Paul calls upon God to witness, after listing the trials he has successfully overcome in executing his apostolic commission, to the truth of his "boasting"; and the interjected doxology refers all credit for these accomplishments to God alone, to whom he owes his vocation as an apostle. It will be observed that it is "the God and Father of the Lord Jesus" to whom Paul addresses his thanks and praise. This expression gives proof of Paul's constant awareness of the profound modification which his notion of God has undergone as a result of his meeting with the glorified Son of God near Damascus. That he characterizes God as he does here also shows how the doxology inevitably evokes in Paul's heart and mind the person of Christ. It is interesting to recall that the only other doxology of this type, which concludes the listing of Israel's privileges, is, it must be confessed, most naturally understood as an intended praise of Christ himself. "There are the patriarchs, from whom sprang the Christ according to the flesh, who is above all things God blessed forever. Amen." (Rom 9:5). The objection to construing the doxology as directed to Christ, however, is a weighty one: Paul nowhere calls Christ God. Hence the more commonly accepted rendering makes the doxology a separate statement. "God, who is above all things, is blessed forever. Amen".

We shall select only two examples of the other form of doxology from several (Rom 11:33-36; 16:27; Eph 3:20-31). These are worthy of citation here because of the information they provide regarding Paul's attitudes in prayer. "My God will fill up every need of yours according to his riches with glory in Christ Jesus. To our God and Father belongs the glory for endless ages. Amen" (Phil 4:20-21). Paul introduces the doxology by a reassuring promise that is solemnly made. The phrase, "My God", characteristic of Paul's prayer, is, as we have noted earlier (Phil 1:3, 1 Cor 1:4; Rom 1:8; Phlmn 4), probably inspired by his familiarity with the psalms, especially since the phrase appears elsewhere in the New Testament only on the lips of Jesus himself (Jn 20:17; Mk 15:34). It is to be noted that Paul does not distinguish spiritual from temporal "needs" (v.19); the promise is all-inclusive. God will make it a reality "in Christ Jesus", who is mediator of the divine bounty as he is the revealer of God's "glory".

The doxology itself is addressed in an unusual fashion for Paul to "our God and Father". The phrase "our Father" is rare in his letters, occurring only in a context of thanksgiving or petition (1 Thes 1:3; 3:11,13: Eph 5:20). Paul has made it clear elsewhere (Gal 4:6; Rom 8:15) that to use this form of address to God the assistance of the Holy Spirit is required. It may well be that his reason for using "our Father" here, instead of the "my God" of the preceding verse, is that Paul wishes to show the Philippian community that he associates each of them with his own praise and thanks to God. This may be a tactful way of thanking them for their benefactions to himself.

The significance of this doxology is rightly seen to lie in its function as the climax to Paul's entire letter to Philippi, so redolent of joy and affection and gratitude. It is an explication in prayer of everything he desires to communicate to this church of his predilection. This brief note, which is (as will be seen later) the fruit of prayer, thus fittingly culminates in a return to prayer.[2]

The letter written to the churches of Galatia contains no formal thanksgiving, a deviation from Paul's usual custom in beginning his letters. It has been replaced by a doxology which terminates an address unique in the Pauline correspondence because of its explicit reference to the work of man's redemption. "Grace to you and peace from God our Father and Lord Jesus Christ, who gave himself up for the sake of our sins to snatch us from the present evil world, in accordance with the will of our God and Father: to him belongs the glory for endless ages. Amen" (Gal 1:3-5).

Paul's grateful praise of God is here prompted by his remembrance of the work of redemption, which originated with

[2] See pp. 140-144.

"God our Father" and was carried out by "Lord Jesus Christ". The phrase, "for the sake of our sins" occurs nowhere else in Paul, who normally says "for our sake". Paul wishes to recall a point that is a cardinal one in his soteriology, that God has revealed himself as "our Father" specifically through Christ's death "for the sake of our sins". In this way he is able to announce the theme of the letter (a function normally performed by the thanksgiving), which is the universal efficacy of Jesus' saving death—a belief imperilled by the doctrines of the judaizing opponents whom Paul confronts in Galatia. This doxology is a summons to a "confession" on the part of "all the brothers" and "the churches of Galatia" (v.2), to glorify and thank God "our Father" as the initiator of man's salvation not through the revelation of the Mosaic Law, but solely through the redemptive death of Jesus Christ. It was this supreme event of history by which God's "glory" was definitively revealed, and Paul appears to suggest that the divine glory continues to be manifested to the individual Christian by God's "snatching us from the present evil world"—a work not yet completed.

That this doxology has taken the place of the formal thanksgiving provides additional evidence, to that already remarked in Rom 1:21, of the close association in Paul's mind of the prayer of praise with thanksgiving. We may also note that we have here an illustration of Paul's invariable practice of addressing the doxology to God the Father. While Christ is included in the prayer-wish which introduces the doxology, he is not named in the ejaculation of praise. There is never mention of the Holy Spirit in any Pauline doxology. Yet it is also characteristic of Paul that the response of loving praise receives an impetus from his attention to the redeeming act of "Lord Jesus Christ", which continues to reveal God as "our Father".

II

Spontaneous Acts of Thanksgiving

By their character as brief ejaculatory prayers these spontaneous expressions of thanks to God resemble the doxologies.

They are also invariably addressed to God alone, usually with some reference to Christ's mediation in man's redemption. However, in contrast with the doxology, the majority of these acts of gratitude is oriented, not to the past historical act of God in Christ, but rather to the ongoing process of salvation in the present epoch of sacred history. They will be found frequently charged with profound emotion. "Thanks to God for his gift beyond words!" (2 Cor 9:15). The feeling evinced here is even more keenly felt in the anguished cry in Rom 7:24-25. "Unhappy man that I am! Who will deliver me from the death-doomed existence in this body of mine?—Thanks to God! [It is God] through Jesus Christ our Lord."

Paul's convincing argumentation in support of Christian belief in the glorious resurrection comes to a triumphant climax in 1 Corinthians 15 with a very moving cry of gratitude. "To God be thanks, who keeps giving us the victory through our Lord Jesus Christ!" (1 Cor 15:57). Paul has urged his readers to look ahead to the day when, by the resurrection of the faithful, the victory will have been snatched from death, and "death's sting" will have been finally removed (vv.54-56). This victory, as he desires the Corinthians to realize, is even now in progress (cf. 2 Cor 3:18): the eschatological hope is becoming a reality in the present. As Hans Conzelmann has observed, this expression of thanks by Paul is "an actualizing of hope for contemporary faith".[3] This hope is based simultaneously upon what God has already effected in the past through the death and resurrection of Christ and upon what he will do through Christ "as first fruits" (1 Cor 15:20) at the close of history. Paul's response of loving gratitude is made for what God is actually doing for his people in the course of history.

As he begins his long apology for the authentic character of his call to be an apostle in 2 Corinthians, Paul again utters a brief and poignant cry of thanks to God. "To God be thanks! who keeps leading us in his triumph in Christ, and spreading in every place the sweet odor of his knowledge through us" (2 Cor 2:14). God is represented as holding a triumph after

[3] Hans Conzelmann, *Der erste Brief an die Korinther* (Göttingen, 1969), p. 350.

the fashion of a victorious Roman general, and Paul associates himself as a veteran in the triumphal procession, because of his union with the risen Christ, through whose death the victory has been secured. It is the thought of the ongoing activity of God in Christ, particularly through Paul's own apostolate, which gives him grounds for gratitude. He is conscious that his union with Christ as he preaches the word of God keeps him continually in the divine presence. "We speak [God's word] from a sincere heart, as something coming from God, in God's presence, through union with Christ" (v.17).

Like the doxologies these brief thanksgivings occur but half a dozen times in all Paul's letters. Their significance lies, as does that of the doxologies, either in their intercalation into a profound theological development, as the last two examples chosen exemplify (cf. also Rom 6:17; 7:25) or, as in 2 Cor 9:15, by their appearance in the middle of a very practical scheme like the organization of a relief fund for the poor of Jerusalem. They thus provide evidence that theologizing, as well as apostolic involvement in activity, are never far removed from the prayer of Paul. Both these absorbing tasks spring from his prayer, and they lead him infallibly back again to prayer.

III
PRAYER AS WISH

The verb commonly used to denote prayer to the gods in the Greek pagan texts of the classical period exhibits the basic sense of "wish". It probably retains something of this original sense in one Pauline text. "I could wish to be cut off from Christ for the sake of my brothers, my natural kinsmen" (Rom 9:3). There is but a single passage in Paul where the word signifies prayer (2 Cor 13:7, 9); and here ambiguity is effectively removed by the addition of the phrase "unto God". 7 "We pray unto God that you may commit no evil—not that we may appear to be vindicated, but that you may do what is right, even though we may seem to be discredited. 8 We have no power to act contrary to the truth, but only on behalf of the truth. 9 We rejoice whenever we are weak and you are strong. This also is our prayer for you: that all may be put right for you" (2 Cor 13:7-9). This beautiful prayer reveals the magnanimity of Paul's apostolic heart, his total forgetfulness of himself, his complete involvment in the interests of the Christians in his charge—even when, as was the case with the Corinthians, they have caused him great pain.

From this single example it is easy to see how profound an act of faith and how much love are required to direct a wish to God, "who is at work in you, inspiring both the wish and the action because of his good pleasure" (Phil 2:13). There are numerous instances of prayer as wish in Paul's letters. Their chief significance arises from their being directed to both the risen Lord and to God the Father at once, or to one or other of them individually. When, in addition to the wishes contained in the body of the letters, those expressed at the beginning or at the close be also taken into account (as they should be), then this kind of prayer is to be found more frequently than any other in Paul's writings.

Perhaps the finest illustrations of prayer as wish are to be found in the first two letters from Paul's pen, 1-2 Thessalonians, where they form a fitting conclusion to the preceding thought-development. They demonstrate the justice of Béda Riguax's observation upon Paul's prayer, "His prayer is the prayer of an apostle." [4] The style of the passages indicates the character of these prayers as solemn invocations.

11 "May our God and Father himself and our Lord Jesus make our route back to you a straight one. 12 May the Lord cause your love for one another, and for all men, to grow, and produce an abundant harvest, like my love for you. 13 Thus will your hearts be staunch and irreproachably holy before our God and Father at the coming of our Lord Jesus with all his holy ones" (1 Thes 3:11-13). The first of the three petitions which this prayer contains is addressed both to God as "our Father" and to "our Lord Jesus", who in his glorified state ranks with God himself. It is important to note that Paul is seen here to pray to Christ as well as to the Father, since he asks to be able

[4] Béda Rigaux, *Les Épitres aux Thessaloniciens* (Paris: Gembloux, 1965), p. 165.

to revisit Thessalonica. Thus in the exercise of his apostolic commission which he holds from both Christ and God (Gal 1:1) he prays to both, or, as in 2 Cor 12:8, to Christ alone. His second petition is presented to Christ, appropriately enough, since it concerns the "new commandment" of fraternal love (Jn 13:34), to whose divine origin Paul will refer in this letter (1 Thes 4:9). His final wish is for the holiness of these Christians, a topic he will take up in the second section of the letter (1 Thes 4:1 ff.). The eschatological perspective which forms the climax of this prayer is seen in the allusion to the divine judgment-seat—"before our God and Father". This perspective, with its references to the parousia, also characterizes the formal thanksgivings. It is significant for Paul's notion of God as judge that he is called "our Father". Pauline spirituality always retains an eschatological orientation, although it is particularly marked in the earlier letters.

The next prayer constitutes a summation of the entire substance of this letter. "May the God of peace himself sanctify you thoroughly, and guard you safe and sound in spirit and soul and body, irreproachable at the coming of our Lord Jesus Christ. He is faithful, the one who calls you; he will surely secure this" (1 Thes 5:23-24). Where the previous prayer was centered upon the gift of fraternal love, here the petition is for "peace", the perfection of holiness. Paul often represents God as "the God of peace" (Phil 4:9; 1 Cor 14:33; 2 Cor 13:11; Rom 15:33; 16:20). This familiar Old Testament conception has been given a new, Christian meaning for Paul. It is that salvation which has become a reality through Jesus' death and resurrection, and is offered to all who accept him in faith. It no longer consists, as it did for Israel, in a this-worldly security and freedom from want or oppression, but has become synonymous with that holiness or consecration to God of every aspect of the Christian's personality, which Paul has described in this letter. Paul's final remark, "He is faithful", reveals the complete confidence with which he breathes his prayer, for it is made to the God who is author of the Christian's call to holiness (4:3). This creative summons by God contains sufficient grounds for trust that it will be realized by God.

Of the three prayers expressed in 2 Thessalonians two are

addressed to Christ, while in the first "our Lord Jesus Christ" is mentioned first. This striking phenomenon has been turned into an argument against the Pauline authenticity of the letter. However, as has been already seen, there is evidence enough elsewhere to show that Paul did actually pray to Christ as well as to the Father. "May our Lord Jesus Christ himself and God our Father, who has loved us and in his graciousness has given us such everlasting encouragement and such a bright hope, grant courage to your hearts and make them staunch in every good work and word" (2 Thes 2:16-17). It is undoubtedly the Christological theme, dominating the paragraph in which this prayer is found (2:13; 3:5), which leads Paul to invoke "our Lord Jesus Christ" in the first place. A striking feature of the prayer is the conviction it manifests of the perfect unity of action between the Father and the Son. It is in Christ's death and resurrection that God has revealed his love of us; and he further demonstrates that love in calling the individual Christian to "an acquisition of the glory of our Lord Jesus Christ" (v.14). It is this which constitutes the "everlasting encouragement" and the "bright hope". What Paul asks for these persecuted Christians is unwavering courage in living and professing their faith.

"May the Lord direct your hearts towards the love of God and the endurance of Christ" (2 Thes 3:5). The awkward formulation of this prayer betrays perhaps the intensity of the emotion with which it was uttered. It is addressed to the glorified Christ, awaited in his parousia, on behalf of a community not only under stress of persecution but also deeply disturbed by false rumors concerning the second coming. It is appropriately addressed to Christ, whose elevation to supreme lordship does not mean any loss of concern on his part for what transpires in this world. He has in fact become more deeply involved in history, especially in the lives of all Christians. Paul calls upon "the Lord" to "direct your hearts towards the love of God", that is, to make them realize more deeply the Father's love for them. The difficult expression, "the endurance of Christ", is probably to be taken to refer in the first place to his unwavering toleration of suffering in his earthly life, particularly in the Passion. Paul knows however (Col 1:24; 2 Cor

4:10) that these persecuted Christians are privileged to share
in the endurance of their Lord by their own staunchness and
courage in resisting for the faith. Their steadfastness is truly
"the endurance of Christ", not only because it is an imitation
of him (1 Thes 1:6), or because their sufferings are borne for
his sake, but also because of their close union with him as members of his body.[5]

"May the Lord of peace himself grant you peace in every
situation and in every way. The Lord be with all of you" (2
Thes 3:16). This final prayer is appositely made to the risen
Lord as the bearer of "peace", or salvation, since his death
has imparted to this traditionally biblical term its Christian
meaning. Paul is accustomed to think of our Lord as mediator
of man's peace with the Father. "Being then justified by faith,
we possess peace with God through our Lord Jesus Christ,
through whom we have come to have the entry by faith to this
state of grace in which we now stand" (Rom 5:1-2). He is also
mediator of that peace between former Jews and pagans, which
creates their fellowship in the Christian community. "For he
himself is our peace, because he has made the two groups one
and has broken down the wall of separation, hatred, by his
own flesh" (Eph 2:14). It is for this reason that Paul speaks
of Christ's redemptive work as "reconciliation" (2 Cor 5:18-
20; Rom 5:10; Col 1:20). Here Paul prays that Christ may be
present among the Thessalonians, since it is his dynamic presence that will keep them united despite disturbances from
within and persecution from without.

Paul ends his angriest letter, that to the Galatians, with a
very solemn wish, which has been called "an authoritative
apostolic blessing." [6] The most remarkable feature of this
prayer is that it makes the acceptance of the law of the cross
(cf. Mk 8:34-37) the essential condition of receiving God's
"peace". Paul interrupts his prayer on this occasion to make
a final retort to his opponents, in which there is a puzzling reference to "the stigmata of Jesus". Paul possibly means the

---

[5] Maximilian Zerwick, *Biblical Greek* (Rome, 1963), #38.
[6] Pierre Bonnard, *L'Épitre de Saint Paul aux Galates* (*Commentaire
du Nouveau Testament IX*) (Neuchatel: Paris, 1953), p. 131.

scars of his former sufferings which he considers a symbol of his belonging to Christ as his "slave".

"And whoever follows this principle—peace be upon them and mercy, and upon the Israel of God! (For the future, let no man cause trouble for me, since I bear the marks of Jesus branded upon my body). The grace of our Lord Jesus Christ be with your spirit, brothers. Amen" (Gal 6:16-18). The "principle" has just been enunciated in a fervent wish on Paul's part, which is really itself a prayer. "As for myself, may God keep me from ever boasting in anything save the cross of our Lord Jesus Christ, on which the world remains crucified for me, as I am to the world. For neither circumcision, nor the lack of it, are of any significance. What counts is a new creation" (vv.14-15). We have here the reappearance of the central issue between Paul and the judaizers that has already been stated earlier in the letter. "Through the Law I died to the Law, in order that I might live for God, that is, I was crucified together with Christ" (Gal 2:19). Since Paul has definitively broken with the religion of the Law, he no longer belongs to the old "world", the fashion of which is "passing off the stage" (1 Cor 7:31). In his view the Law is a symbol of that old, outmoded world-order in which sin reigns. The radical character of Paul's "principle" should not be missed. He follows the teaching of Jesus who replaced the merely human goal of self-fulfilment by the evangelical idea of self-transcendence. Thus to accept the call to be a Christian becomes nothing less than a "new creation".[7] Man's acquiring the grace of justifying faith is wholly dependent upon God's graciousness, since it is he alone who gives man the capability of saying "Yes" to the call. Paul never forgets that "he is faithful, the one who calls you: he will surely secure this" (1 Thes 5:24), and hence God's fidelity forms the basis of Paul's "boasting", that is, his grateful praise and confidence. The divine faithfulness is now symbolized, since Christ's resurrection, by "the cross of our Lord Jesus Christ", the death of him who is risen from death forever.

[7] The application of the creation-motif to the New Testament reality is to be credited to Paul's originality: see D. M. Stanley, "Paul's Interest in the Early Chapters of Genesis", *Analecta Biblica* 17 (1963), 241-252.

This apostolic blessing of Paul is given to all Christians who "imitate" himself (2 Thes 3:9; 1 Cor 4:1) [8] by their awareness that their Christian existence hangs upon the thread of the graciousness of God. Paul prays that they may experience the divine "mercy", and so be granted "peace", salvation together with "the Israel of God". This unusual phrase probably indicates the communion of faith which Paul recognizes to exist between the Christian Church and those members of Israel who exhibit the faith of Abraham (Rom 4:11-12).

A very beautiful wish for peace is inserted towards the end of the letter to the Romans. It is noteworthy for its mention of the Holy Spirit. "May the God of peace fill you with all joy and peace in the practice of your faith, so that by the power of the Holy Spirit you may overflow with hope" (Rom 15:13). Paul invokes "the God of peace" upon the Roman community, since he has been discussing a problem which he knows has tended to strain relations within the church itself (Rom 14:1 —15:13), the question of scruples about dietary regulations. The practice of the Christian faith should produce nothing but "joy and peace". Moreover, the Christian should not allow himself to become too much immersed in the past, but look forward expectantly to the future. The *élan* which moves the believer forward, by enabling him to put into their proper perspective the trials of the present, is an effect of the presence of the Holy Spirit and of his power. Paul made this clear earlier in his letter, when describing the process by which hope is generated (Rom 5:3-4). What proves that our hope is authentic and "does not disappoint" is the fact "that God's love has been poured forth in our hearts through the gift of the Holy Spirit to us" (Rom 5:5). Paul has elsewhere ascribed the creation of hope to the operation of the Spirit. "But we look for the hope of justification by the work of the Spirit through faith" (Gal 5:5). As the present prayer indicates, Paul cannot conceive of a life of real faith from which hope is absent.

---

[8] D. M. Stanley, " 'Become Imitators Of Me': The Pauline Conception of Apostolic Tradition", *Analecta Biblica* 11 (1959), 291-309.

IV
INTRODUCTORY AND FINAL WISHES

The wish that accompanies the opening of the Pauline letters consists basically of "grace be to you and peace" (cf. 1 Thes 1:1). After this first letter however the formula appears more fully developed. "Grace be to you and peace from God the Father and Lord Jesus Christ" (2 Thes 1:2). With one further modification the expression becomes almost invariable throughout Paul's correspondence. "Grace be to you and peace from God *our* Father and Lord Jesus Christ" (Phil 1:2). Only in Galatians does Paul expand this stereotype in a remarkable way, as we have already seen earlier in this chapter. "Grace to you and peace from God our Father and Lord Jesus Christ, who gave himself up for the sake of our sins to snatch us from the present evil world, in accordance with the will of our God and Father" (Gal 1:3-4). A much simplified form of the wish appears in Col 1:2: "Grace to you and peace from God our Father."

The development which the wish for "grace and peace" receives in Galatians provides help in determining how Paul understands the reality which these terms represent. "Grace" (*charis*) may contain an echo of the usual Greek epistolary greeting "hail" (*chaire*). It is however no more than a faint echo. "Peace" (*eirēnē*) is the well-known Hebrew greeting (*shālôm*). For Paul these words have acquired a totally new significance from the redemption in which God the Father and Christ collaborated in closest unity. As has been pointed out, this twofold event, Jesus' saving death and resurrection, has disclosed the love of the Father (Rom 5:8) and of Christ (Gal 2:20) for sinful and rebellious man. It has also revealed Christ's love as Son for the Father by his filial obedience (Phil 2:8; Rom 5:19), as well as the Father's love for his Son, who as man's redeemer is "his own dear Son" (Col 1:13). In fact, for Paul the redemption has revealed God *as Father* and Christ as *the*

Son (Gal 4:4; Rom 8:3,32). Indeed, it proves that God is *our* Father whose saving designs Christ carried out "in accordance with the will of our God and Father'" (Gal 1:4).

For Paul the redemption is also an act of the graciousness of God. "But God being rich in mercy, on account of the great love with which he loved us, even though we were dead by our transgressions, brought us to life again together with Christ —it was by grace that you have been saved!" (Eph 2:4-5). The redemption was no less an act of graciousness on the part of Christ. "For you know the graciousness of our Lord Jesus Christ, how being rich, he became poor for your sake, in order that you by his poverty might be made rich" (2 Cor 8:9).

Béda Rigaux has rightly observed that "in the New Testament we may consider grace as a Pauline term".[9] The word is not found in Matthew, Mark, or—apart from the Prologue—in John and 1 John. It is rare (four times only) in Luke, although it appears more frequently in Acts. Paul may not have been the first to employ the term and give it its Christian significance, but it held a great appeal for him. This was because of the constant and very deep sense of gratitude to God and to Christ, which characterizes his prayer. He recognizes the graciousness of the Father as the source of his own apostolic vocation (Gal 1:15). Like the author of the Fourth Gospel (Jn 1:14), Paul knows that it has become incarnate in Jesus Christ: this "graciousness of God has been given to us in Christ Jesus" (1 Cor 1:4). "By God's graciousness I am what I am! Indeed, his graciousness towards me has not been ineffectual" (1 Cor 15:10). The universality and abundance of the grace of God never ceases to be a cause for wonder to Paul. "Where sin abounded, grace immeasurably surpassed it" (Rom 5:20). "All this has been done with you in mind, that grace already abounding might swell the chorus of thanksgiving, as more men share it, that ascends to the glory of God" (2 Cor 4:15).

Paul has also given the Old Testament concept of "peace" a new content. This is the result, in part at least, of his distinctive view of the redemption as "reconciliation" (2 Cor 5:18-20; Rom 5:9-10; Col 1:20; Eph 2:16). Christ is the agent of peace

---

[9] Béda Rigaux, *op. cit.*, p. 352.

(Eph 2:14-16), and it is his peace that must rule in Christian hearts (Col 2:15). He is "the Lord of peace" (2 Thes 3:16). Peace appears prominently among the harvest produced by the Spirit (Gal 5:22). "The kingdom of God consists . . . of uprightness, and peace, and joy inspired by the Holy Spirit" (Rom 14:17). God the Father remains the author and initiator of this peace. It is he who "in Christ was reconciling the world to himself" (2 Cor 5:19), who has "made peace through his blood [shed] on the cross" (Col 1:20). As a consequence it is chiefly with God that "once justified by faith, we possess peace" (Rom 5:1). He has in fact summoned the Christian by his vocation "to live in peace" (1 Cor 7:16). It is a matter of some importance to Paul that the cultus reflect this salient feature of God, "for he is a God, not of confusion, but of peace" (1 Cor 14:33). Except for the title Father, no designation of God is so common in Paul as "the God of peace" (1 Thes 5:23; Phil 4:9; 1 Cor 14:33; 2 Cor 13:11; Rom 15:33; 16:20).

Thus Paul's opening prayer-wish, inspired as it undoubtedly was by his reflections upon the meaning of man's redemption, is seen to exhibit a depth of Christian meaning. It may well be, as Joseph Fitzmyer has discerningly remarked,[10] that the combination of grace and peace in Paul was originally inspired by the very ancient priestly blessing in the book of Numbers, which juxtaposes covenant favor (grace) with peace. "The Lord bless you and keep you! The Lord let his face shine upon you, and be gracious to you! The Lord look upon you kindly and give you peace!" (Num 6:24-26).

We must now say a word about the concluding prayer-wish, which evinces, with minor variations, the basic form Paul has given it in his first letter: "The grace of our Lord Jesus Christ be with you" (1 Thes 5:28). Two formulations which have been notably expanded (2 Cor 13:13; Eph 6:23-24) will be discussed presently. The formula with which Paul terminates his letters is considered by many commentators a kind of apostolic blessing which Paul imparts in closing. The very interesting

[10] Joseph A. Fitzmyer, "New Testament Epistles", *The Jerome Biblical Commentary,* p. 224.

suggestion has been made that it is actually a borrowing from the primitive Christian liturgy. That this view was current in antiquity may be inferred from the addition in several ancient manuscripts of the word Amen.

In fact Ernst Lohmeyer [11] has made the not implausible surmise that the opening and closing wishes have been taken over by Paul from the formulae with which the earliest Christian public worship began and ended. As is well known, Paul twice expresses the command (1 Thes 5:27; Col 4:16) that his letters be read to the community assembled for the liturgy. The heart of Christian cultus was of course to be found from the beginning of the Church in the Eucharist. Whatever instruction or readings may have been included were necessarily related to this supreme act of worship through which the risen Lord Jesus became present sacramentally in the midst of the community. There is no compelling evidence from the New Testament, it must be admitted, for the view that there was ever a Christian service consisting solely of what might nowadays be called the liturgy of the word. On the other hand, there are indications (Acts 2:42-47; 1 Cor 11 and 14) that instruction was generally combined with the celebration of the Eucharist. Pierre Benoit [12] has proposed the attractive hypothesis that the Lucan narrative of the post-resurrection appearance of Jesus to the two disciples at Emmaus was constructed after the pattern of the cultus of the apostolic age. The explanation of "the Scriptures" by the risen, but as yet unrecognized Jesus (Lk 24:25-27) created for the disciples the atmosphere of faith (v.32) through which he finally "became known to them in the breaking of the bread" (v.35). This is not to suggest that the risen Lord celebrated the Eucharist with these favored disciples. It does suggest that Luke has seen and presented this episode as illustrative of what occurs in the Church's Eucharist celebrations. The faithful are summoned to hear the word of God proclaimed, in order that they may better recognize the

---

[11] Ernst Lohmeyer, *Die Briefe an die Philipper, an die Kolosser und an Philemon* (Göttingen, 1964), p. 191.

[12] Pierre Benoit, *The Passion and Resurrection of Jesus Christ* (New York: London, 1969), pp. 278-282.

presence of the glorified Christ in that word and in one another, so that with newly sharpened eyes of faith they may perceive more readily his real presence in the sacrament of faith.

We are now able to suggest an answer to a problem which arises from the marked contrast perceptible between the formulation of the opening and closing wish in Paul's letters. It will have been noted that the wish which terminates the letters makes no mention of God the Father, but only of "the grace of our Lord Jesus Christ". The form of the prayer presents a second problem. Throughout his letters Paul speaks frequently of "the grace of God", but—apart from one doubtful reading at Gal 1:6—there is but a single instance in the body of his letters which exhibits the phrase, "the grace of our Lord Jesus Christ" (2 Cor 8:9; cf. 12:9). Once also, as in the opening wishes, grace is associated with Christ and the Father (2 Thes 1:12). In view of Paul's almost inveterate custom, this final wish that the grace *of Christ* be present with the community appears to demand some explanation. I suggest that the formula is quite comprehensible if Paul was aware that the reading of his letter in community formed part of the preparation for the Eucharist, the sacrament of the grace of Christ. It is interesting to observe that the final wish in 1 Corinthians is immediately preceded by the phrase *Marana tha,* "Come our Lord", commonly thought to have been a Eucharistic acclamation, or perhaps an *epiklesis.* "If anyone does not love the Lord, may he be anathema. *Marana tha!* The grace of the Lord Jesus be with you" (1 Cor 16:22-23).

The relevance of this practice of ending his letters with the wish that Christ's grace may abide with the community for our investigation into Paul's prayer should not be overlooked. It provides another instance of a conviction we have already found in Paul, that it is in the risen Christ that God has drawn near to us: in "the grace of Christ" we are privileged to possess the grace of God.

It remains to take notice of two examples of this Christological prayer-wish with which Paul concludes all his letters, where there is a significant variation on the ordinary formula. In 2 Cor 13:13 the wish is expanded into a triadic expression, which

will constitute one of the most important Pauline sources for
the later Trinitarian doctrine. "The grace of the Lord Jesus
Christ, and the love of God, and the participation in the Holy
Spirit be with all of you!" Hans Lietzmann is of the opinion that
"in the ancient liturgies this triadic greeting always follows the
'kiss of peace'; hence the supposition is plausible that this
connection is old and has its origins in the rite of the Pauline
communities. The letter is read aloud in the community as-
sembly, then the kiss of peace follows with the Lord's Supper
introduced by the liturgical greeting." [13]

The fact that this enlarged formula begins in the usual way
with "the grace of the Lord Jesus Christ" shows that it had
developed naturally out of the basic form of the prayer-wish. It
also reflects perhaps the manner in which the revelation to
Paul of the identity of the risen Christ near Damascus brought
him to a new realization that the God of Israel he had always
worshipped was in reality "the Father of our Lord Jesus
Christ" (2 Cor 1:3). "The participation in the Holy Spirit" is to
be taken as similar in meaning to the parallel expressions
"participation in the blood of Christ", "participation in the body
of Christ" (1 Cor 10:16), which are employed by Paul to
designate the Eucharist. The dynamic presence of the Holy
Spirit, who dwells in the Christian so that his body is a true
"sanctuary" (1 Cor 6:19), effects his sanctification and justification (1 Cor 6:11). As "the Spirit of Christ" he causes
the Christian to belong to Christ (Rom 8:9); as the Spirit of
the Father, "of him who raised Jesus from the dead", he will
have a part in the future revivification of the Christian (Rom
8:11). The role of the Spirit in Christian prayer Paul considers of the highest moment. While reserving for the next
chapter a fuller discussion of this topic,[14] we may remark here
that it is the Holy Spirit who presides over the Christian's
continuing growth in self-identity as an adoptive son of God
(Gal 4:6).

The concluding wish in the letter to the Ephesians breaks

---

[13] Hans Lietzmann, *An die Korinther I/II* (*Handbuch zum Neuen
Testament* 9) (Tübingen, 1949), p. 162.
[14] See pp. 102-103, 119-121, 124, 127-130.

radically with the pattern consistently preserved by Paul in his other letters. Here God is named as well as Christ, and the wish is for peace, love, faith, as well as grace. "Peace to the brothers, and love with faith from God the Father and Lord Jesus Christ. Grace be with all those who love the Lord Jesus Christ unto life immortal" (Eph 6:23-24). A rereading of this letter will reveal that peace, love, and faith are its dominant themes, and each of these gifts is related to Christ as well as to the Father.

V
PRAYER AS CONFESSION

The two longest passages in the Pauline letters, which by reason of their nature as "confessions" must be considered true prayers, are found at 2 Cor 1:3-11 and Eph 1:3-14. The category of "confession", with its evident liturgical character is found in the Old Testament, especially in certain psalms (Ps 144:1 ff.). The Lucan *Benedictus* (Lk 1:68-79) exemplifies this type of prayer, which is found elsewhere in the New Testament (1 Pt 1:3 ff.). The "confession" is a solemn, public act of praise and thanksgiving proclaimed before other believers with the purpose of eliciting their collaboration in "blessing" God for his wonderful works. The Pauline confession in 2 Cor 1:3-11 stands in marked contrast to that in Ephesians by reason of its less formal, more spontaneous quality. It does not maintain the rhythmic and hymnic traits so consistently as does the second passage. On the other hand, it gives a better insight into Paul's personal prayer by the fact that it is less inhibited by the conventions of liturgical and poetic form, and also because it is a very individual reaction to a concrete situation, which affected Paul deeply. It enunciates Paul's joyous, grateful praise at being delivered from a recent and very grave crisis, the threat of which still hangs over him. This is the "tribulation in Asia" reviewed in the last chapter.[15] Perhaps the most significant difference between the two confessions is that pointed out by Heinrich Schlier.[16] They are responses to two distinct

---

[15] See pp. 69-72.

[16] Heinrich Schlier, *Der Brief an die Epheser* (Düsseldorf, 1957), pp. 41-42.

kinds of theophany, or manifestation of God's presence. The
prayer in 2 Corinthians has arisen from Paul's experience of
God in the midst of danger, and in this it resembles the reaction
of the psalmist in Ps 28:6-7. The confession in Ephesians reflects a theophany communicated by a vision or oracle, similar
to that which occasioned Zachary's *Benedictus*. In it Paul un-
folds the revelation of the mystery of God (Eph 1:9) that has
been granted to him through the divine gift of "full wisdom
and insight" (v.8).

One value which the confession in Corinthians holds for our
inquiry is the indication it gives that Paul was little inclined to
draw a distinction between public and private prayer. This
moving example is both liturgical (it is a summons to his addressees to pray for him and to give thanks with him) and at
the same time intensely personal (it is totally related to Paul's
own critical situation). Another value is to be seen in the testimony it gives to Paul's persuasion that his sufferings and con-
solations were in fact a participation in the sufferings and
triumph of Christ himself (Col 1:23), and that these are of salutary significance for the Church. Thus the confession illustrates
Paul's conviction that Christ did not die and rise "instead of us",
in the sense that he excused or excluded us from suffering
with him (Rom 8:17) and experiencing "the power of his
resurrection" (Phil 3:10) in our own Christian existence. Indeed, for Paul baptism has meaning as a ritual anticipation of
our sharing throughout life in Christ's death, burial, and (ultimately) resurrection to new life with him (Rom 6:3-8). Thus
this sacrament sets the pattern for the entire life of the believer.

Paul's purpose in this confession is to solicit the prayers of
his Corinthian Christians in helping him to live with the "death-
sentence" he knows to be unrelenting in its inevitability. But
he wishes perhaps even more to increase the chorus of praise
and gratitude to God "for his act of graciousness towards me"
(2 Cor 1:11). Thus he begins his confession with an invitation to bless God, who has revealed himself to him as "Father
of our Lord Jesus Christ". God has indeed revealed himself
to every man with Christian faith through the continual saving
experience of "tribulation" and "consolation". This latter term,
it must be confessed, presents difficulties for the translator. It

denotes consolation, or comfort in the literal sense of that word. It signifies encouragement, if by that is understood courage to endure. The robust spirituality of Paul challenges us not to permit any version of his text to give the impression that he is seeking deliverance from the harsh realities of life.

It is in keeping with the nature of the confessions that Paul should inform his correspondents of the desperateness of the situation in which he faced death at Ephesus. His candid admission that he came close to despair, as well as his magnanimous avowal that he was at the time still far from putting his trust completely in God, cannot but win our admiration and respect.

3 "Blessed be the God and Father of our Lord Jesus Christ, our compassionate Father, our God who is all encouragement! 4 He keeps encouraging me in every one of my tribulations, so that I am able to encourage other people in each tribulation they suffer, through the comfort I myself experience from God. 5 It is because Christ's sufferings overflow in me that I in my turn overflow with consolation through Christ. 6 So when I suffer tribulation, it is in view of your encouragement and salvation: when I am comforted, it is in view of the encouragement you may feel in staunchly enduring the kind of suffering I myself bear. 7 And my hopes for you remain undaunted, because I know that since you are sharing in these sufferings, you will also be given a share in the [divine] consolation.

8 I do not wish you to be ignorant, brothers, of the tribulation I experienced in Asia. I was crushed by an excessively heavy burden, beyond my power to bear, so that I even despaired of living. 9 In fact, in my heart I have accepted the death-sentence. It was intended to teach me, not to put my trust in myself, but in the God who raises the dead. 10 He it is who rescued me from such grave perils of death, and so it is he who will continue to rescue me. Upon him I have set my hope irrevocably: he will rescue me yet, 11 provided you too will join in helping on my behalf by prayer. Thus gratitude will radiate from many faces, as thanks are offered to God on my behalf for his act of graciousness towards me" (2 Cor 1:3-11).

Perhaps the most precious feature of this prayer is its revelation of how completely human Paul actually was. The almost exclusively supernatural content of his prayer which his letters attest, his seeming lack of concern for the everyday needs of the temporal order, may at times discourage the more ordinary Christian. In this confession Paul bares his heart as he prays for a reprieve from the doom he knows awaits him eventually. We can be grateful for this rare glimpse of his humanity, which permits us some sense of Christian solidarity with this great-souled apostle.

The confession in Ephesians begins with the same Christian formula which headed the passage in 2 Cor 1:3: "Blessed be the God and Father of our Lord Jesus Christ". Immediately however it directs our attention to the manifold meaning Paul has discerned in the phrase "in Christ". The risen Lord, by his exaltation to heaven, has become the sphere in which "every spiritual blessing" for the Christian people is located. The Christian conception of "peace" is thus distinguished from the Old Testament *shālôm,* which always retained a measure of the earthy in its articulation of the messianic blessings. The "blessings" of which the passage speaks are "spiritual", that is, dominated by the dynamism of the Holy Spirit. The paradigm for the sum of all these blessings is the risen and glorified Christ, who as "last Adam" has become "life-giving Spirit" (1 Cor 15:45). His presence, through union with the Christian people as his body (Eph 4:11-16) *is the great theophany* which brings to the Church "full wisdom and insight" (Eph 1:8). The glorified Lord is in the fullest sense the "recapitulation" (v.10) of every blessing the Father has conferred upon us. He is the first and most fundamental "spiritual blessing" that has been bestowed on the Church.

Paul in the course of this confession goes on to enumerate six other "spiritual blessings", which are really various aspects of the first. There is the specifically Christian gift of holiness, or consecration to God, the divine sonship (v.5). There is the blessing of the historical event of man's redemption (v.7). When it is viewed with the fulness of "wisdom and insight" the "spiritual blessing" is seen as "the Mystery" par excellence (vv.8-9), the epiphany of God's saving plan of the recapitulation in Christ of the entire cosmos. A fifth aspect is to be found in the "election" of Israel as God's "portion" (*segūllāh*), or acquisition (v.11; cf. Deut 9:29). The divine call of the pagans to the gospel presents the sixth aspect (v.13). The crowning blessing is the gift of the Holy Spirit, whose indwelling in the heart of the Christian and in the Church constitutes a kind of "first instalment" of our ultimate inheritance. The Trinitarian character of this deeply theological hymn of praise and thanksgiving is striking. This essentially Christian revelation, as the passage clearly indicates, has been given us "in Christ". Perhaps there is no other passage in all Paul's letters that so profoundly testifies to the Trinitarian orientation of his prayer as does this confession.

3 "Blessed be the God and Father of our Lord Jesus Christ, who has blessed us in Christ with every spiritual blessing in the heavenly sphere. 4 In him God chose us before the creation of the world that we might be holy and irreproachable in his service by love, 5 since he destined us, of his own free and loving choice, as his adopted sons through Jesus Christ, 6 in order that the glory of his graciousness might redound to the praise of the grace he has bestowed on us in his beloved Son. 7 In him it is that we possess the redemption through his blood, the remission of our transgressions. That [event] demonstrates the riches of God's graciousness, 8 lavished on us by the gift of full wisdom and insight. 9 For he has made known to us the mystery of his purpose. It was, according to his good pleasure, determined beforehand in Christ, 10 to become a reality in the fulness of time: his plan to recapitulate in Christ all that exists in heaven or on earth. 11 It is in Christ that we [the Chosen people] have been granted our share in the inheritance, being destined thereto by the untrammelled decision of him, who brings all to realization in accordance with the design of his will. 12 We, the first to have placed our hope in Christ, have been destined to praise his glory. 13 It is in Christ that you too [the pagans], on hearing the word of truth, the good news of our salvation, and putting your faith in him, have been sealed with the Holy Spirit, promised by God. 14 He is the pledge of our inheritance, leading to our redemption as God's own portion, to his praise and glory" (Eph 1:3-14).

Of all the prayers which appear in Paul's letters none provides such impressive testimony to the Trinitarian character of his prayer. Here God appears as the "Father of our Lord Jesus Christ" (v.3), the initiator by his completely "free and loving choice" (v.4) of man's redemption (v.7), the divine "mystery" (v.9) of the recapitulation in Christ of Jew and Gentile (vv.11-13), announced in "the word of truth, the good news of our salvation" (v.13). This new status conferred by God's graciousness upon the Christian is conceived in characteristically Pauline fashion as constituting us "his adopted sons through Jesus Christ" (v.5) through the gift of the Holy Spirit, "the pledge of our inheritance" (v.14).

This confession displays another value, of considerable moment for our investigation, by centering attention upon the risen Christ, thus emphasizing the central position which he always held in Paul's prayer. By focussing upon Christ in this way the passage indicates the role played by Paul's meeting on the Damascus road in revealing the mystery of the Trinity. His understanding of God as Father and of the Spirit's presence in us as "the pledge of our inheritance" (v.14) became a reality for Paul as a result of his initial Christian experience. Through this magnificent profession of faith we are given an insight into the prominent place which the truth of our adoptive sonship held for Paul in the Christian life of prayer. As will become clear from a review of his instructions, prayer is the principal means by which the believer can continually progress in this life towards a deeper consciousness of his own self-identity "as his adopted sons through Jesus Christ" (v.5), "sealed with the Holy Spirit" (v.13) who brings us an awareness of "our inheritance" "as God's own portion" (v.14).

Chapter 4
Paul's Observations
Concerning Prayer

We began our inquiry into the meaning of prayer for Saint Paul by collecting and reviewing those passages scattered through his letters which may be judged to be genuine prayers. They were discovered to fall into four categories: the doxology, the brief, spontaneous act of gratitude, the wish directed to God or to Christ, and the confession. Three passages which are generally regarded as hymns (Phil 2:6-11; Col 1:15-20; Eph 5:14) were not included since there is a well-grounded consensus that Paul did not compose them. Our examination revealed certain qualities and directions which may be taken as characteristics of Paul's manner of prayer. The praise of God, gratitude for his "wonderful works", as well as for his gracious favors bestowed on Paul personally, a marked joyousness in responding to the divine initiative, a certain uninhibited candor and wonder with regard to his own shortcomings and God's fatherly concern, are so many indications of Paul's profound faith and hope, and of his intense love of God and of Christ. As regards the priority of certain of these attitudes over others, it is too early to make a definitive judgment because of the somewhat haphazard way in which these prayers, for the most part brief ejaculations, are scattered through the letters. Yet we have found certain directions taken by Paul's prayer. If the examples are mainly addressed to God the Father, it became clear that Paul also prays to Jesus Christ risen. If there is no prayer to the Holy Spirit, some evidence was found of Paul's awareness of the significance of the Spirit's activity in Christian prayer.

With a view to discerning more accurately and concretely the shape of Paul's prayer, the place it occupied in his own Christian life and in his apostolic ministry, his pedagogy in teaching others how to advance in this necessary art, we propose now to examine the observations he makes about prayer. These assume the form either of exhortations or of descriptions of prayer. In both instances it may be assumed that Paul speaks out of his own personal experience; hence his remarks can be taken to shed light upon his own prayer-life.

I

JOY, PRAYER, THANKSGIVING

We have already drawn attention to the elements of joy and thanksgiving contained in the Pauline conception of "boasting", in which the prayer of petition was also present by implication in the expression of loving confidence in God. Petition was also implied in the brief thanksgiving in Rom 7:25, which is so redolent of joy. This threefold attitude will be seen to characterize the formal Pauline thanksgiving, when it is examined in the next chapter. It is instructive to observe how these three qualities appear in combination in Paul's instructions on prayer to the communities under his charge.

The first instruction which emphasizes the necessity of maintaining this triple element in all genuine Christian prayer occurs in the second part of 1 Thessalonians, devoted to a description of Christian living in accordance with the will of God, who has given the believer his vocation. For Paul the goal of Christian existence is epitomized in the single word, "sanctifying", which he repeats three times in his exhortation (1 Thes 4:3; 4, 7). The term indicates the ongoing process of the Christian's consecration to God, the goal of which is "eternal life" (Rom 6:23). "This is the will of God—your sanctifying" (v.7). The duty of growing in holiness, being devoted more completely to

God, is the imperative arising out of the divine gifts of faith and baptism, and hence it represents God's will for him as a person.

In the sequel Paul takes up the various issues involved in being a Christian about which he feels the Thessalonians need further schooling, among them, instruction in prayer. 16 "Be joyful always, 17 pray without ceasing, 18 give thanks in every eventuality. This is God's will in Christ with regard to you. 19 Do not quench the Spirit, 20 do not belittle prophetic utterances—21 test everything about them: hold onto what is good, 22 shun every appearance of evil [in them]" (1 Thes 5:16-22). The triad, joy, prayer, thanks, is presented as a unity: the three are considered simply so many aspects of "God's will in Christ", which Paul has already called "your sanctifying" (1 Thes 4:3), the process initiated by the divine call to Christians (1 Thes 4:7). "Sanctifying" is a peculiarly Pauline word, found elsewhere in the New Testament only at Heb 12:14 and 1 Pt 1:2. It is related to the action of the Holy Spirit (2 Thes 2:13) and to the risen Christ, "who became our wisdom from God, uprightness, and sanctifying, and redemption" (1 Cor 1:30). If Paul regards the Father, Christ, and the Spirit as involved in furthering the sanctifying of the Christian, it is to be expected that he will be aware of their activity in the Christian's response to the will of God by joy, prayer, and thanksgiving.

By asserting that the Christian response is "God's will *in Christ* with regard to you", Paul is probably thinking, not so much of Christ's mediation of the divine action, as of the union between the Christian and the risen Lord, the basis upon which the threefold reply of the believer rests. Joy, prayer, and thanksgiving are three significant manifestations of the new life, "*the* charism of God in Christ Jesus our Lord" (Rom 6:23), communicated through Christ in the Spirit from the Father. The triad is central to the Pauline conception of being a Christian. What aspects of this reality do these three graces denote?

The joy of which Paul speaks is not a kind of natural optimism, but a divine gift. Not only is it not incompatible with suffering, but, as the Thessalonians themselves have demonstrated, its presence in "tribulation" is proof of the presence of the Holy Spirit who causes it (1 Thes 1:6). This joy is the opposite of "anxiety" (Phil 4:4-6), preoccupation with concerns other than "pleasing the Lord" (1 Cor 7:32-33). It is incompatible with the hopeless grief displayed by the pagan in the face of death (1 Thes 4:13), although not incompatible with that "grief related to God" which "produces a change of heart leading to salvation, while the grief of the world leads to death" (2 Cor 7:10).

This Christian joy is frequently associated by Paul with the Holy Spirit, who produces it (1 Thes 1:6). With love, joy is among the first fruits of the Spirit (Gal 5:22): with justice and peace, "joy in the Holy Spirit" is an element in "the kingdom of God" (Rom 14:17). It is "the power of the Holy Spirit" that makes "joy and peace abound in hope through believing" (Rom 15:13). Paul credits his joy in his imprisonment to the prayers of the Philippians and "the assistance of the Spirit of Jesus Christ" (Phil 1:18-19).

By his recommendation to "be joyful *always*" Paul indicates that joy is to be a permanent attitude on the part of the Christian, stimulated by attention to the true nature of joy as a gift of God in the Holy Spirit. By prefixing this directive to the command to "pray always" Paul implies that joy is the context in which prayer can flourish.

The term for prayer employed here is a general one: Paul regards the Christian life as a life of prayer, indeed of *incessant* prayer. He urges his addressees to "persevere in prayer" (Rom 12:12; Col 4:2), and in this he himself leads the way. He prays "always" for the Thessalonians (2 Thes 1:11), "day and night" and "beyond all measure" (1 Thes 3:10). In Paul's summons to the Christian to engage in "the holy war", constancy in prayer is given due place as one of the most effective spiritual weapons. "Give yourselves wholly to prayer and petition by praying at every opportunity in the Spirit: and to the same end, keep vigils with total perseverance and constant petition for all the saints and for me" (Eph 6:18-19). As Heinrich Schlier notes, "prayer in the Spirit" does not suggest glossolalia, nor is a contrast intended between "interior" and "vocal" prayer.[1] It recalls the operation of the Spirit in Christian prayer, which is like the Spirit's activity in erecting upon Christ as its foundation the Ephesian community as "a dwelling-place for God" (Eph 2:22), or like his operation in communicating "the Mystery" to Christ's apostles and prophets (Eph 3:5).

Paul's exhortation to the Thessalonians to "pray without ceasing" reveals his conviction, manifested elsewhere, that there is no time, or place, or circumstance in life that is not to be accompanied by prayer. At the same time it is to be noted that he does not command his Christians to "say prayers" always. What he urges is the cultivation of an attitude, after the example of Jesus himself (Lk 18:1), the apostles (Lk 24:53), and the primitive church of Jerusalem (Acts 12:5). The attitude is perhaps best described as a constant attention to God, which is assisted by a deepening awareness of the nearness of Christ and of the action of the Spirit within the heart. The various eventualities and crises of daily living help to alert the Christian to this reality and his own reactions to his circumstances prompt him to specify this general attitude of prayer by acts of praise, petition for his own needs and those of others, joyful thanks for the divine assistance. This probably explains why Paul, who shows in his letters a great familiarity with the many forms prayer can assume, has here chosen to employ the most general and comprehensive word for prayer at his disposal.

Moreover, as with the joy to be displayed "always" in the Christian life, Paul knows that incessant prayer is a gift of God, forming as it does part of that concrete reality, "his will in Christ with regard to you". Whatever form the prayer at times may take, the essential is that the Christian pray unremittingly. Only in this way does he remain open to the divine will for him by virtue of his union with Christ. Finally, it should be observed that Paul does not specify that the prayer be addressed to God. We have already seen that his own

[1] Heinrich Schlier, *Der Brief an die Epheser* (Düsseldorf, 1965), p. 301.

prayer was at times directed to "the Lord" (2 Thes 2:16-17; 3:5). Indeed, this was especially so in the one narrative he has left of an experience (2 Cor 12:7-10), which he regarded as marking a major advance in his own attitude to prayer. And in fact his remark that the Amen (one of Paul's favorite prayers) is always said through the risen Christ (2 Cor 1:20) is itself evidence of how frequently Paul turned in prayer to Christ while praying to God. One has only to recall that the Lord Jesus was the most real, as well as the person closest to Paul's life, to be aware that to pray *through him* could only mean that an intensely personal communication with Christ was presupposed as the condition *sine qua non* of any prayer to the Father.

"Give thanks in every eventuality" (1 Thes 5:18) is the third aspect of Christian living, or Christian consciousness vis-a-vis the will of God, which Paul inculcates. There is no term for prayer, including the most general word he has just employed, which occurs in Paul's writing with anything like the frequency of the verb or noun expressing thankfulness. Moreover, it has in Pauline usage become a technical term for offering thanks to God, and thus it can be used, as here, without explicit mention of God (1 Cor 14:17). Only once is it used of gratitude to human beings in the Pauline letters (Rom 16:4). It is a hellenistic word, originally meaning "do a favor for", "oblige"; in late Greek it came to mean "be grateful", "give thanks". In the Greek Bible it appears rarely, and exhibits both the secular and the religious (Jud 8:25; 2 Macc 1:11; 10:7) signification.

Paul undoubtedly received the term from the tradition of the early Christian community, where it was employed to express the sentiments of Jesus at the Last Supper (1 Cor 11:24). He uses the noun, "act of thanksgiving" (*eucharistia*), to denote a prayer or attitude of thanks (1 Cor 14:16; Eph 5:14), not however with reference to the Eucharist. In this sense it appears very early in the sub-apostolic Christian literature (*Didachē* IX, I, 5), particularly in the letters of Ignatius of Antioch.

It may be said that in Paul the word becomes charged with

new significance by contrast with Jewish usage, where it was used for praise of God. The development is due to Paul's profound sense of indebtedness to the divine graciousness for everything he has and for all that happens to him. As Béda Rigaux observes, the term "voices Paul's feeling of complete indebtedness and, at the same time, it frees the heart from a duty".[2] Paul employs the word to denote the direction of his gratitude to God alone; nowhere does he speak of giving thanks to Christ, or to the Spirit. We shall see from a study of the formal thanksgivings that Paul had the habit of expressing his thanks to God in the course of his prayer, where it is interwoven with petition. Thus he appears to have regarded gratitude, like joy, as the climate favorable to prayer.

In our passage (1 Thes 5:18) Paul urges that thanks be expressed "in every eventuality". There is no gift of God, no circumstance of life, so insignificant as be allowed to pass without thanks. This attitude of constant, universal gratefulness is regarded by him as an aid to perseverance in prayer: "Persevere in prayer, remaining wakeful at it by thanksgiving" (Col 4:2). The command to "remain wakeful" is the Christian watchword for the second coming of Christ (Mk 13:37). Paul who is not unfamiliar with it (1 Thes 5:6) urges thanksgiving as a means of keeping this eschatological hope alive.

Like constant joy and unremitting prayer, this capacity for gratitude at all that happens to the Christian constitutes the concrete expression of "the will of God in Christ". Thus it is primarily a divine gift which elicits and supports the continual response of the man with faith. Paul's keen sensibility of his indebtedness to God for all that he has and is, and his extraordinary sense of the limitlessness of the divine bounty demand that these directives for Christian living be taken at their face-value and not discounted as an exaggeration. It may not be irrelevant to cite the perceptive observations of Jerome D. Quinn on this point. "The language is, of course, hyperbolic, but only in the sense that to believe always, to hope always,

---

[2] Béda Rigaux, *Les Épitres aux Thessaloniciens* (Paris: Gembloux, 1956), p. 359.

to love always is hyperbolic. The exegesis of these passages
(not to mention our acting on their imperatives) has tended
to be 'hyperbolic' (if I may coin a term), and to that extent
we have not really seen the heart of Paul the apostle, totally
concerned with 'the Lord's affairs' (1 Cor 7:32) and 'anxiety'
for all the churches (2 Cor 11:28)." [3]

It is impressive to find this same threefold injunction recurring again in Philippians. "Rejoice in the Lord always. I shall
say it again, rejoice! Let your magnanimity be known to all men.
The Lord is near. Stop worrying; rather, in every prayer let
your requests be made known with gratitude. And the peace of
God, which surpasses all understanding, will guard your hearts
and your thoughts in Christ Jesus" (Phil 4:4-7). Here the joy
to be constantly elicited is specified by "in the Lord". It is to
radiate to "all men" through Christian "magnanimity". The
term Paul employs is a borrowing from Stoic terminology, but
it has been christianized by being founded upon the sense of
the nearness of the risen Christ, not necessarily however in a
chronological sense (the imminence of the parousia). While
the phrase "the Lord is near" might be a variant of *Marana
tha!*—"Come, our Lord!" (1 Cor 16:22), it is more probably
an allusion to Ps 144:18-20 in the Greek version of the Septuagint. "The Lord is near to all who call upon him, to all who
call upon him in uprightness. He will do the will of those who
fear him, and he will hear their request, and save them. The
Lord will guard all who love him . . .". For Paul it is the risen
Lord who embodies the nearness of God. When Paul's inter-
jection of the thought of Christ's nearness as the basis for Christian joyfulness is understood as an allusion to Ps 144, it explains the transition in our text to the exhortation about prayer.

"Stop worrying" echoes the sayings of Jesus recorded in the
Sermon on the Mount (Mt 6:25, 27, 28, 31, 34). Excessive
concern is the negation of Christian joy, revealing as it does a
want of faith in the fatherly care of God. It is also an insidious
form of ingratitude. Untiring prayer "with gratitude" is here
proposed as the remedy for troubled anxiety.

[3] Jerome D. Quinn, "Apostolic Ministry and Apostolic Prayer" *Catholic Biblical Quarterly* 33 (1971), 489-490.

Three nouns here designate prayer. Bishop J. B. Lightfoot [4] characterizes the first term as "the general offering up of the wishes and desires to God". It is found frequently enough in Paul. The second word "implies special petition for the supply of wants", and it is characteristic of Paul. With the third word, not occurring elsewhere in the letters, attention is focussed on the content of petitionary prayer. Paul's point is that whatever form prayer may assume, it is crucial to display thankfulness in addressing God. Paul's own personal practice, as has been pointed out, confirms the fact that this is his deep conviction about the necessity of giving thanks always in prayer.

Paul shows his belief in the infallible efficacy of prayer by appending a word about God's reply to the pleas of the Christian. "And the peace of God, which surpasses all understanding, will guard your hearts and your thoughts in Christ Jesus" (v.7). One of the effects of prayer is to maintain the union of the Christian with Christ. "The peace of God" (a phrase found nowhere else in Paul) bestowed in response to prayer is pictured as a cordon of soldiers thrown round the intimate personal relationship between Christ and the praying believer, to "guard" those powers ("your hearts and your thoughts") which are employed in prayer. The military metaphors suggest the continual struggle with evil that accompanies Christian existence. The struggle is elsewhere presented as war between Christian love and the powers of evil (Rom 12:9-21). Among the weapons to be relied upon are two members of the triad we have been considering: "Rejoicing through hope, standing firm in tribulation, persevering in prayer" (v.12).

II
"IN THE NAME OF OUR LORD JESUS CHRIST"

The author of the Fourth Gospel designates Christian prayer as asking "in the name of Jesus", when he teaches the infallible nature of petition either to Christ himself (Jn 14:13-14), or to the Father (Jn 15:16). "The name" here signifies that revelation of Jesus' self-identity which, in this Gospel, is com-

[4] J. B. Lightfoot, *Saint Paul's Epistle to the Philippians* (London, 1881), p. 160.

municated by Jesus' glorification. The believer's response of
faith and love to Jesus, "the Vine" (Jn 15:1 ff.), inaugurates
and sustains that mutual "abiding" in the glorified Jesus which
is "eternal life". When the Christian addresses the Father with
attention to his union with the incarnate and risen Son, he prays
"in Jesus' name", and such prayer is universally efficacious.
"And on that day you will not ask me for anything. I solemnly
assure you that whatever you ask the Father in my name he
will give you. Until now you have asked nothing in my name:
ask and you will receive, in order that your joy may be fulfilled
. . . On that day you will ask in my name, and I do not promise
you I shall ask the Father on your behalf, because the Father
himself loves you, since you have loved me and have put faith
in the fact that I am come forth from the Father" (Jn
16:23-27).

The corresponding Pauline phrase is "the name of our Lord
Jesus Christ". When Paul prays that the Thessalonians become
worthy of their God-given vocation by the fullest living out of
the Christian life, his purpose is "that the name of our Lord
Jesus may be glorified in you, and you in him, according to the
graciousness of our God and of Lord Jesus Christ" (2 Thes
1:12). The mention of glorification in connection with "the
name" indicates that it is question of God's revelation of the
person of Jesus Christ. He is thinking of the deepening in
the Christian of the awareness of *who Christ is*, rather than of
that eschatological glorification he has just spoken of (2 Thes
1:10). As Christ reveals himself more intimately to the Christian, he is increasingly "glorified" in him: as the Christian re-
sponds with increased love and "activity of faith" (v.11), he
is "glorified" in Christ. Paul speaks in similar fashion of this
continual process of the deepening of the Christian's knowledge of Christ in 2 Cor 3:18: "All of us, as with unveiled
face we behold the glory of the Lord in a mirror, are being
transformed into the same image from glory to glory, by the
Lord who is Spirit". Christ himself is the mirror, it would
appear,[5] in which the believer contemplates his "glory" as

[5] A. Feuillet, *Le Christ Sagesse de Dieu d'après les Épitres Paulini-
ennes* (Paris, 1966), pp. 135-144.

Lord, thereby growing more and more in the experiential knowledge of *who Christ is*. This progress in learning Christ's identity in a more personal, intimate fashion is something which concerned Paul all his Christian life, and is to be considered a salient feature of his spirituality.

There are two passages concerned with the purpose of public worship, which speak of this constant acquiring of the knowledge of Christ through prayer "in the name of our Lord Jesus Christ". "May the word of Christ dwell among you in all its riches, as you teach and admonish one another by songs, hymns, and spiritual canticles, singing gratefully to God in your hearts. And whatever you do by word or action, [do it] all in the name of the Lord Jesus, giving thanks to God the Father through him" (Col 3:16-18). The Christian liturgy, in which "the word of Christ" is particularly operative, is intended to increase the community's awareness of Christ and lead to thanksgiving—its dominant motif, soon to be explicitly articulated by its designation as the Eucharist. This public expression of thanks, arising out of growth in the knowledge of "the word of Christ", is mediated by him to the Father. Christ's mediation of the liturgical action and its articulation in words makes it prayer "in the name of the Lord Jesus".

How does the community actually pray to the Father *through* Christ? It is enough to recall the profoundly personal character of Paul's relationship to the risen Christ to realize that prayer through him to God demands that the believer first approach Christ *as a person,* not as some kind of instrument of communication, employed simply as a means. The passage in Ephesians which is a parallel to that just cited clarifies this question admirably. "Do not get drunk on wine—that is simply dissoluteness! Rather be filled with the Spirit, as you speak to one another by songs, hymns, and spiritual canticles. Sing and make music in your hearts *to the Lord,* giving thanks always for everything in the name of our Lord Jesus Christ to God, who is also Father" (Eph 5:18-20). The *liturgical* character of the chanting of hymns, whose deeply Christological and theological character (cf. Phil 2:6-11) contains instruction for the church, demands that these prayers be in a real sense also addressed to the assembled community. Their character *as prayer* however demands that they be addressed "to the Lord", and ultimately as thanksgiving to the Father. This prayer of gratitude through Christ to God is prayer "in the name of our Lord Jesus Christ".

Thus it becomes very clear that Paul did actually pray to Christ, who was so intensely real as a person in his life. That prayer, Paul was well aware, did not terminate with Christ, but came to rest ultimately, "in the name of" Christ, with the Father.

III

PRAYER AS STRUGGLE: A MISUNDERSTANDING

There are several passages in Paul, as is well known, in which metaphors deriving originally from those athletic exercises so dear to the Greeks make their appearance (1 Cor 9:24-27). One of these was cited in the discussion of Paul's conversion (Phil 3:12-14).[6] Two other passages employing the image of athletic contests have been commonly interpreted as indications that Paul described prayer, which he considered an efficacious means of exercising his apostolate, under the image of an athletic contest (Rom 15:30; Col 4:12). Is it in fact accurate to say that he wished thereby to illustrate the function of his "apostolic prayer", to assert his conviction that it was "a struggle in which the apostle engaged with God on behalf of the very mission that had been confided to him"?[7]

Before attempting to answer the question, we should give some thought to the very curious phenomenon, the appearance of athletic images in a writer who remained culturally so Jewish in outlook as Paul. Frequenting the hellenistic gymnasium was one of the features of Hellenism held in horror by the Jews, because of the bodily nakedness, which was a concomitant feature of Greek athletics (cf. 2 Macc 4:10-14). Moreover, the

---

[6] See pp. 18-21.

[7] Stanislas Lyonnet, "Un Aspect de la 'Prière Apostolique'" *Christus* 5 (1958), p. 229.

Greek games, held under the patronage of the gods, were a manifestation of the Greek, and therefore pagan, religious spirit. Finally, by Paul's day the great hellenistic athletic contests of three or four centuries before had fallen into a sorry state of degradation and corruption.[8]

How then explain the appearance of these sporting images in Paul? A careful study even of those passages, where the metaphor is deliberately and consciously used by Paul, will reveal a lack of concrete detail such as would not be expected in a man who had been a spectator at the games. On the other hand, the kind of comparisons made was current in the popular philosophy of the time. They were also literary commonplaces in hellenistic Jewish writers like Philo. It seems more plausible then to consider these as the sources of Pauline athletic imagery rather than any personal interest Paul may be thought to have taken in Greek athleticism. Indeed, it may well be that this kind of imagery had already passed into common parlance, and hence could be employed at times by Paul without adverting to the games, which had given rise to the transferred sense of the terms.

There are passages in the letters which show that Paul often represented this apostolic ministry as an athletic contest. For one thing, it expressed the opposition against which he had often to struggle. "Having suffered injury and outrage at Philippi, as you are well aware, with the help of our God we fearlessly declared to you the gospel of God—and what a struggle it was!" (1 Thes 2:2). The term "struggle" in this text could be applied as well to suffering and persecution for the sake of the faith and the gospel. Thus Paul compares the sufferings endured by the Philippian community to his own situation in prison. "To you the grace has been given [by God] for the sake of Christ, not only to believe in him but also to suffer for his sake. You are engaged in the same contest as you once saw me involved in, and in which, as you hear, I am still engaged" (Phil 1:29-30).

Paul uses the same figure to describe for the Roman church

8 Victor C. Pfitzner, *Paul and the Agon Motif* (Leiden, 1967), p. 187.

his projected visit to Jerusalem, during which he anticipates
trouble from the Jews, who regard him as a renegade, and perhaps also, suspicion or mistrust on the part of the Jewish Christians there. In this "contest" which concerns the gospel, Paul
asks urgently for the assistance of prayers. "I implore you,
brothers, by our Lord Jesus Christ and the love of the Spirit,
to join the contest on my side by your prayers on my behalf to
God, that I may be rescued from the unbelievers in Judea and
that my service to [the community of] Jerusalem may find acceptance by the saints,—and further, that by God's will I may
ultimately visit you joyously and enjoy some rest together with
you" (Rom 15:30-32).

The "contest" Paul faces for the sake of the gospel includes
opposition from his enemies, and suspicion (at least) from his
fellow-Christians of Jerusalem. He invites the members of the
Roman community to support him by their prayers, thus providing them an opportunity of participating in the contest. This
is the sense of the compound verb "struggle together with",
which is correlative to the second compound verb "enjoy rest
together with". There is consequently no suggestion that Paul
thinks of prayer as a "contest". It is regarded rather as the
means of permitting the Romans to share in the contest, which
Paul faces in defending his gospel and safeguarding his life.

The contest-imagery recurs in Colossians. "He [Christ] it
is we proclaim by admonishing every man and instructing each
one by wisdom of every kind, in order that we may present
each as a mature person in Christ. To this purpose also I labor
by engaging in the [present] contest with that energy Christ
creates in me by his power. For I desire you to know of the
strenuous contest I am carrying on for your sake and that of the
Laodiceans, and for all who have never set eyes on me" (Col
1:28–2:1). Paul intends to "proclaim Christ" by means of
this letter he is actually writing to Colossae. But he is anxious
to have these Christians realize that by suffering imprisonment,
as he is, he has not ceased to engage in the contest on behalf
of the gospel. His sufferings *are* the sufferings of Christ, and
they are efficacious for the entire Church (Col 1:24), Christ's

body; and hence, they are Paul's present means of carrying on the contest for the Colossians and Laodiceans.

Among those who are near the prisoner (though not actually imprisoned with Paul) is a member of the Colossian community, Epaphras, their founder (Col 1:7). In forwarding the greetings of Epaphras Paul speaks of him as also involved in the "contest" on their behalf by his prayers for their perseverance, the sole means left to Epaphras at the moment of "working" for them. "Epaphras sends you his good wishes, that servant of Christ who is one of you. He is continually engaged in the contest by his prayers on your behalf, that you may stand fast . . . " (Col 4:12).

The consideration of these texts shows that Paul does not conceive prayer as a struggle, but as one means among others of taking part in the "contest" for the faith and the gospel, to which as an apostle he is pledged. Insofar as the metaphor of contest affects the Pauline notion of prayer, it may be said to imply great earnestness and devotion in thus sharing in the apostolic struggle. Nowhere does Paul give any indication that he considered prayer itself as a "contest".

IV
Prayer and the "Building Up" of the Church

There can be no doubt of the high esteem in which Paul held prayer as a means of fostering the growth of the Church. His constant references to his own unremitting prayer for the communities to which he writes are too numerous to mention (cf. 2 Cor 13:7-10). Moreover, he frequently asks for assistance by their prayers for himself and his work, from his correspondents (1 Thes 5:25; 2 Thes 3:1; 2 Cor 1:11; Rom 15:30; Col 4:3).

In his discussion of that type of prayer which he calls "speaking with tongues" (1 Cor 14:2 ff.), Paul evaluates it in function of the development of the congregation, especially towards unity. "Now with regard to your own situation, since you are eager for spiritual gifts, seek to excel in those conducive to the building up of the church" (1 Cor 14:12). The highest priority is given to fraternal love; next in value is prophecy (14:11). He displays considerable reserve with regard to prayer "with tongues". He acknowledges indeed that it is a gift of the Spirit (v.1), that it is prayer (v.14), of personal benefit to him who possesses it (v.4). Paul admits that he himself possesses the charism to a high degree (v.18). However, he places a far greater value on prayer which engages the mind (vv.13-19). Praying with tongues has no sign-value for other Christians. For those without faith it is indeed a sign (v.22), but a *menacing* sign, as the Old Testament shows (Is 28:11-12; Deut 28:49).

Paul does not forbid such prayer at public worship, but he limits its exercise severely (vv.27-28). The principle he applies to prophesying within the community is applicable *a fortiori* to prayer with tongues: "God is a God of peace, not of confusion" (v.33).

What was the nature of this prayer with tongues? Paul does not provide sufficient data to enable the question to be answered with any degree of probability. Since the Corinthians were acquainted with the experience, there was no need to describe it to them. Professional scripturists remain divided on whether this kind of prayer was the same as that ecstatic prayer described by Luke as occurring on Pentecost (Acts 2:2-13). Nor can any historical tradition be recovered that might settle the issue. Saint John Chrysostom, one of the greatest exegetes of the Antiochian school, asserts in the fourth century that already in his day all historical memory of the nature of prayer in tongues had been lost. He remarks a-propos of 1 Corinthians chapter 14, "The entire passage is very obscure. This ambiguity arises from our lack of knowledge of a phenomenon that happened in that era, but no longer occurs in our times".[9] It must, in consequence, be admitted that the identification by some present day Pentecostalists of an experience, designated as speaking or praying with tongues, with what happened among first century Corinthian Christians

---

[9] Homily 29, XII, 1, cited by E.-B. Allo, *Première Épitre aux Corinthiens* (Paris, 1956), p. 377.

rests on an assumption that would be very difficult, not to say impossible, to demonstrate either exegetically or historically.

V

PRAYER AS AWARENESS OF ADOPTIVE SONSHIP

We come now to the theme which, I venture to suggest, must be said to express the dominant motif in Paul's conception of Christian prayer. In reviewing the passages which exhibit the fruit of Paul's reflections on the sense of his initial meeting with the risen Christ by the Damascus road, we pointed to Gal 1:15-16 as the text which best discloses what this experience held for Paul personally, and how it affected permanently his entire approach to God in Christ.[10] "When it pleased him who set me apart from my mother's womb and called me through his graciousness, *to reveal his Son in me* . . .". However crucial this confrontation might in Paul's mind be for his commissioning as an apostle, endowing him with an authority equal to that of the Twelve, however radical its formative influence on his new views as a Christian regarding justification by faith, his conversion remained principally in his eyes—and this above every other consideration—the disclosure of the Father's predilection for himself because it was God's revelation of "his Son in me".

The correctness of this judgment, we have also seen, is borne out by the most personal disclosure in all Paul's writings of what living as a Christian had come in the course of years to mean for him. "It is no longer that I live—Christ lives in me. With regard to my present bodily existence, I live my life by *faith in the Son of God,* who loved me and handed himself over for my sake" (Gal 2:20). To be a believer means for Paul, above all else, to maintain a loving interpersonal relationship with the risen Christ, dwelling within him as the Son of God. This confession illuminates in a concrete way what Paul meant by describing the purpose of his own conversion to the Chris-

[10] See pp. 33-40.

tian life as "that I might live for God" (Gal 2:19). His new-found relationship to God as Father was created by God's revelation of "his Son in me". Accordingly he can characterize their new Christian life for the Thessalonians as an "awaiting his Son from heaven, Jesus our rescuer from the wrath that is coming" (1 Thes 1:10). He will designate the Father as the source of the Corinthians' vocation by saying, "God is faithful, through whom you were called into the fellowship of his Son Jesus Christ our Lord" (1 Cor 1:9). The goal of Christian life is a return to God as Father through the Son, "through whom we both have access in one Spirit to the Father" (Eph 2:18). "For us there is one God, the Father, from whom all [has come] and to whom we all [return], and one Lord, Jesus Christ, through whom everything [came] and through whom we [return to the Father]" (1 Cor 8:6). "Those whom he knew beforehand he destined to be remolded in the image of his Son, so that he [the Son] might be the eldest of a large family of brothers" (Rom 8:29).

It is striking how congenial Paul found it to express the roles played by God and by Christ in man's redemption in function of their relationship as Father and Son. God "did not spare his own Son, but handed him over for the sake of us all" (Rom 8:32). It was "God the Father who raised him from the dead" (Gal 1:1); "We were reconciled to God through the death of his Son" (Rom 5:10); "Giving thanks to the Father, who has readied you to share the inheritance of the saints in the realm of light. He it is who rescued us from the power of darkness and has transported us into the kingdom of his own dear Son" (Col 1:12-13). Christ "was constituted Son of God in power by resurrection from the dead" (Rom 1:4), since "he was raised from the dead by the glory of the Father" (Rom 6:4).

Thus it is no accident that Paul should employ a term to designate the relationship of the Christian to God in Christ, which is found nowhere else in the New Testament: adoption, adoptive sonship. It was God who "destined us, of his own free and loving choice, as his adopted sons through Jesus Christ" (Eph 1:5). "We are God's children" (Rom 8:16,

21; Phil 2:15; Eph 5:1). We are "God's sons" (Gal 3:26; 4:7; Rom 8:14, 19). It is interesting to observe how Paul, by a free adaptation of certain Old Testament texts (2 Sam 7:8, 14; Is 43:6; Jer 31:9) makes even more explicit than it was the divine promise, "I will be like a father to you, and you will be as sons and daughters to me" (2 Cor 6:18).

It is in Galatians that Paul first speaks of Christian prayer in terms of this divine adoptive sonship. It will be recalled that the third chapter of that letter is devoted to solving the problem raised by Paul's judaizing adversaries in the minds of these former pagans. How can the Gentiles be heirs of the promise made by God to Abraham, when they cannot claim any relationship to the patriarch of Israel? Paul gives a preliminary answer, "The men of faith—they are Abraham's sons" (Gal 3:7), since it was precisely in view of the justification by faith of the Gentiles that God's *proto-evangelium* announced to Abraham is worded by Scripture, "In you will all the Gentiles [nations] find blessing" (v.8). Indeed "Christ redeemed us [Jewish-Christians] from the curse of the law, in order that Abraham's blessing might by Christ Jesus pass to the Gentiles" (vv.13-14).

Paul advances a further argument. The divine promises were pledged "to Abraham and to his offspring" (v.16); but Christ alone is truly Abraham's offspring, and hence his sole heir. Faith in Christ Jesus has made all Christians "God's sons", while baptism has united them so closely to Christ as to be "one man in Christ Jesus" (vv.26-28). To belong "to Christ's party", as these Gentile Christians now in fact do, means they "are Abraham's offspring, heirs by promise" (v.29).

The mention of the word "heir" leads Paul by free association to characterize the era before Christ's coming as a time when mankind, Jew as well as Gentile, was a minor, "in no wise different from a slave" (4:1), and indeed all "were enslaved by subjection to the elements of the world" (v.3). By this last mysterious phrase, Paul clearly means the Mosaic Law so far as the Jews were concerned (3:22-24). Whatever corresponded to it in the case of the Gentiles is very difficult to say. Perhaps it was so obviously their ignorance and degradation as pagans, that Paul considers precision unnecessary. Christ's entry into human history meant that mankind, Jew and pagan, had attained its majority.

We have now reached the passage which is of particular interest to our theme. 4 "When the fulness of time came, God sent forth his Son, become [man] of a woman, become subject to the Law, 5 in order that he might redeem those under law, in order that we might receive the adoptive sonship. 6 To show that you are sons, God sent forth the Spirit of his Son into our hearts, crying *'Abba,* dear Father!' 7 So that each one of you is no longer a slave: he is son; but if son, also heir by act of God" (Gal 4:4-6).

"The fulness of time" signifies the climax of sacred history, "the fulfilment of the ages" (1 Cor 10:11). For Paul it is the breaking in upon man's history of the future age: the end-time has become a matter of human experience. The initiative in accomplishing the turning-point of history belongs of course to God. It is to be observed however that for Paul the divine initiative is deployed in *two acts,* each with its own specific purpose. "God sent forth his Son", the pre-existent Christ: "God sent forth the Spirit of his Son", the Holy Spirit.

In describing God's sending forth of his Son Paul underscores the reality of the incarnation: "become [man] from a woman", and also the historicity of Jesus Christ: "become subject to the Law". The aim of this mission was the universal redemption of mankind. This was accomplished (although Paul does not stop here to mention it) by Jesus' death and resurrection (Rom 4:25). What is often called the "objective redemption" meant the coming of age of the entire human race, now given the possibility of freedom from "the elements of the world". For Christians, whether former Jews or Gentiles, the redemption meant something more specific: "that we might receive the adoptive sonship", through faith which creates man's receptivity for this gift of the Father. Paul does not pause to mention faith (and baptism), since he has already spoken of both (Gal 3:26-27) in his preceding paragraph. Nor does he take time to explain this "adoptive sonship". In the interest of his principal argument he is content here to present the adoption of man by God as the actual liberation of the Christian, whether pagan or Jewish, from all regime of law. In Romans 9:4 he lists among the privileges of Israel that "adoptive sonship" of which the Mosaic Law articulated the responsibilities for the chosen people. It has now been replaced by a totally new "adoptive sonship" in Christ Jesus.

However, it is not enough in the plan of the Father that the Christian should have been graciously raised to this totally undeserved status as his son in Christ. The Christian must in addition be made conscious of his precious, new dignity. And for this, the sending forth of the Spirit, the gift of the risen Christ, was necessary.

It may not be irrelevant to say something here about the significance of the Holy Spirit for Paul. As in the Old Testament, the Spirit is associated with divine power. He operates particularly through the gospel, "the power of God leading to salvation" (Rom 1:16). "The gospel", Paul writes to Thessalonica, "did not come to you by word alone, but also in power and by the Holy Spirit with deep conviction" (1 Thes 1:5). Thus he is source of that joy in persecution which is the hallmark of an authentic Christian vocation (v.6), and also the source of Christian hope (Rom 15:30). He is the bearer of divine revelation (1 Cor 2:10), and is operative in baptism (1 Cor 6:11; 12:13). He is the antithesis of the "letter" of the "old testament"—the phrase is Paul's invention (2 Cor 3:14), and the source of the newness of the New Testament (2 Cor 3:6; Rom 2:29).

The Spirit is the gift of God to the Christian people (1 Thes 4:8; Gal 3:5), and constitutes the pledge or earnest of eternal life (2 Cor 1:22; 5:5; Eph 1:14). As God's gift, he is the one through whom "the love of God has been poured out into our hearts as a gift" (Rom 5:5); hence he is the well-spring of Christian "communion", or fellowship (Phil 2:1; 2 Cor 13:13; Rom 15:30). The Spirit dwells within the Christian and the Christian community as in his sanctuary (1 Cor 3:16; 6:19; Rom 8:11). Thus he is active at the very heart of the Christian life of prayer by his divine assistance (Phil 1:19): he "comes to the aid of our weakness" and "intercedes" for us when at prayer.

It is evident however that Paul's conception of the Holy

Spirit and his role in Christian living has been mediated to him through his experience of the risen Christ. Consequently, one finds Paul predicating most of these activities and attributes of the Spirit also of the glorified Christ. Apart from the very obscure remark, "The Lord is the Spirit" (2 Cor 3:17-18), there is the statement that "the last Adam has become life-giving Spirit" (1 Cor 15:45). Christ is "the power of God and the wisdom of God" (1 Cor 1:24). Like the Spirit (1 Cor 6:11), Christ "has become for us . . . justification and sanctifying" (1 Cor 1:30). Like the Spirit, Christ is associated with God's love (Rom 8:35-39). He dwells within us (Rom 8:10; 2 Cor 13:5; Gal 2:20; Col 1:27); he intercedes for us (Rom 8:34).

The phenomenon we have been describing provides an important insight into Paul's prayer-experience. One might say that all he knows about the Holy Spirit as a person, whatever he has grasped of the function of the Spirit in Christian life, have been revealed to him through his experience of the dynamic presence of the risen Christ in his own personal history. But the mystery of the Spirit remains always involved for Paul in the mystery of Christ's own identity—a mystery that he continued to plumb until the end of his life.

To return to Gal 4:6, the second great act of God in conferring upon the Christian his adoptive sonship is to make him aware of his true self-identity. "To show that you are sons, God sent forth the Spirit of his Son into our hearts, crying 'Abba, dear Father!' " This second gift is identified by Paul as "the Spirit of his Son", since his presence involves the revealed presence of the risen Christ within us (Rom 8:9-10). If the Son is the incarnation of the divine power (1 Cor 1:24), the Spirit makes us aware of that power (1 Thes 1:5). As the Son has demonstrated the Father's love of sinful man by his death on behalf of all (Rom 5:8), the Spirit enables the believer to experience that divine love in his own heart as a gift of God (Rom 5:5), and so drives out fear (Rom 8:15).

This is the meaning of Christian prayer for Paul. It is nothing less than an experience of our filial relationship with God. This astonishing revelation of the mystery of man's identity would be impossible except for the Father's gift of the Spirit, who enables us to recognize God as our Father. The intensity and the continuing character of the dynamic presence of the Spirit in the prayer of the Christian is indicated by Paul's repetition of the term "Father", first in Aramaic, then in the vernacular Greek.

It will be recalled that *Abba* was the familiar form of address in the Palestinian families of Jesus' day. Out of reverence, no Jew ever dared address God with the informality and intimacy suggested by the word. In the Gospels only Jesus during his mortal life is represented as addressing God in this manner (Mk 14:36). Evangelical tradition however had preserved the memory of Jesus' precious gift to the disciples, his own familiar way of speaking to the Father. The *Our Father* has come down to us in two formulations, both probably of liturgical provenance (Mt 6:8-13; Lk 11:2-4). It seems plausible, from the variations already observable in these two versions of the dominical prayer that the early Church understood Jesus to provide an example or "blue-print" rather than a set formula from which the Christian might not deviate. What was understood to be significant was Jesus' gift of *his own personal attitude towards the Father* in prayer to his followers. Imbued with these dispositions evinced by the incarnate Son of God, the believer might confidently approach God "in Jesus' name" as his own adoptive Father with the assurance of being infallibly heard.[11]

Paul, who has undoubtedly in mind this manner of approaching God bequeathed by the Lord Jesus, points to the intervention of the "Spirit of his Son" in each attempt by the Christian to speak to God as Father. To pray in the spirit in which Jesus prayed, with the filial dispositions which Jesus had enjoined on the disciples, is, Paul tells us, to experience the dynamic action of the Holy Spirit. It seems clear from the whole context (as well as that of Rom 8:15) that Paul is convinced that this experience is shared by every sincere Christian in his prayer. There is no question of any privileged, mystical experience.

[11] We wish to draw attention to the beautiful article by Jacques Guillet, "Le Christ prie en moi," *Christus* 5 (1958), 150-165, an admirable explanation of the significance of Jesus' gift of the Lord's prayer to his disciples.

Paul concludes his description of the Christian's experience by insisting upon the very individual and intimate nature of each believer's filial relation with God his Father. This is seen in his use of the second person singular, "thou" (which unfortunately for the clarity of recent versions is now obsolete in English). To remedy this poverty of the modern idiom, "thou" has been rendered "each one of you". "So that each one of you is no longer a slave: he is son; but if son, also heir by act of God" (Gal 4:7). With this statement Paul reaches the climax of his entire development. The human race in tutelage to "the elements of the world" (vv.1-3) had formerly been in the condition of a slave. The sending forth by God of his Son meant man's attaining of his majority, his being given the capacity, through faith, of adoptive sonship. The sending forth of the Spirit of God's Son has endowed the Christian with a totally new self-consciousness, the intimation of his identity as a son of God. This growth in awareness of *who he is* remains an ongoing process throughout the life of faith with the assistance of the Spirit. It frees the Christian from man's old attitude as slave, replacing it with the realization that as God's son he is provided with an undreamed of heritage. The essential clue to this profound mystery has been reserved for the emphatic position at the very end of the sentence: it is "by act of God" the Father that this metamorphosis, not only of man's essential condition, but of his Christian consciousness, has been effected. The unprecedented has occurred through the presence of the Spirit, as well as by the redemption through the Son's death and resurrection. Paul's appreciation of the depth of this mystery of God's predilection provides an answer to his constant insistence upon the Christian's need for uninterrupted prayer to the Father. None is more acutely aware than Paul that God's gift implies our need of a never-ending schooling by the Holy Spirit in what it means to be a son of God. This divine pedagogy will only cease when such a son enters fully upon his inheritance beyond this present existence.

The letter to the Romans resumes in chapter eight this sequence of ideas, in order to develop more explicitly the Pauline teaching concerning the prayer of the Christian. The passage begins with a description of Christian existence couched in juridical terms. "Therefore, at present there exists no condemnation for those in union with Christ Jesus, for the law of the spirit of life in Christ Jesus has freed me from the law of sin and of death" (Rom 8:1). The author of the Fourth Gospel often borrows the terminology of law to offset the impression, which his use of symbolism (light, life, truth) may give, of merely mythological language. Juridical terms like judgment, conviction, witness, serve to focus upon the radical realism with which he intends his imagery to be comprehended. Paul similarly uses the Mosaic Law here as a paradigm in presenting the realities of Christian life. It is a "law" with everything that word implies, for "men who are versed in law" (Rom 7:1), of stability, order, permanence, and reality. Because however it is founded upon "union with Christ Jesus", it is a "law of life", not a dead "letter" (Rom 2:29), and it is to be characterized by "the Spirit".

The Christian has been freed from the condemnation imposed by "the law of sin and death" (Paul thinks concretely of the Mosaic Law) by God's overriding divine act of condemnation "of sin in the flesh"—of his Son sent "in the likeness of sinful flesh" (v.3). This juridical presentation of Christ's death and resurrection permits Paul to describe the resulting Christian life as the fulfilling of "the just claim of the Law", the accomplishing of the will of God (v.4), under the impulse of "the spirit" (vv.5-8), a kind of personification of that new reality in the Christian, which is the antithesis of "the flesh". The reality behind this personification is the indwelling "Spirit of God", so intimately involved with the presence of the risen Christ in the Christian, that it appears to be a matter of indifference to speak of "the Spirit of Christ", or of "Christ in you" (vv.9-11). Both the risen Christ and the Holy Spirit are dynamically involved in Christian existence. Hence the responsibilities incumbent upon the believer, who knows his indebtedness to the Spirit for this divine indwelling, become clear. To maintain the new life within him so as finally to enter upon his full inheritance without succumbing to death (which for Paul means fundamentally separation from the living God), the Christian must live a "spiritual" life (vv.12-13). What does this mean for Paul?

14 "All who are moved by the Spirit of God are God's sons. 15 It is not a spirit of slavery you have received, [leading you back] once again into fear: you have received the Spirit of adoptive sonship. By the fact that in him we cry '*Abba,* dear Father!', 16 the Spirit himself adds his testimony to that of our spirit that we are God's children. 17 But if his children, also his heirs: heirs indeed of God, hence coheirs with Christ, provided we suffer together with him in order that with him we may also be glorified" (vv.14-17).

Paul now enucleates more explicitly the phenomenon of the conscious Christian life, which he had hinted at in Gal 4:6-7. The dynamic element is the Holy Spirit without whose aid man could not discover his true identity as God's son. The Spirit, however, who is divine power, "moves" (literally, "drives") the believer in a manner consonant with his human dignity and responsibility as a person. He acts (Paul is well aware) in a way diametrically opposed to those forces of frenzy that seized the devotees of pagan orgiastic rites. Paul had warned against such irrational religious delirium in writing to the Corinthians "about spiritual gifts" (1 Cor 12:1-3). To alert them to the dangers inherent in any uncontrolled indulgence in religious enthusiasm, he reminded them of their former experiences in certain mystery-cults. "You know that when you were pagans you were led astray after dumb idols—however you happened to be driven". The Spirit of the God, who is "a God, not of confusion but of peace" (1 Cor 14:33), "moves" the believer in a very different manner, for he has been redeemed from the status of slave and rescued from the harrowing of fear by the Spirit who makes him conscious of his divine "adoptive sonship".

The Spirit is moreover the one who stands at the heart of all Christian affectivity in prayer: "in him we cry, 'Abba, dear Father!' " (v.15). Paul employs the word "cry" here, as in Rom 9:27, to suggest the intensity of the loving, filial gratitude to which the Christian is moved by the Spirit in his address to God his Father. Within this profoundly personal testimony in

the depths of the Christian's "spirit", Paul observes, there is to
be caught, by the man who becomes attuned to it, the accom-
panying, supportive testimony of the Spirit himself. This
prayer, arising from the innermost being of the believer, brings
a more conscious realization of what his "adoptive sonship"
truly means: "we are God's children" (v.16). By his use of this
term Paul insinuates the divine reality of the Christian's status
that exceeds the sense suggested by the legal term "adoptive
sonship". God has, in fact, begotten him by faith and baptism.
And because he is truly God's child, he is God's heir, endowed
with the capacity to share in the very heritage of Christ, the
unique Son of God.

Christ however has entered upon his inheritance by his passion and glorification. Thus to be "coheirs with Christ" means to
participate in his passion and ultimately, his glory (v.17). Paul's
Christian realism and his fidelity to the gospel, which proclaims
the essential duty of "saying 'No' to self" (Mk 8:34-37), do not
permit him to gloss over the harsh realities attendant upon the
Christian life in this world. He reminds his readers at this point
of the value and necessity of exercising Christian hope. "I am
convinced that the sufferings of the present era are not worthy
of comparison with the coming glory that is to burst in revelation over us" (v.18). He summons as witness the material
creation, that itself is to share in its own way in man's future
destiny, since it too has been the object of Christ's redemptive
work. "The creation itself will also be freed from the slavery of
corruption [to enter] upon the freedom of the glory of the children of God" (v.21). Meanwhile the irrational creation evinces
a solidarity in the hopes of the Christian: "the whole creation
groans together with us and endures with us the pangs of child-
birth until now" (v.22).

This groaning which expresses the "hope" of the material
universe resonates in Christian hearts endowed with "the first
fruits of the Spirit", that adoptive sonship in its initial stage of
which Paul has already spoken. Now (v.23) he discloses its
inchoate character: "we look forward in expectation to [that]
adoptive sonship, the redemption of our body". There is a further stage in our becoming sons of God—and this, in virtue of

the truth that we are "coheirs with Christ" (v.17): the glorious resurrection of the just. Jesus Christ himself, whose relation to God as his Father is unique, had (Paul remarked at the beginning of this letter) his divine sonship deepened and enhanced by rising from death. He was "constituted Son of God in power by the spirit of holiness through resurrection of the dead" (Rom 1:4). By Christ's death and resurrection we were indeed saved, but "we were saved in hope" (v.24).

It is the same with our adoptive sonship. Paul had already pointed out (Gal 4:5) that Christ's redemptive act had given us, through faith and baptism, the receptivity for adoptive sonship, and "the Spirit of his Son" produced in us the awareness of this privileged state (v.6). He has, as we have seen, restated this truth in this letter to Rome (vv.14-17). Now he points out that in a very real sense we are for the present "sons of God"—"in hope". As a consequence, the awareness of our divine filiation to which the Spirit increasingly leads us will never, in this life, enable us to *see* this reality even in its present, germinal state. It remains, as does its fulfilment through resurrection, an object of Christian hope. "Now a hope that is already being seen is no hope at all. Who hopes for what he has before his eyes? While if we do not see, we go on hoping: we keep up our expectation through endurance" (vv.24-25).

These remarks have a carefully calculated purpose: they lead up to what for Paul is the most important lesson in prayer the Christian in this world can learn. He has indicated earlier (vv.14-16) that our prayer-life must be centred upon our growing consciousness of our adoptive filiation, since that is the intent of the Spirit's testimony in our hearts. Given however the incipient nature of this adoptive sonship, the Spirit has an even more significant role to play. He plays the decisive role in sustaining our hope *while at prayer,* that God will hear our cry to him as our Father. The "example" (so to say) of the material creation with its transparent sense of expectancy and our own groaning anticipation are calculated to sustain our hope at prayer.

"Likewise also the Spirit comes to the aid of our weakness. (For we do not know how to pray as it is necessary). Indeed, the Spirit himself is interceding through our inarticulate groaning. And he who searches men's hearts knows what is the Spirit's intent: that he intercedes according to God's will on behalf of the saints" (vv.26-27).

Christian prayer in Paul's eyes is largely an exercise of hope, without which prayer would be quite meaningless—as in fact it was for the Stoic with his strong belief in the determinism governing history. Nor is prayer a means of exerting pressure upon God, nor does its effectiveness lie in the more subtle methods of persuasion. Much less is it a kind of spiritual exhibitionism. The oratorical virtuosity and the self-centred smugness of the Pharisee in the Lucan parable (Lk 18:11-12) is presented as an exercise in futility. Jesus himself had warned his disciples against the superficiality of praying "so as to be seen by men", on the grounds that this was to seek reward elsewhere than with the heavenly Father (Mt 6:5-6). He had also pointed out that to employ rhetoric in approaching God was tantamount to denying that "your heavenly Father knows what you need before you ask him" (Mt 6:7-8).

Paul points out the paramount importance of the very element which is a matter of universal experience in prayer: "our weakness". It is this, which more than anything else, gives rise to discouragement and leads to the abandonment of prayer. Yet it is this very sense of our own ineptitude, of frustration in seeking God, of our utter poverty when we stand in his presence, which provides the occasion for the intervention of the Holy Spirit. It will be recalled that Paul confessed to having learned this supreme lesson in his single account in all his letters of his own prayer. The answer he received to his earnest supplication to be relieved of "the thorn for the flesh" was to remain with him the rest of his life. "And he has given me his response, 'My graciousness is all you need, since [my] power is being brought to its perfection by [your] weakness'" (2 Cor 12:9). The vacuum created by our own weakness permits the untrammelled activity of the Holy Spirit. Only in this situation is our prayer transformed into the exercise of Christian hope, which alone makes it authentically Christian prayer. "May the God of hope fill you with complete joy and peace in your life of faith by hope through the power of the Holy Spirit" (Rom 15:12).

Consequently, the essential point of departure for all efficacious prayer is a deep consciousness that "we do not know how to pray as it is necessary" (v.26). In Christianity the iron inexorability of Fate, which for the pagan Greek pervaded the destiny of both men and gods, has been replaced by faith in the will of God our Father. Thus the New Testament expression "it is necessary" is the equivalent of "according to God's will". The deepest cause of our weakness at prayer is our ignorance of the divine will. "Who among men knows what a man is really like except that man's own spirit within him? Likewise no one knows what God is really like except the Spirit of God" (1 Cor 2:11). This sad consequence of our present human condition is, in Paul's mind, bound up with the incomplete character of our Christian adoptive sonship which he has just alluded to.

The grounds for hope are not far to seek, if only we realize that "the Spirit himself is interceding through our inarticulate groaning". The Greek word "intercede" originally means to "interrupt". It suggests the intervention of a third party in a dialogue between two persons. The Spirit is here pictured as interjecting himself between God and our stammering, disjointed attempts to speak to him. He makes our "inarticulate groaning" his own, and so creates for us the possibility of effectual discourse with him "who searches men's hearts". For God recognizes the finality of this "interruption" on the part of the Spirit, who employs the only thing we can call our own in prayer—"our weakness", expressed by "our inarticulate groaning"—to "intercede according to God's will on behalf of the saints" (v.27). Authentic Christian prayer must exhibit that dialectic of suffering and glory, which is the heritage of every true adoptive son of God. It consists of weakness, inarticulateness, ignorance of God's will on our part, and, on the part of the intervening Spirit, the creative power that transforms our bumbling efforts into his own intercession "according to God's will on behalf of the saints". This is what Paul meant earlier by his statement, "By the fact that in him [the Spirit] we cry '*Abba,* dear Father!', the Spirit himself adds his testimony to that of our spirit that we are God's children" (vv. 15-16). Paul had moreover immediately alerted his reader to a further consequence *for the Christian life of prayer* of this inchoative sonship. "But if his children, also his heirs: heirs indeed of God, hence coheirs with Christ, provided we suffer together with him in order that with him we may also be glorified" (v.17).

Paul concludes his remarks appositely, in view of the central position assigned by him in Christian prayer to the function of hope, in view of the as yet unfulfilled nature of our filial relationship to God, by expressing the Christian hope in the ultimate completion of this adoptive sonship. "Now we know that for those who love God he makes all things work together for their good, as they have been given their vocation according to his design. [We know,] that is, that those he knew beforehand he has already predestined to be remolded in the image of the Son, in order that he might be the eldest of a large family of brothers" (vv.28-29). The very inability which the Christian experiences in his attempts at prayer is a mark of God's fatherly love for his imperfect sons and daughters. Indeed all the difficulties and the frustration we feel in our efforts at speaking with our Father have been foreseen in his plan. Provided only we love God, we know he will make the very things that thwart our well-intentioned, if ill-informed efforts conspire together for our good. We have come to know this because it is a matter of common Christian experience in prayer that the Spirit's aid is given only in view of "our weakness". We are continually being taught new lessons in hope, just because "we do not know how to pray as it is necessary". We have, although we may be in large measure unaware of it, actually been granted the grace to sense that "the Spirit himself is interceding through our inarticulate groaning", which is so like the "groaning" of the irrational creation! (v.22).

In fact, so intimately one with our own expression of our misery at our inarticulateness in prayer is the intercession of the Holy Spirit, that a question arises. Is it possible to distinguish in our reactions what is truly his divine activity from those tendencies and desires that spring simply from our own self-will and sinfulness? and if so, what criteria lie at hand to assist us in finding the will of God in any concrete situation? The answer to such questions is to be found in Paul's teaching on discernment and (perhaps more clearly) in his practice of this Christian activity, to which he attached such importance.

VI

THE PAULINE CONCEPTION OF DISCERNMENT

Paul's approach to the Christian life may be characterized as eminently rational and practical, provided such a qualification be understood within the context of faith and love and hope. The gift of faith, while it enables the Christian to transcend the natural powers of reason and acquire, in his maturity, "God's wisdom by [the revelation of] mystery" (1 Cor 2:6), does not destroy his reason, nor lessen his obligation to act as a responsible person. Paul can qualify Christian life as "your rational worship" (Rom 12:1), by which he clearly intends to signify "spiritual worship". In urging the Roman community to avoid conceit, he tells them "to think your way to a reasonable self-esteem proportionate to the measure of faith that God has given each one" (Rom 12:3).

Paul fully appreciates man's unique position as a self-conscious being, and it is to his usage that we owe the semantic development of the Greek term for consciousness, which has come to express the phenomenon we call "conscience". For Paul it usually denotes the Christian from the viewpoint of his awareness of his self-identity; hence it necessarily includes a relationship to faith and the truths of revelation. His discussion of the "weak conscience" and the strong (1 Cor 8:7-13; 10:25-29) not only shows the need of the correct formation of a Christian conscience, but also discloses the sense of liberation as well as of obligation to Christ and one's neighbor, which it effects. Paul is not unaware of the existence of authentic conscience among pagans, who live without benefit of positive divine revelation (Rom 2:15-16). His sensitivity in dealing with the consciences of others springs from the delicacy of his own conscience (2 Cor 1:12), from his constant awareness of the divine mercy to himself and of God's presence (2 Cor 4:1-2), and from "the fear of the Lord" (2 Cor 5:11). Above all, Paul is aware of the dynamic assistance which the Holy Spirit gives to the testimony of the Christian conscience (Rom 9:1).

In these circumstances it is no surprise that the expression "the discernment of spirits" comes from Paul's pen (1 Cor 12:10), although indeed 1 John 4:1 speaks of the need of "testing the spirits".[12] It is to be noted that in the text cited Paul regards discernment as a spiritual charism, and he relates it in a special way to prophetic utterance, as he had done earlier in writing to Thessalonica. "Do not quench the Spirit, do not belittle prophetic utterances—test everything about them: hold onto what is good, shun every appearance of evil [in them]" (1 Thes 5:19-22). The spiritual perceptiveness necessary to distinguish true from false prophecy is such a delicate matter that it requires the special charism of "discernment of spirits" (1 Cor 14:29). This extraordinary gift belongs to the "spiritual man", that is, the Christian who is fully mature and delicately attuned to the Spirit. "The merely natural man does not accept those things belonging to the Spirit of God. They are follies in his eyes, and he cannot know them, because they are to be investigated spiritually. But the spiritual man investigates them all, while he himself is not subject to anyone's investigation . . . Now we possess the mind of Christ" (1 Cor 2:14-16). To qualify for the practice of Christian discernment one must, like Paul himself, participate in the mentality of Christ, which is bestowed only by the Spirit. "I believe that I too have the Spirit of God" (1 Cor 7:40).

Each Christian however, to the extent that he is able, is

---

[12] For a solid historical introduction to this difficult subject, see *Discernment of Spirits* (Collegeville, 1970), a translation of the article by French experts in the *Dictionnaire de Spiritualité*, edited by Edward Malatesta (translation by Sister Innocentia Richards).

called upon to practice discernment in the concrete circumstances of everyday life, since he is under obligation to seek
God's will in all he does. There are several reasons for this in
Paul's view. The individual and indeed the whole Christian
people face ultimately the divine judgment (1 Cor 3:13).
Diligence in discerning the value of one's own conduct anticipates the divine judgment. "If we were to investigate ourselves, we should not be being judged; but when we are judged,
we are disciplined by the Lord lest we be condemned with
the world" (1 Cor 11:31). Moreover, Christian existence is
constantly exposed in this life to tribulation; hence discernment is necessary to react with endurance and true hope, (even
joy) to this situation (Rom 5:3-4).

What demonstrates the need for discernment most clearly
is the very ambiguity of the Christian life. The believer is indeed an adoptive son of God, but only inchoatively; he is in the
present life only "saved in hope" (Rom 8:24). His person is
the "sanctuary of the Holy Spirit" (1 Cor 6:19), but he must
take constant care "not to grieve the Holy Spirit of God, with
whom you have been sealed for the day of redemption" (Eph
4:30). Because of his deep sensitivity to the ambivalence of
Christian existence and the contrast between "the already" and
"the not yet", Paul has given to the Greek word "to test" a
religious and Christian meaning which it did not exhibit before his time; and it is this word (apart from his own practice of
discernment) which provides the clues to his understanding of
this necessary Christian activity.

It is love which founds the possibility of discernment. "May
your love yield an ever richer harvest of true knowledge and
apperception of every kind, so that you may test what is most
worthwhile. Thus you will be sincere and without blame in
view of the day of Christ" (Phil 1:9-10). "Do not conform to
this present age, but become transformed by the renewal of
your mind, so that you can test what is God's will, the good
and pleasing and perfect" (Rom 12:2). "Conduct yourselves
as children of light . . . by testing what is pleasing to the Lord"
(Eph 5:8, 10).

Attention to the truths of divine revelation, as Paul indicates when apostrophizing the Jew, is necessary for authentic discernment. "You know his will and can test what is most worthwhile, because you have been instructed in the Law" (Rom 2:18). To act against the conviction of faith is always sinful. "Happy the man who does not condemn himself through his testing. He who eats while in doubt has been condemned because [he acted] contrary to his faith. Whatever is contrary to faith is a sin" (Rom 14:22-23). Discernment is above all necessary in one's preparation for the reception of the Eucharist. "Each one must test himself: only then let him eat the bread and drink from the cup. The man who eats and drinks without discerning the body eats and drinks judgment for himself" (1 Cor 11:28-29).

From the evidence of his letters Paul is continually engaged in this work of discernment. He mentions various criteria for judging the authentic character of spiritual gifts and in estimating their relative importance. "No one speaking with the Spirit of God can say, 'Cursed be Jesus:' and no one can say 'Jesus is Lord,' except by the Holy Spirit" (1 Cor 12:3). It is ordinarily by "the fruit of the Spirit" that the activity of the Holy Spirit may be perceived and assessed; and it is important to note, in the list of these Paul gives, that account is taken of their priority. "The fruit of the Spirit is love, joy, peace, endurance, kindliness, goodness, fidelity, gentleness, self-control" (Gal 5:22-23). The "building up" of community is the criterion for judging the hierarchy of charisms (1 Cor 14:5). There is also the principle that "God is not a God of confusion but of peace" (1 Cor 14:33).

We may conclude this rapid survey with a text which illustrates Paul's attitude to the Christian duty of discernment. "Keep examining yourselves to see if you are living the life of faith. Keep testing yourselves! Surely you perceive that Christ Jesus is among you—unless of course you prove unequal to the test" (2 Cor 13:5).

Chapter 5
The Shape of
Paul's Prayer

We are finally in a position to undertake a study of what are called the formal thanksgivings in the Pauline letters. As is well known, there is a section towards the beginning of almost all Paul's letters which contains an account of his prayer for the communities to which he writes. It is to be noted that this "thanksgiving" is not a prayer, even in the sense in which the opening wish may be considered prayer, but *a narrative of Paul's prayer*. The significance of this fact for our investigation will become evident presently. Not every letter contains the formal thanksgiving, although where it is omitted, in 2 Corinthians and Galatians, something else has been substituted in its place. There is a "confession", which is a true prayer of praise and gratitude, inviting the collaboration of the Corinthian community in 2 Corinthians 1:3-11. That this does not necessarily eliminate the thanksgiving may be gathered from the phenomenon in Ephesians, where the "confession" (Eph 1:3-14), introduced by the identical formula found in 2 Corinthians ("Blessed be the God and Father of our Lord Jesus Christ"), is immediately followed by an account of Paul's thanksgiving prayer for this community (Eph 1:15-23). The omission of a formal thanksgiving in Galatians has been compensated for by an extended prayer-wish (Gal 1:3-5), the most fully developed instance of this type in Paul's correspondence, terminated by a doxology.

I
PAUL'S CREATIVITY IN THE THANKSGIVING

At a first approach to these formal thanksgivings, whose structure will become readily apparent as we study them, one might conclude that the very formality to which they consistently conform makes them less capable of revealing the shape of Pauline prayer than other, more seemingly spontaneous passages, like those reviewed in Chapter Three. We did in fact begin our study by examining those brief prayers because their very spontaneity and brevity appeared more apt to disclose what was characteristic of Paul's attitudes in prayer. If however, as I venture to suggest is the case, the Pauline thanksgiving is not dependent upon a conventional form within which he must confine himself, but is rather a literary creation of Paul himself, then we should gain a real insight into Paul's prayer from a study of it.

Béda Rigaux [1] points out that Paul was not bound by the conventions of letter-writing in his day as regards the thanksgiving to the extent that many commentators have thought. In the first place, as we have said, he does not always insert a formal thanksgiving at the beginning of his letters, substituting a "confession" for it, or expanding the opening prayer-wish. Secondly, in the letters that have survived from antiquity many do not contain a prayer, while the number of those that do appears, from the third to the first centuries before the Christian era, to decline sharply. Moreover, Paul has developed the thanksgiving in an original manner so that it is no longer linked with the address and opening greeting, but orientated to the body of the letter through its presentation of the principal themes to be treated.

If one recalls that Paul intended his letters to be part of the public worship of the Christian community, which included "the breaking of the bread" in obedience to Jesus' injunction to

---

[1] Béda Rigaux, *Les Épitres aux Thessaloniciens* (Paris: Gembloux, 1956), p. 357.

the disciples at the Last Supper, it becomes possible to suggest a further reason for the evolution of the Pauline thanksgiving. While, so far as is known, the name "Eucharist" was not applied to the Christian liturgy until after the apostolic age, the formulae of the words of institution preserved in the New Testament (especially that recorded in 1 Cor 11:24) show that the eucharistic action was from the beginning regarded as a gesture of thanksgiving to God after the example of Jesus himself (cf. also Mk 14:23; Mt 26:27; Lk 22:19). If the Fourth Gospel contains no narrative of the institution of the Eucharist, its author has nonetheless taken pains to underscore the eucharistic significance of Jesus' feeding of the crowds in a way that is clearer than any of the Synoptic evangelists (cf. Jn 6:11), especially by the insertion of the phrase, "the Lord having given thanks" (Jn 6:23).

II

THE THANKSGIVING, REFLECTION OF PAUL'S PRAYER

But the most significant reason for the creative use Paul has made of the thanksgiving in his letters, is to be discovered in the structure of his own prayer. We pointed out earlier in Paul's instructions on prayer the presence of the triad, joy, petition, and thanksgiving (1 Thes 5:16-18; Phil 4:4-6). It is very striking how frequently this triad reappears in the Pauline thanksgivings. The constellation is present in Paul's first extant letter. "What kind of *thanks* can we give to God for you on account of the deep *joy* we experience because of you in the presence of our God? Night and day with utmost earnestness *we ask* to see your faces again, and to strengthen your faith where it is deficient" (1 Thes 3:9-10). "I *give thanks* to my God . . . always in every *petition* of mine for all of you. It is *with joy* that I make the petition . . ." (Phil 1:3-4). Even in the brief note to Philemon the triad is to be observed. "I *give thanks* to my God always as I make a memento of you in *my prayers*. . . for I have had *much joy* and consolation from your love . . ." (Phlmn 4-7). The second half of the thanksgiving in

Colossians exhibits an interesting variation in its presentation of the triad. (It is taken in part from the hymn quoted.) "For this reason we also . . . do not cease *praying* and *petitioning* on your behalf that you may be filled with the recognition of his will . . . with *joy! Giving thanks* to the Father . . .'" (Col 1:9-12).

Thus it would seem that we have uncovered in this consistent accompaniment of petition by the sentiments of joy and thanksgiving an attitude of heart and mind, which may be taken as fundamental in Paul's prayer. Whether there is any relation between this triad and the trio faith, love, and hope, which makes its first appearance in Paul's letters with the first thanksgiving (1 Thes 1:3) and recurs in others, either expressly (Col 1:4-5) or by implication (2 Thes 1:3-4; Phlmn 5), we shall investigate in the course of this chapter. One might moreover ask whether there is any perceptible connection between the three-fold attitude of joy, petition, and thanksgiving, and the direction of Paul's prayer to the Father through Christ in the Holy Spirit (Eph 2:18).

We have spoken of the formal thanksgiving as a narrative describing to the addressees Paul's prayer on their behalf. It is important to note how frequently he sets his expression of gratitude, as well as the mention of his petitions for his correspondents *in the context of his prayer*. "We give thanks to God always, whenever we make a memento on behalf of all of you in our prayers . . ." (1 Thes 1:2). "I give thanks to my God for each of your remembrances [of me] always, in every petition of mine on behalf of all of you . . ." (Phil 1:3-4). "First of all, I give thanks to my God through Jesus Christ for all of you . . . God is my witness . . . how unremittingly I make a memento of you always in my prayers . . ." (Rom 1:8-10). "We pray on your behalf . . ." (Col 1:3). "I give thanks to my God always, whenever I make a memento of you in my prayers . . ." (Phlmn 4). The frequency with which Paul alludes to the spontaneous and constant feeling of gratitude in the course of his prayer, for those to whom he writes, shows that the epistolary thanksgiving in his letters derives much of its special character from his prayer. Accordingly, it should disclose certain salient features of Paul's personal prayer.

III
EPISTOLARY FUNCTION OF THE THANKSGIVING

There is a functional feature of the Pauline thanksgiving which merits attention. In his perceptive monograph on this subject, Paul Schubert has observed that "the Pauline thanksgivings, with the exception of 1 Thessalonians, serve as a rather formal introduction to the body of the letter." [2] Paul's purpose in writing to Philemon is to persuade him to accept back the runaway slave Onesimos as a brother in Christ (v.16) for the love Philemon bears to Paul. Because of this, love is mentioned before faith, an inversion unusual for Paul, and he declares that he has been praying that the faith they possess in common may become operative by enabling Philemon to recognize, in view of his relation to Christ, the essential goodness of reconciliation with Onesimos.

4 "I give thanks to my God always whenever I make a memento of you in my prayers, 5 because I hear of your love and faith which you have towards the Lord Jesus and towards all the saints. 6 [I pray] that your fellowship in the faith may become active in recognizing every blessing we share in our relationship to Christ. 7 For I have had much joy and consolation because of your love, since the hearts of the saints have been refreshed through you, my brother" (Phlmn 4-7). Not only does Paul reverse the usual order in mentioning faith and love; he also relates the exercise of faith to "all the saints" as well as to Christ, which is somewhat extraordinary, because he is thinking of Philemon's reception of Onesimos.

His use of the expression "my God" deserves special attention, since outside the Pauline letters it occurs only once in the New Testament on the lips of Jesus himself (Jn 20:17). The phrase is found in the thanksgiving of the two most intimate letters (Phil 1:3; Phlmn 4) in the Pauline corpus, but it is also

[2] Paul Schubert, *Form and Function of the Pauline Thanksgivings* (*Beihefte zur Zeitschrift für die Neutestamentliche Wissenschaft* 20) (Berlin, 1939), p. 24.

found in the thanksgiving of Paul's two most formal letters (1 Cor 1:4; Rom 1:8), where however there is some uncertainty in the manuscript tradition about its authenticity. Of the two other instances where it occurs, one is a kind of prayer (Phil 4:19), while the other is set within a deeply emotional passage. "(I fear) that when I come again my God may humiliate me before you" (2 Cor 12:21). This arresting phrase, "My God," which is often said to illustrate the influence on Paul's prayer of the Psalter, provides precious evidence of Paul's awareness of the deeply personal nature of his relationship to God. This should be the more carefully noted as Paul is most discreet always in his care to disclose as little as possible about his own religious feeling towards God the Father.

That Paul's account of his prayer, by way of the formal thanksgiving at the beginning of his letters, should contain a preview of the theme or themes he proposes to treat is proof that what he writes is really the fruit of his own prayer. His letters were written out of his prayer for those whom he thus addresses. This is at once an indication that, for Paul, these communications were an important means of discharging his responsibility towards his addressees as their apostle, and a sign of the "practical" orientation of Paul's prayer, habitually directed towards his apostolate.

Not all the thanksgivings in the Pauline letters, however, will provide the same insight into Paul's prayer. The reason for this lies in the variations they display in length, complexity, and especially personal intimacy. The letter to the Romans, which most approximates a formal treatise, contains a thanksgiving (Rom 1:8-17), which reflects Paul's lack of immediate knowledge of the Roman community. And the fact that he writes to a church, in which he himself is unknown, in order to expose "his gospel" in anticipation of his intended visit, explains its formal tone. For a different reason, the thanksgiving occurring in 1 Cor 1:4-9 discloses little of Paul's real concern about the troublesome Corinthian community. The impression is definitely given that, without being insincere, Paul has confined himself carefully in a very formal way to the little he can at this point be grateful for. No mention is made of their faith, which he knows to be weak, much less of their love, the deficiency of which is evidenced by the cliques existing among them. He contents himself with references to "knowledge", "expression" (terms which the letter will show to be ambivalent) and their lack of "no charism" (v.7). Yet he does reveal his own high hopes for their "strengthening" by Christ so that they will be "blameless" (v.8), and so by implication their need of correction. The one revealing phrase, a favourite with Paul, occurs at the very end: "God keeps faith" (v.9).

IV
THANKSGIVING IN PHILIPPIANS

Apart from Philemon, the only extant example of a note written by Paul to an individual, the letter to Philippi is universally acknowledged to be the most personal and, doctrinally speaking, the simplest of the Pauline writings. We shall in consequence examine the thanksgiving of this letter in order to see what it discloses concerning the character of Paul's own prayer. The fact that in spite of its well structured arrangement, which renders it easily distinguishable from the opening greeting and the body of the letter (Phil 1:3-11), Paul's affection for this community of his predilection radiates throughout the passage, gives hope that we shall be able to discern in it the reflection of Paul's prayer.

Attention is drawn to two divergencies from most modern translations in the version which we have made of the passage. "I give thanks to my God *for each of your remembrances* [of me] always . . ." (v.3). The justification for this departure from the more customary renderings can be seen in the exact parallel in the Greek between this prepositional phrase and that (v.5) which follows, "for your participation in the gospel". Paul gives two motives for his expression of gratitude to God: the gifts sent him by this community on various occasions, and their participation by faith, love, and hope, and prayer in his apostolic commission to preach the gospel.

The second departure occurs in the ambiguous phrase in v.7, which could be translated "because I hold you in my heart". Preference is given here to the equally possible rendering, "because you hold me in your hearts", since this makes better sense, particularly in a letter written chiefly to thank these Christians for their benefactions to the imprisoned Paul. Moreover, this version agrees with that found in the *New English Bible,* a most accurate translation by a group of eminent New Testament scholars in England.

3 "I give thanks to my God for each of your remembrances [of me] 4 always in every petition of mine on behalf of all of you. 5 And I make this petition with joy, because of your participation in the gospel from the first day until now, 6 since of one thing I am certain—that he who began the good work in you will bring it to perfection by the day of Christ Jesus! 7 Indeed, it is right that I should adopt this attitude towards all of you, given that you hold me in your hearts. For all of you are sharers in the grace that is mine, as I lie in jail or take the stand to defend and affirm the gospel. 8 God is my witness how I long for all of you in the heart of Christ Jesus!

9 And this is my prayer [for you]: may your love yield an ever richer harvest of true knowledge and apperception of every kind, 10 so that you may test what is most worth while. 11 Thus you will be without flaw, blameless in view of the day of Christ, exhibiting in abundance that fruit of uprightness through Jesus Christ, to the glory and praise of God" (Phil 1:3-11).

Perhaps the most striking feature of this account of his prayer is Paul's total direction of his gratitude to God. He does not directly thank the community of Philippi, since he realizes that their love for himself, symbolized by their gifts to him, is really a gift of God to them. It is in reality God who has allowed them to share in "the grace that is mine" (v.7), the apostolic witness Paul gives to the gospel by his imprisonment and his "affirmation of the gospel" at his coming trial.

The fundamental nature of this prayer of Paul, however, from which its designation as a "thanksgiving" must not be allowed to distract us, is that it is a *petition* to God through

Jesus Christ in the Holy Spirit for the Philippian church. He himself states that it is "in every petition on behalf of all of you" (v.4) that he gives thanks to God and experiences joy. It is by this prayer of petition, in fact, that he expresses the gratitude he feels to these benefactors of his. He asks God to increase abundantly their love shown towards himself (for he recognizes that love as a divine gift), in such a way that it may benefit them. In Paul's eyes love is the source of that "real knowledge" (v.9) that is a basic principle in Christian living. "Mere knowledge breeds arrogance: it is love that builds. If a man is of the opinion he knows something, he has not yet come to know as it is necessary. If however a man loves God, [it is a sign that] he has become known by him" (1 Cor 8:1-3). To know "as it is necessary" is to know the will of God, to recognize true moral and religious values. Such knowledge comes from God's having "known" a man, which in the biblical sense means knowing through experience, and is ultimately love in its highest form. The creative love of God for man, as St. Augustine remarked, has made man lovable, thus capable of loving God. Hence, as Paul observes (Gal 4:9), it is more correct to say a man "is known by God" than to say a man "knows God".

Thus this divine gift to man of love endows man with the capacity to "test what is most worth while" (v.10), for this love which has its source in God is in fact "poured forth in our hearts by the gift of the Holy Spirit" (Rom 5:5). "No one can say 'Jesus is Lord' except by the Holy Spirit" (1 Cor 12:2). He is at the root of that "renewal of your mind, so that you can test what is God's will" (Rom 12:2).

It is important to see that, while in his account of his prayer for the Philippians Paul has not named the Holy Spirit, he does in fact allude to his presence. He speaks of the joy he experiences in praying to God for the community. Such joy, he is well aware, is the effect of "the power of the Holy Spirit" (Rom 15:13) and stands high among the fruits of the Spirit (Gal 5:22). In this very letter he will shortly ascribe his joy to "the assistance of the Spirit of Jesus Christ" (Phil 1:18-19). Moreover, in thanking God for "your *participation* in the gospel" (v.5) and in acknowledging that "you are *sharers* in the grace that is mine" (v.7), Paul alludes to the Holy Spirit, the source of all such participation or "fellowship" (2 Cor 13:13). He will speak in fact of this as "participation" or "sharing of the Spirit" (Phil 2:1) to his beloved Philippians. Accordingly, if Paul prays here to the Father, he is not unconscious of "being led by the Spirit" (Rom 8:14).

Similarly by implication Paul makes his petition through the risen Christ to the Father. What he asks for these Christians is an abundance of "that fruit of uprightness" which comes only "through Jesus Christ" (v.11). Indeed one might say that Paul makes his petition "in the heart of Christ Jesus" (v.8), since it is there that he reciprocates their love for himself by asking through him that their love be increased to overflowing. Paul's spontaneous cry, the sincerity of which he summons God to attest, "How I long for all of you in the heart of Christ Jesus", shows how profoundly the risen Christ represents for Paul the nearness of God. It is moreover the Christ of the parousia who dominates the entire perspective of Paul's prayer, which reaches its climax with the coming of Christ as judge. Yet he who will judge the community is not someone unknown to these Christians. He has been involved deeply in their progress as the mediator of their growth in "uprightness", guiding it in view of "the glory of God" (v.11). This "glory" signifies the revelation of God, not as some abstract truth, but as that experiential knowledge of God and his will that comes through faith and love and hope. The "praise of God" includes every aspect of the Christian's reaction to God's self-revelation, which may be summed up as an attitude of prayer.

"God" the Father is given the place of privilege at the beginning and the conclusion of this prayer of Paul, since he is the initiator and the end of Christian existence. "For us there is one God the Father", Paul will write to Corinth, "from whom all [has come] and to whom we all [return]" (1 Cor 8:6). "He who began the good work in you will bring it to perfection by the day of Christ Jesus" (v.6). It is God who is author of "your participation in the gospel from the first day until now" (v.5), as he has made the Philippians "sharers in the grace that is mine" (v.7). God alone can testify to Paul's love for this community "in the heart of Christ Jesus" (v.8), since he has created that love in Paul, as he has also created the love which the Philippians have manifested to their apostle. Consequently it is God whom Paul thanks for this gift of love (v.3): it is to God Paul addresses his petition for the development of this love (v.9). Paul's entire prayer has been orientated "to the glory and praise of God" "through Jesus Christ" in whose heart God's gifts of love to Paul and to the Philippians find their concrete expression. And through the joy Paul feels, as he makes "every petition" with gratitude, he knows that he prays in the Holy Spirit. The Trinitarian direction revealed in Paul's account of his prayer in this formal thanksgiving is a characteristic feature of his spirituality.

Another quality has also become manifest in Paul's expression of his faith and love sustained by hope. It is his faith and love which bid him thank God the ultimate giver of all gifts, instead of directly thanking his benefactors (v.3). The joy Paul feels provides evidence of his faith and hope in the Philippians' "participation in the gospel" (v.5). His love for them "in the heart of Christ Jesus" is expressed by his petition for their best interests (v.9). He displays his faith and hope through his avowal that he is "certain that he who began the good work in you will bring it to perfection by the day of Christ Jesus" (v.6). He again voices his hope at the climax of the thanksgiving as he anticipates the eschatological salvation of the Philippian community (v.11).

Paul's joy, petition, and thanksgiving thus expressed through faith, love, and hope imply, when they do not expressly assert, the many faceted relationship of his prayer to God, to Jesus Christ, and to the Holy Spirit. Our analysis of this formal thanksgiving has provided evidence that it is not a product of any epistolary convention, but is capable of yielding a deep insight into the shape of Pauline prayer.

V

DETERMINING THE LENGTH OF OTHER THANKSGIVINGS

The extent of the formal thanksgiving in Philemon (4-7), 1 Corinthians (1:4-9), Romans (1:8-17), and Philippians

(1:3-11) is fairly easy to determine. This is also true of 2 Thessalonians (1:3-12), which however exhibits a second thanksgiving after the warning about speculations concerning the date of the parousia (2:13-17). The letter to the Ephesians, which begins like 2 Corinthians with a "confession" (Eph 1:3-14) as we have seen, has also a formal thanksgiving (1:15-23).

There are two lengthy thanksgivings. That in Colossians (Col 1:3-20) appears to extend to include the hymn to the cosmic Christ (Col 1:15-20) which constitutes its climax. A particularly instructive example occurs in Paul's first extant letter, 1 Thessalonians, in which the body of the letter is really an extended thanksgiving (1 Thes 1:3–3:10), which comes to a climax in a prayerful wish (3:11-13). Because of the extraordinary length of this thanksgiving, the formula of gratitude is repeated twice at 2:13-16 and at 3:9-13. Paul Schubert has convincingly shown by arguments drawn from a stylistic analysis that "the thanksgiving itself constitutes the main body of 1 Thessalonians".[3] I suggest that the same conclusion may be reached by considering, as we have, the formal thanksgivings in the Pauline letters as accounts written for the benefit of his addressees of Paul's own prayer. We have already observed that one feature of these accounts is the consistent appearance of the triadic constellation joy, prayer, and thanksgiving. Another characteristic of these passages, arising from their nature as accounts of his prayer related for his correspondents, is the intercalation of personal remarks and personal reminiscences, which give them a cachet of intimacy. Examples of this have been seen in the thanksgivings extensively cited. "The hearts of the saints have been refreshed through you, my brother" (Phlmn 7). "God is my witness how I long for all of you in the heart of Christ Jesus!" (Phil 1:8). This personal note is not absent when, as in the case of Romans, Paul addresses himself to a community with which he is unfamiliar. "For I long to see you in order to share with you some spiritual gift to make you strong; or rather I should say, to be encouraged together with you through our mutual faith, yours and mine" (Rom 1:11).

---

[3] *Ibid.*, pp. 17-26.

We have moreover noted that Paul's purpose in narrating his prayer, made on their behalf, to a particular group of Christians, is (from the epistolary point of view) to introduce the theme of his message to them, *which is the fruit of his own prayer*. Thus the burden of his letter to Philippi is to exhort that church to greater Christian fellowship (Phil 2:1 ff.; 4:2-3) through growth in love. Accordingly, he tells them he is praying earnestly that "your love yield an ever richer harvest of true knowledge and apperception of every kind, so that you may test what is most worth while" (1:9-10). For Philemon, whom he wishes to persuade to accept Onesimos "no longer as a slave, but as more than a slave, a beloved brother" (v.16), Paul asserts that he is praying "that your fellowship in the faith may become active in recognizing every blessing we share in our relationship to Christ" (v.6).

What is Paul's purpose in writing his first letter to the church in Thessalonica? He is deeply concerned about their perseverance in the faith, particularly because they have had to face persecution since his departure, and perhaps most of all, because he is conscious of the incomplete nature of their instruction in the gospel. Luke's account of Paul's evangelization of Thessalonica (Acts 17:1-10) makes it clear that his work of founding this community had been interrupted. Paul himself displays an intense desire to return to these neophytes (1 Thes 2:17-18). His sending of Timothy was a substitute measure, when he could not go himself (3:1-5). In his letter he attempts to fill some of the lacunae in the community's scanty knowledge of Christianity (4:1–5:22). But his chief concern—and this consequently occupies the body of his letters—is for their fidelity to the gospel, which involved in Paul's eyes loyalty to himself. At the same time he is overjoyed (3:8-10) at Timothy's good news of their courageous profession of their faith in the face of the threats to their own lives, and of their deep affection for Paul himself (3:6-7).

Because then of the situation in which Paul finds himself, thwarted in his efforts to return in person to complete the Christian formation of his Thessalonians, yet overjoyed at Timothy's heartening reports of their constancy, he allows himself

twice to dwell at greater length than usual in his formal thanksgiving upon the personal reactions of his addressees in the past
and upon his own feelings of the moment. That the mood of
intimacy is characteristic of the Pauline thanksgiving has been
seen from our study of Philippians and Philemon. Here in his
first extant letter he reminisces first (1:5b—2:12) about his
community's remarkable conversion from paganism despite
persecution, and the loving, detached singleheartedness of his
fellow-missionaries and himself. The terminology of thanksgiving reappears at 2:13 briefly, but the thought of the sufferings borne by the young church reminds Paul of his desire to
visit the foundation he has made in Thessalonica (2:17-20),
and he expresses his joy at the good news brought by Timothy
(3:1-8). He then takes up the expression of thanks a final
time (3:9), and brings the whole thanksgiving to a climax, as
is his habit, with the articulation of his petition for the Thessalonians (3:11-13). It is this delay in stating the content of
his prayer, an integral part of the formal thanksgiving, which
forms the chief reason for asserting that the thanksgiving extends through the body of the letter.

If this contention is correct, it has some significant implications for our understanding of the nature of Paul's prayer.
Firstly, it indicates that the Pauline thanksgiving, which we have
seen owes more to Paul's creativity than to contemporary epistolary conventions, reflects profoundly the nature of his prayer.
His concern to exercise his responsibility towards the communities from which he is separated has led him to employ prayer
as the first means of assisting them. Whatever instruction, ad-
monition, or exhortation he may set forth in his letters are the
direct result of the joy, intercession, and thanksgiving he has
experienced and voiced in the course of his prayer. Secondly,
since Paul regards prayer as one supremely important function
of his apostolic commission, his prayer is habitually focussed
upon his apostolic work. Thus we see, particularly in the
thanksgiving of 1 Thessalonians, how he does not hesitate to
bring before God the contemporary condition of the communities under his charge, their problems as well as their Christian
achievements. Indeed it is in the course of his prayer that he

works out the solutions to the difficulties which beset his Christians. This is apparent from a reading of the fourth and fifth chapters of 1 Thessalonians, where Paul attaches as a conclusion to the body of his letter the explanations in the light of the gospel to the problems with which they are wrestling. Thirdly, the realism and "practical" nature of Paul's prayer provides the motivation to pray "beyond all measure", "day and night", "always", and "without intermission" for his neophytes. His constancy at prayer is assisted by the alternation of request, joy, and thanksgiving, so characteristic of his dealings with God and Christ. Fourthly, the exercise of faith and love together with Christian hope for the future constitute the core of his prayer just as they insure, in Paul's view, the vitality of Christian existence. It is obvious that he has taught the Thessalonians the superlative value of this triad for Christian living, since in this first letter of his he refers to them early in the thanksgiving without explanation or apology. Finally, if his expression of thanks is addressed solely to God (1 Thes 1:2) as the originator of their "election" (v.4), and if he experiences joy "in the presence of our God" (3:9), his petition is directed both to "our God and Father and our Lord Jesus" (3:11). For it is the risen Christ, who gave the commandment concerning "brotherly love" (4:9), to whom Paul looks for the growth and "abundant harvest" of their "love for one another and for all men" (3:12). That Paul has not neglected to affirm the significance for Christian prayer of the dynamic presence of the Holy Spirit may be inferred from his explicit references to the Spirit (1 Thes 1:4, 6).

VI
A SYNOPSIS OF THE THANKSGIVING IN
1 THESSALONIANS

The three principal passages of the thanksgiving in 1 Thessalonians are here set down side by side, with the intention of etching more clearly the shape of Paul's prayer which this narrative discloses. It should not be forgotten however that the personal recollections with which the intervening paragraphs are filled formed a very real and characteristic feature of Paul's prayer. It may not be irrelevant to recall during a reading of the entire passage that Paul is here employing what has been called an epistolary plural when he uses "we". In fact these first person plurals might more effectively be rendered "I", since the thanksgiving here as elsewhere is an account by Paul of his personal dialogue with God through the risen Lord Jesus. The first section is 1:2-5.

2 "We give thanks to God always for all of you, whenever we make a memento of you in our prayers, 3 because we recall incessantly the active quality of your faith, and the labor of your love, and the enduring character of your hope in our Lord Jesus Christ, in the presence of our God and Father. 4 For we recognize, brothers beloved of God, the [genuineness of] your election, 5 in the fact that our gospel did not touch you by mere force of words, but also by the power of the Holy Spirit, leaving deep conviction."

(2:13) "This is why we also give thanks to God unceasingly, since when you received the word of God from our lips, you accepted it for what it truly is—no mere human communication, but the word of God, who is continually at work in your hearts as believers."

(3:9-13) "What kind of thanks can we give to God for you on account of the deep joy we experience because of you in the presence of our God? 10 Night and day, beyond all measure, we ask to see your faces again, and to strengthen your faith where it is deficient!"

11 "May our God and Father himself and our Lord Jesus make our route back to you a straight one. 12 May the Lord cause your love for one another and for all men to grow, and produce an abundant harvest, like our love for you, 13 so that your hearts may be staunch and irreproachably holy in the presence of our God and Father, at the coming of our Lord Jesus with all his holy ones".

It only remains to draw attention to one further feature of Paul's prayer attested by this first formal thanksgiving: his awareness that at prayer he stands "in the presence of our God and Father" (1 Thes 1:3; 2:9). This representation of the divine presence, as the repetition of the same phrase in his concluding prayer (3:13) shows, Paul has drawn from the image of the final judgment, where God appears in the role of eschatological judge as "our God and Father". Thus Paul reveals his attitude in prayer as one of profound awe and reverence, and of filial familiarity. He expressly mentions that his thanksgiving is made before "our God and Father" (1:2-3) and that it is here also he experiences "deep joy because of you" (2:9). His account of his intercession for the Thessalonians discloses that it is also made to "our God and Father" (3:11).

That this phrase "our Father" reflects an habitual stance of Paul during his prayer is indicated by the fact that with a single exception it always occurs throughout his letters in a context relating to prayer. Thus it is found in several of the opening wishes (Phil 1:2; 1 Cor 1:3; 2 Cor 1:2; Gal 1:3-4; Rom 1:7; Col 1:3; Phlmn 3; Eph 1:2), and in other brief prayers (2 Thes 2:16; Phil 4:20). This relatively rare formula in Paul's writing appears only once apart from these instances (2 Thes 1:1).

It should be noted, by way of concluding our discussion of the thanksgiving in 1 Thessalonians, that we are probably here assisting at Paul's first attempt (or at any rate, one of his earliest attempts) to create the highly individual form of the thanksgiving, which will become the hallmark of his letters. We should be grateful that this initial sketch, with its sprawling length and its twice repeated recapitulations of gratitude, does not display the rigorous abnegation and craftsmanship exhibited by the thanksgiving in Philippians. For in this somewhat clumsy example we are provided with a better insight into the actual prayer of Paul as a kind of continuing *Te Deum* of gratitude to "our Father", expressive of the intense joy experienced at prayer and prompted by every new petition Paul makes out of his "day-to-day burden, the concern for all the churches" (2 Cor 11:26).

It would be difficult to miss the apostolic character of such prayer. Paul is deeply involved in the lives of those whose apostle he is, and he brings their problems into "the presence of our God and Father". This prompts him to petition on their behalf for the gifts they need, while their steadfast practice of the Christian life through faith and love, above all by hope, provides continual motivation for spontaneous, unremitting expression of thanksgiving. And whether he is confronted with questions requiring theological reflection on the meaning of faith in God's saving act in Jesus Christ, or those involving Christian worship as well as those arising from Christian living, or the more painful and delicate issues that demand vindication of his authority as apostle or reconciliation on the personal level, Paul experiences through the power of the Holy Spirit a deep joy which he never appears to lose. For this joy is grounded upon his ever-growing esteem of God's graciousness to himself and to his churches, and upon a lively and realistic sense of his own weakness.

The Pauline thanksgivings reflect also the paradoxical nature of Paul's relations in prayer with God, with Christ, and with the Holy Spirit. In none of them (apart from 1 Thessalonians) does the name of the Spirit appear, yet they are redolent with a loving awareness of the Spirit's activity with their repeated references to joy, hope, fellowship, love. Very rarely indeed (Phil 1:8) do we catch any more than a fleeting glimpse of the intensely personal, affectionate attitude towards the risen Christ which Paul elsewhere so movingly avows (cf. Gal 2:20; Phil 1:21). Paradoxically it is in one of the most reserved and formal of all the thanksgivings, that of 1 Corinthians, that Paul gives a hint of how much his relationship to Christ means to him, thanking "my God for the graciousness of God that has been given in Christ Jesus" (1 Cor 1:4), and recalling that it is through God "you have been called into the fellowship of his Son Jesus Christ our Lord" (v.9). Paul's account of his petition for the community in 1 Thessalonians is the single instance of his mentioning prayer addressed to Christ (1 Thes 3:9, 10), although it is surely obvious from Paul's candid confessions of how much Christ meant to him, representing as he did the nearness of God, how constant his intercourse with him in prayer must actually have been. This astounding reluctance, which Paul displays, to refer except very seldom to this "conversation with Jesus" (as the Imitation of Christ describes prayer) recalls the apparent contradiction in Paul's preference for describing his relation to Christ as a "slave" (2 Col 4:5; Phil 1:1; Rom 1:1) to his "Lord", when that relationship was one of such loving intimacy. This appears to be the more inconsistent in the light of his approach to God as "our Father", and his reminder to every individual in the Galatian communities that "each of you is no longer a slave but a son" (Gal 4:7).

In certain respects Paul reveals more about his attitude to God in prayer through the accounts he gives in the formal thanksgiving. It is to God that he exclusively voices his gratitude, to him almost invariably that he presents his petitions. His first extant letter at least shows that he addresses God as "our Father" (1 Thes 1:3; 3:11, 13), and the loving, "my God" (Phil 1:3; 1 Cor 1:4; Rom 1:8; Phlmn 4) is proof of the affection and intimacy of this relationship. Were it not however for certain of his observations on prayer (Gal 4:6-7; Rom 8:14-29), the depths of Paul's familiarity with God in prayer, his sense of union with the Father through the presence of his risen Son would not be as palpably discernible.

These reflections may serve as a necessary reminder that one must be wary of drawing conclusions of too sweeping a nature from the examination of one particular source—even a specially fruitful source like the formal thanksgivings—of information about Paul's personal prayer. Indeed even when the complete data have been assembled and examined, it is salutary to bear in mind that the veil which Paul has so successfully drawn over his personal religious life has been pierced only partially. To employ a metaphor that was congenial to Paul himself—"now we behold only puzzling reflections in a mirror" (1 Cor 13:12). It is of considerable help to a balanced judgment as to what Paul actually reveals of his own prayer-life through the formal thanksgivings, to keep constantly in mind that these are *basically narrative accounts of his prayer*. As a consequence they will yield no small insight into that prayer, yet an insight circumscribed, generally speaking, by what Paul intended to convey about the manner and content of his prayer.

VII
Thanksgiving in Colossians

The thanksgiving in Colossians (Col 1:3 ff.) must be considered to include the celebrated hymn to Christ (Col 1:15-20), with which it comes to a climax. The most convincing reason for this can be readily seen from the structure of the sentence in which Paul narrates the nature of his petition for this community. The Greek text containing his prayer, which begins with v.9 extends, without any full stop, grammatically speaking, to embrace vv.12-14 which form the immediate introduction to the hymn. These verses in fact are so intimately connected with the Christological hymn that they may well have formed an integral part of it "prior to its use in Colossians." [4] Accordingly, there is no apparent reason for excluding the entire hymn from the thanksgiving passage (Col 1:3-20).

Indeed, there is another reason why it should be included, when we recall that one function of the formal thanksgiving in the Pauline letters is to give a preview of the principal theme of the development which follows it. As Pierre Benoit has rightly observed, Paul's principal purpose here is to present "the person and work of Christ no longer from a merely soteriological viewpoint, but from a *cosmic* viewpoint. Christian salvation assumes the dimensions of the universe. Christ is not only Head of the Church, whose members are his and form his body; he is the head of the entire creation, including every being in it, celestial as well as earthly". [5]

Because of this purpose in writing to a church, in which the uniquely divine honor rendered to the risen Christ in primitive Christianity appears to have been in jeopardy through an exaggerated cult of the angels, Paul has chosen to include in his thanksgiving a hymn, very probably not of his own composi-

---

[4] Bruce Vawter, "The Colossians Hymn and the Principle of Redaction", *Catholic Biblical Quarterly* 33 (1971), 70.

[5] Pierre Benoit, *Les Épitres de Saint Paul aux Philippiens, à Philémon, aux Colossiens, aux Ephésiens* (Paris, 1949), p. 50.

tion. We may here conveniently adopt the opinion of Bruce Vawter, following Ernst Käsemann, that the hymn (from v. 12 to v.20) had been already adapted for use in the Christian baptismal liturgy, and so quite familiar to Paul's addressees. "As such it contains a theology which . . . turns up elsewhere in the NT canon. It is by no means the theology of Paul . . ." [6] "This christology of glorification would, it is true, occur more readily to a Johannine than a Pauline author. Yet it is hard to imagine Paul repudiating it altogether . . . [It represents] a development, surely. But a development that it is not impossible to imagine Paul himself making, and certainly one that has not betrayed Pauline thought".[7]

What is of moment for our investigation of Paul's prayer is the evidence that the presence of this citation within this Pauline thanksgiving provides that, as he prayed for the Colossian church, Paul recalled this magnificent hymn, extolling Christ's cosmic supremacy as reconciler of the entire world and now risen from death as head of the Church. For this indicates that Paul strove in his prayer, because of doctrinal problems confronting his correspondents, to gain a deeper Christian understanding of various aspects of the faith, in order better to enucleate these beliefs for his perplexed or erring neophytes. We have constantly to remind ourselves that in the early years of the life of the Church, when Paul wrote, relatively little of what we would call "theological thought" was available as resource material. What little there was (and its profundity is most impressive) had been elaborated in hymns like this one in Colossians, or that in Philippians 2:6-11. Paul himself through his letters was, thanks to his religious genius, to provide a most precious addition to this as yet limited theological treasure. In the following chapter we shall suggest that there was an important relation between what may be called the main theses of Pauline theology and the apostolic prayer of Paul.

The singular significance for Christian spirituality of the Colossians thanksgiving has been beautifully attested by Dr.

---

[6] Bruce Vawter, *art. cit.*, pp. 73-74.
[7] *Ibid.*, p. 77.

C. F. D. Moule, the distinguished New Testament scholar of
the University of Cambridge. We wish to cite it here as an
appropriate introduction to the passage itself. "It is immensely
valuable for anybody who desires to learn how to pray to
take careful note of the substance of the great prayer indicated in these verses, and of its structure, and of its parallels
elsewhere." [8] We have sought to throw some light on the structure of this magnificent narrative of Pauline prayer by presenting our version of it in three paragraphs, which lead on to
the hymn with which it reaches its climax. The first paragraph
(vv.3-6a) contains Paul's expression of gratitude for the divine gifts accorded in Christ to the community. The second,
so typical of other thanksgivings as we have seen, presents
with charming informality some brief reminiscences (vv.6b-8).
The third paragraph gives an account (vv.9-11) of Paul's
prayer for the Colossians. The hymn has been set out in sense
lines to recall its rhythmic and poetic quality.

3 "We give thanks to God the Father of our Lord Jesus
Christ always when we pray on your behalf. 4 For we have
heard of your faith, born of your union with Christ Jesus, and
the love you have for all the saints, 5 through that hope, stored
up for you in heaven, of which you first heard by the word of
truth, the gospel, 6 when it became present in your midst.

Yes, it continues to yield its harvest and to grow the
world over, just as it has done among you. The first day you
heard it, you recognized it for what it truly is—the graciousness
of God. 7 For of course you learned it from Epaphras our
dear fellow-slave, who is Christ's faithful servant in your service. 8 It is he who has made clear to us your love engendered
by the Spirit.

9 That is precisely why, from the day we heard the news,
we do not cease to pray for you. And we ask that you may be
filled with the true knowledge of God's will through perfect
wisdom and spiritual understanding, 10 so that you may live

---

[8] C. F. D. Moule, *The Epistles of Paul the Apostle to the Colossians
and to Philemon (Cambridge Greek Testament Commentary)* (Cambridge, 1958), p. 47.

lives worthy of the Lord, fully pleasing to him. We beg that you may continue to yield a harvest rich in every good work, thus growing in the true knowledge of God, 11 being imbued, by virtue of the might of God's glory, with ample power leading to endurance and steadfastness in every contingency.—And all this, with joy!

12   Giving thanks to the Father who has readied you
       To share the inheritance of the saints in the realm of light.
13   He it is who rescued us from the power of darkness,
       And has transported us into the kingdom of his own dear Son,
14   In whom we possess the redemption, the remission of our sins.
15   He is the Image of the unseen God, first born of all creation,
16   Since in him the entire universe has been created:
           What exists in heaven and on earth,
           What is visible, what is unseen,
           Thrones and sovereignties, principalities and powers.
       The whole universe has been created through him and for him.
17   Indeed, he exists before all else:
       The universe is sustained and embraced by him!
18   He is the Head of the Body—his Church!
       He is Beginning: first born among the dead,
       That he might hold the primacy in everything.
19   In him it pleased God that creation's fulness might reside,
20   That through him he might reconcile the universe unto himself:
       (For he has made peace through his blood shed on the cross.)
       Yes, reconcile whatever is, in earth or heaven!"

Paul begins his account of his prayer, as is his habit, by

noting his repeated acts of thanks to God as "the Father of our Lord Jesus Christ". For as the citation of the Christological hymn will indicate, his gratitude springs from his contemplation of the divine work of the redemption occasioned by his realization of the remarkable manner, in which the community accepted the gospel preached by Epaphras and now lives the Christian life. His thanks go to "the Father", since it is precisely this relationship to "our Lord Jesus Christ" that has been revealed by God's initiative in accomplishing man's redemption (Gal 4:6; Rom 8:3, 32). Once again God has revealed himself as Father in bestowing on the Colossians the capacity to accept the gospel, "the word of truth" (v.5), that is, the revelation of God's relationship to man through Christ. This revelation is not merely a matter of communication, even of the good news of salvation, as a kind of theological knowledge. It is "the power of God [leading] to salvation" (Rom 1:16). It is then a matter of the deepest spiritual experience, which Paul here describes (see also 1 Thes 1:3) under its threefold aspect of faith, love, and hope. It is to be carefully noted that Paul, who has made his name among some Christians as the theologian of justification by faith alone, can only adequately describe the grace which readies a man to accept the gospel in terms of this triadic unity. Moreover, this threefold gift, which establishes their relationship with God as Father, describes their new and intimate union "with Christ Jesus", the risen Lord, who mediated the divine action in the redemption of man and who, as the nearness of God, mediates the filial relation of the Christian with his Father. When Paul speaks of the gospel "becoming present in your midst" (v.6), he is thinking of Christ's new presence in the community.

As he did in the passage in 1 Thessalonians (1:5), Paul names hope last, partly because of its eschatological character (it is the glorified Christ of the parousia who is "that hope stored up for you in heaven"), partly also to emphasize here the contemporary function of hope as supportive of faith and love. Commentators express surprise at Paul's view that these two are in a sense dependent upon hope. Dr. Moule's observation is particularly apt. Hope, "the Christian confidence that in Christ, God's way of love 'has the last word', is not only future: already it is the source of steadfastness, of active concern for fellow-Christians . . . Precisely because it is 'stored up in heaven' . . . it is a potent incentive to action here and now".[9] In point of fact Paul has already laid stress upon the close interdependence of this triad in his "hymn" to Christian love (1 Cor 13:7): "(Love) can bear anything, believe anything, hope for anything, endure anything". Paul will return to this role of hope in contemporary Christian existence, when he describes the nature of his petition for the community (v.11), to associate it with the activity of the Holy Spirit as "ample power leading to endurance and steadfastness in every contingency" and with "joy".

With his usual informality and chattiness Paul introduces a personal note into his description of his own prayer (vv.6b-8). The unusual order ("yield its harvest and grow") in the comparison he employs to depict the spread of the gospel, as Professor Moule has observed,[10] also appears in the Marcan version of the parable of the Sower (Mk 4:8). Indeed this inversion of harvest and growth also appears in the little parable about invisible growth which is peculiar to Mark. "Automatically the earth bears fruit: first the blade, then the stalk, then the full ear of grain upon the stalk" (Mk 4:28). This curious transposition, appearing as it does in Paul several years before the writing of Mark, may well be an echo of the words of Jesus himself, with which Paul was, like the evangelist, familiar from its preservation in the oral tradition. If so, it deserves to be ranked with the other interesting allusions to the parables of Jesus in Paul;[11] and its presence here in Paul's account of his prayer may be a precious indication of his use of the sayings of Jesus in prayer.

Paul describes the Christian formation of the community as

---

[9] *Ibid.,* pp. 49-50.

[10] *Ibid.,* pp. 49-50.

[11] D. M. Stanley, "Pauline Allusions to the Sayings of Jesus", *Catholic Biblical Quarterly* 23 (1961), 26-39.

"learning" (v.7), a word which in the Gospels (Mt 11:29; Jn 6:45) denotes becoming a disciple of Jesus. To Paul it suggests the apprenticeship in living the Christian life by the reception of tradition (Phil 4:9), of "the teaching" (Rom 16:17), by "learning Christ" (Eph 4:20). It is a helpful reminder of the "practical", experiential meaning which he attaches to knowledge of Christ and of God's will. This is here suggested by the equivalence of this "learning" with "your love engendered by the Spirit" (v.8).

Paul's petition, "that you may be filled with the true knowledge of God's will through perfect wisdom and spiritual understanding" is similar to that in the thanksgiving in Philippians. "May your love yield an ever richer harvest of true knowledge and apperception of every kind . . . that you may be filled with the fruit of uprightness through Jesus Christ" (Phil 1:9-11). Here however Paul draws attention to the reciprocal interaction between the divine gift of "the true knowledge of God's will" and the living out of the Christian commitment. The gift is given "that you may live lives worthy of the Lord" (v.10), the risen Christ. But the "harvest rich in every good work" in its turn enables the Christian to "grow in the true knowledge of God." I venture to suggest that this conception reflects the alternation in Paul's own life between contemplation and action. The divine gifts bestowed on him through prayer result in his carrying out the duties of his apostolic commission: his apostolic activity makes him return to prayer to thank God and to beg for his continuing assistance. It is a noteworthy feature of Paul's life, filled to an extraordinary degree with activity, involvement in the lives of others, personal confrontations, reverses, risk and achievements, which in other men so frequently spell activism, that all these become grist for the mill of contemplation, of "boasting" (2 Cor 10:7–12:10), that joyous "confession" which elicited from himself and others thanksgiving and praise of God.

As he prays for this gift of contemplation in action for the Colossian community, he is keenly aware that it stems from two sources: "the might of God's glory", the self-revelation of

God in Jesus Christ through the gospel which is "God's power
[leading] to salvation" (Rom 1:16), and "ample power"
through the active presence of the Holy Spirit. It is these alone
that produce "endurance and steadfastness in every contingency" (v.11), that is, Christian hope, that (as he has already
asserted) sustains and develops faith and love. As Paul remarked
to the Thessalonians (1 Thes 1:6), such a "reception of the
word in tribulation with joy" is to be attributed to the work of
the Holy Spirit. In his presentation here of his petition, he has
set the word "joy" in the place of prominence by reserving it
to the very end of his narrative.

It may not be unhelpful, before turning to the baptismal
hymn with which Paul's thanksgiving concludes, to take note of
the presence of the various polarities which give shape and content to his prayer. The presence of the three triads observed
in the thanksgiving in Philippians and in Thessalonians is un-
mistakably clear. There is the Trinitarian orientation: the Father to whom thanks (v.3) is given, to whom by implication
(v.9) the petition is made; Christ risen, with whom the Colossians' gift of faith (v.4) and hope (v.5) is associated, as
well as their Christian existence "worthy of the Lord" (v.10);
the Spirit, source of love (v.8), and power and joy (v.11).
There is the triad faith, love, and hope, which in addition to
being related to the Trinity, is connected with the reception of
the gospel. As "the word of truth", the gospel elicits hope
(v.5); as "the graciousness of God" (v.6), it produces the
recognition of faith; as something "learned" (v.7), it brings
forth "your love engendered by the Spirit" (v.8). For the gospel that contains God's self-revelation as "the Father of our Lord
Jesus Christ" is truly "the might of God's glory", that imparts
through the Holy Spirit "ample power" (v.11). There is finally
the triad of thanksgiving (v.3), petition (vv.9-11), and joy (v.11).

Throughout this narrative of Paul's prayer the focus of attention has been directed to the divine activity in history on
the part of the Father, Christ, and the Spirit in the lives of the
Colossian community. In citing the liturgical hymn Paul con-
centrates upon what has thus far been heard only as a kind of
counterpoint, the central event of sacred history in the death

and exaltation by the Father of his incarnate Son. The ode speaks of the action of the Father in history, "who has readied you to share the inheritance of the saints" (v.12), "who rescued us from the power of darkness" (v.13). To God also is ascribed the vocation to the Christian Church, designated by the somewhat unusual phrase "the kingdom of his own dear Son". Paul himself had employed similar language however in writing to Corinth, when he described "the end" of sacred history as occurring when the risen Christ "will hand over the kingdom to God his Father" (1 Cor 15:23). Meanwhile "he must reign" in the Church (v.25). The resurrection of Christ is mentioned as the central event of history through which, as "first-born among the dead", Christ has acceded to universal "primacy" (v.18).

It is very probable that Paul has intercalated, in v.20, the statement which breaks the rhythm of the poem: "For he has made peace through his blood shed on the cross". He has undoubtedly done this to show more explicitly how the reconciliation of the cosmos has been effected in history. Probably also it was Paul who added as a gloss the phrase "his Church" in v.18. If so, this represents a development of his celebrated image of the Church in his earlier letters (1 Cor 12:21-27; Rom 12:4). There however it had been employed to explain the union of each Christian with the risen Lord as a member of his body. Now the Church as the body of Christ is distinguished from the exalted Lord who is her head.

Yet it cannot escape notice that, for all the attention paid to the historical activity of God through the redemption of mankind in Christ, the theology which inspired this magnificent hymn lays more emphasis upon the mystery of salvation *as the present possession of the Christian* than Paul was accustomed to do in his theology. The Father already "has rescued us" (v.13), where Paul habitually considers this event an eschatological one reserved for the future (Rom 7:24; 1 Thes 1:10). Because of their present union with Christ Jesus, it is possible for the unknown author of the hymn to assert of all Christians in this life that "we possess the redemption" (v.14). Throughout all his earlier letters Paul relates the fulfilment of man's redemption to the second coming of Christ, as the cause of the glorious resurrection of the body (Rom 8:23; cf. Rom 6:4). It would appear, as Pierre Benoit has observed,[12] that the Christian's participation in "the inheritance of the saints in the realm of light" (v.12) is regarded as an actual reality of contemporary Christian existence, not simply as celestial beatitude. Father Vawter's balanced judgment deserves to be quoted here. "This christology of glorification would, it is true, occur more readily to a Johannine than a Pauline author. Yet it is hard to imagine Paul repudiating it altogether . . . The difference in the Pauline emphasis, which accounts for the Pauline adaptations, we conceive to be one of eschatological perspective. It should not be minimized, but neither should it be exaggerated".[13]

Certainly the hymn's conception of the exalted Lord is not incompatible in any respect with that presented elsewhere in Paul's writings. The fact of Christ's pre-existence, as we have seen, is asserted at Galatians 4:4 (as it is at 2 Cor 8:9; 13:4; Rom 8:3). The part played by the pre-existent Christ in creation has not gone unnoticed (1 Cor 8:6). At least in one passage Paul has presented the risen Christ as "the image of God" (2 Cor 4:4), where however it denotes his mediatorial role as the bearer of revelation through "the gospel of the glory of Christ". In the hymn under consideration it is as "first-born of all creation" that Christ is "the image of the unseen God", since he appears as the cause and focus of a primordial unity within the whole cosmos (v.16). That this original harmony reigning in creation has been at some point in sacred history disturbed and even destroyed is presupposed by the reference to God's gracious decision to "reconcile the universe unto himself" by the death of Christ, who "has made peace through his blood shed on the cross" (v.20). This portrayal of the redemptive event as a divine act of reconciliation is quite typical of Paul's thought (2 Cor 5:18-20; Rom 5:1, 10). Nor is the idea of the redemption in Christ of the material creation alien to Paul (Rom 8:18-22). It does however receive a new emphasis in this excerpt from the Christian liturgy.

[12] Pierre Benoit, *op. cit.,* p. 54.
[13] Bruce Vawter, *art. cit.,* p. 77.

Here we wish to direct attention to our rendering of v.19 which reflects an interpretation not universally admitted. "In him it pleased God that creation's fulness might reside". The Greek term for "fulness" (*plērōma*) denoted in Stoic terminology the entire world, and was later to form part of the Gnostic vocabulary of the second century. At the same time the conception of the universe filled with the creative power of God is not unfamiliar from the Old Testament (Jer 23:23-24; Ps 139:7-12; Wis 1:7). Many commentators interpret this "fulness" in the light of the remark at Colossians 2:9: "In him [Christ] all the fulness of the divinity dwells incarnate". In our opinion however it seems more in keeping with the context of the hymn to regard v.19 as a description of the eschatological restoration in Christ of the original harmony of the universe.

Paul has included this hymn in his thanksgiving, although it evinces a theological conception palpably different from his own mode of thought, in the first place because it must have been familiar to his addressees from a liturgical service at which they had often assisted. He has also woven it skilfully into his own text (with some modifications) because it extolled the primacy of the exalted Christ above the whole creation, including those "thrones and sovereignties, principalities and powers" (v.16), which appear to have been the occasion of a danger in faith to the Colossian community. The principal motive on Paul's part for the inclusion of this hymn in the thanksgiving, I venture to suggest, is that he had already contemplated it in prayer as part of his preparation for writing to Colossae, and had found its Christological presentation a fresh aid to his offering of thanks to God and his petitions for these Christians, as well as a congenial stimulus, by its very divergence from his own thought, to his prayerful reflection upon the work of Jesus Christ.

The Colossians thanksgiving is important in our project of discovering the shape of Paul's prayer because it exemplifies, through the inclusion of this liturgical hymn, an aspect of his contemplation which has only appeared previously as a muted accompaniment to his formal thanksgivings, that is, the prayerful reflection upon the mystery of Jesus' earthly career, which for Paul was recapitulated in his death and resurrection. One catches a discreet hint of it perhaps when Paul thanks "my God" in writing his first letter to Corinth "for the graciousness of God that has been given you in Christ Jesus" (1 Cor 1:4). It underlies the references in the long thanksgiving in 1 Thessalonians to the imitation "of the Lord" (1 Thes 1:6; cf. 2:14-15). An understanding of the evangelical traditions concerning what Jesus had said and done during his life on earth is a presupposition for the acceptance of the gospel, "the graciousness of God" (Col 1:6), the proclamation in human speech (1 Thes 1:5) of the merciful act of God through the life and death of Jesus Christ. Hitherto however the Pauline thanksgiving passages, considered as narratives of Paul's own prayer, have been almost entirely engaged with his contemplation of the contemporary Christian existence of his addressees. Apart from the thanksgiving in Colossians they provide less evidence regarding Paul's contemplation of Jesus' earthly life and the central event of Christian redemption than is perceivable in other passages in the letters dealing with prayer. In the following chapter we shall inquire to what extent Pauline theology may be considered as the fruit of Paul's prayer and how far that theology may be judged to have determined the manner and the content of Paul's approach to God in Christ.

Chapter 6
Pauline Prayer
and Pauline Theology

Saint Paul has left no extensive collection of prayers. Had he produced something like the Psalter, it would be possible to reconstruct from such a compilation the distinctive Christian vision that inspired it. Moreover, our study of what Paul has written on prayer has revealed more than once his great reluctance to speak of his own prayer-life. Only rarely, as in the "confessions" (2 Cor 1:3-11; Eph 1:3-14), do we catch a glimpse of the quality and depth of his prayer. It is accordingly difficult to diagnose in any specific way the effects of his prayer as a catalyst in his theological reflection. Nor did Paul compose a Gospel like the four evangelists. Thus it is not feasible, as it is for instance with the author of the Fourth Gospel, to delineate the structure of his prayer from a presentation of Jesus' earthly history. Although Paul was favored with "visions and revelations by the Lord" (2 Cor 12:1) and while he states that he received his gospel "through an 'apocalypse' of Jesus Christ" (Gal 1:12), Paul did not, like the seer of Patmos, write an apocalypse through whose bizarre and exotic visions the contemplative character of his spirituality might have been discerned.

In this final chapter we propose to consolidate and broaden what we have learned about the phenomenon of Pauline prayer by examining certain parallels between it and his theological reflection with a view to discovering any discernible interaction there may be between the two. We shall attempt to extend the range of our knowledge of Paul's prayer in a quite concrete

165

manner by taking cognizance of certain passages in his letters which evince a particularly deep personal conviction about the realities of Christian existence (Phil 1:18b-26; 2 Cor 4:7-15; Rom 8:31-39). The passages selected do not exhibit the features that would make them recognizable as being in Paul's formal prayer-style, yet they will be found to stand in marked contrast by their character as "confessions" with other passages, where the same themes are enucleated in more formally theological language or in a polemical context. While these sections are not prayer, they appear to be reflexes or echoes of prayer, prolegomena to prayer, or possibly, a transposition of prayer into another manner of discourse.

I
THE DYNAMICS AND STRUCTURE OF
PAULINE THEOLOGY

Before venturing to delineate the salient characteristics of Pauline theology, we must point out a fairly obvious but highly significant feature it displays. While Paul reflected vigorously and in a most original manner upon the events which mediated the Christian revelation, he did not create, in any formal sense, a theological system. What is correctly designated as Pauline theology has been quarried from the same source we have used for our investigation of Paul's prayer—his letters.

Paul appears to have regarded the letter as another mode of fulfilling the commission given him by Christ "to preach" (1 Cor 1:17), both towards those foundations he had himself made, and towards other communities, like Rome or Colossae, with which he was personally unacquainted. One principal purpose of these communications was to confront crises, answer questions, solve problems arising out of the day-to-day living of the gospel. The churches to which he wrote were not yet equipped with what would eventually come to be acknowledged as authoritative Christian literature, yet they were in possession of the essential traditions of the faith communicated at least orally by Paul or others. Consequently there is, in the Pauline letters, a certain incomplete, often disparate, sometimes un-balanced quality to be detected in the theology they present.

These letters were, as we have seen, also designed by Paul to fulfil another primary function. He ordered them to be read to the community assembled for public worship (1 Thes 5:27; Col 4:16); hence they had a role in the cultus of the church. The setting in which he desired them to be heard was a liturgical one. With the possible exception of some pre-Gospel Passion narratives,[1] there were probably no other specifically Christian readings available for use in the cultus. This cultic purpose of the Pauline letters may also be seen to be reflected in the credal formulae (1 Cor 8:6; 5:3 ff.; Rom 1:2-4), dox-ologies, and hymns (Phil 2:6-11; Col 1:12-20), which appear sporadically in them. Paul's not infrequent use of metaphors borrowed from worship (Phil 2:17, 25, 30; 3:5; 4:18; 2 Cor 9:12; Rom 1:9; 5:2; 12:1-2; 15:16, 27) is further evidence of this same intention. Moreover, as has been observed earlier,[2] the prayer-wish with which each letter opens, together with that which concludes it, appear to suggest that the entire com-munication was designed as a preparation for the central act of Christian worship, the Eucharist, which "announced the death of the Lord until he comes" (1 Cor 11:26). Hence the inference seems valid that Paul saw a relationship between his theological reflection and the prayer of the community.

We observed in our discussion of the formal thanksgiving[3] as a narrative of Paul's prayer for his addressees that the letters also bore a real relationship to his personal prayer. That these accounts contained the themes to be developed in the body of the communication indicated the apostolic quality of Paul's prayer that could embrace the problems faced by his churches. These forced him, in the course of his prayer, to reflect upon the theological implications of the gospel for Chris-tian existence. That such reflection was not alien to prayer in Paul's view may be gathered from his trenchant remark in

---

[1] X. Léon-Dufour, article "Passion", in the *Supplément, Dictionnaire de la Bible,* vol. VI (Paris, 1960), col. 1432.

[2] Cf. pp. 80-92.

[3] Cf. pp. 135-137.

criticizing the phenomenon of glossolalia at Corinth. "I shall pray with my spirit, but I shall also pray with my mind" (1 Cor 14:15). Also significant in this connection is his observation in the course of a discussion of Christian wisdom. "We have not received the spirit of the world, but the Spirit who comes from God, in order that we may know those things God has graciously given to us" (1 Cor 2:12). He insists, as he terminates the section, "But we have the mind of Christ" (1 Cor 2:16).

To draw attention to Paul's appreciation of the element of Christian understanding in prayer is not however to suggest the sweepingly general and too facile conclusion that Paul's theology came exclusively from his prayer. Yet I venture to submit that there are certain resonances between the two, and even a degree of similarity in pattern. Before taking up this question in detail, it is necessary to attempt a summary description of Pauline theology.

The dominant perspective in Paul's thought is the cross illuminated by the glory of the risen Christ. It is the glorified Lord Jesus, remaining forever "the one who has been crucified" (1 Cor 2:1), who is operative at the heart of Pauline theology. The conception, the fruit of Paul's experience on the Damascus road and of additional formative influences in his apostolic career, may be said to constitute the heuristic principle guiding him in his exploration of the mysteries of Christianity.

Thus the God of Israel was manifested to Paul as "the Father of our Lord Jesus Christ" (2 Cor 1:3), "the God of our Lord Jesus Christ" (Eph 1:17). The "Spirit of God", already known in the Old Testament as a manifestation of the divine power of Yahweh (cf. 2 Cor 3:16-17), is revealed as "the Spirit of Jesus Christ" (Phil 1:19), "the Spirit of his Son" (Gal 4:6), "the Spirit of adoptive sonship" (Rom 8:15). The risen Christ with whom Paul is aware he is constantly united represents for him the presence of God, the nearness of the Father (2 Cor 2:17; 12:19). The indwelling of the Spirit is recognized as the presence of Christ within the Christian (Rom 8:9-11), for Christ as "the last Adam has become life-giving Spirit" (1 Cor 15:45). Yet if Paul's new knowledge of the Father and the Spirit was mediated through the self-revelation of the Son, the three are not confused in his mind (2 Cor 13:13).

It is moreover in terms of the risen Christ that Paul reflects upon the significance of what he has called the "redemption" (1 Cor 1:30; Rom 3:24; Col 1:14; Eph 1:7, 14). It was "in Christ" that "God was reconciling the world to himself" (2 Cor 5:19), and it is "through our Lord Jesus Christ" that "being justified by faith we possess peace with God" (Rom 5:1). The "redemption" exists "in Christ Jesus" (Rom 3:24); it is "in him we possess the redemption" (Col 1:14). "Through faith in Christ Jesus you are all sons of God;" and through baptism "into Christ you have been clothed with Christ": hence "you are all one person in Christ Jesus" (Gal 3:26-28). Baptism "into Christ Jesus" means baptism "into his death" (Rom 6:4). To celebrate the Eucharist is to "announce the death of the Lord until he comes" (1 Cor 11:26); it is "communion with the blood of Christ", "communion with the body of Christ" (1 Cor 10:16). The only authentic uprightness is "that justification through faith in Christ, the justification from God because of faith" (Phil 3:9).

"Living" in Paul's words "*is* Christ" (Phil 1:21), and to die means simply "to be with Christ" (Phil 1:23). To be "at home in this bodily existence" is "to be in exile from the Lord", while "to leave our home in this bodily existence" means "to make our home with the Lord" (2 Cor 5:6, 8). In fact, "to live for God", in Paul's eyes, actually signifies that "It is no longer I that live—Christ lives in me. With regard to my present bodily existence, I live my life by faith in the Son of God . . ." (Gal 2:19-20). To exist "in union with Christ" can only be adequately described as "a new creation" (2 Cor 5:17). Paul has coined a series of neologisms to emphasize the Christian's participation in the various phases of Christ's redemptive work: he suffers with Christ (Rom 8:17), is crucified with Christ (Gal 2:19), dies with him and is brought to life with him (2 Cor 7:3); he will be glorified with him (Rom 8:17). The Captivity letters speak of the Christian as "raised with Christ" (Col 2:12; Eph 2:6), even "seated together with him" in heaven (Eph 2:6).

It is of considerable importance to note what, in all this,

is *not* being said. It never occurred to Paul to suggest that Christ had replaced God as creator (Rom 1:25), as initiator of man's reconciliation (2 Cor 5:19), as author of the Christian's vocation (1 Cor 1:9) and instigator of his every good action (Phil 2:13; 1 Cor 4:7; 10:13), as the ultimate goal of man's existence (1 Cor 8:6). It is from God that Paul's personal call to apostleship came (Gal 1:15); it is God's "graciousness" that has made Paul what he is (1 Cor 15:10; 2 Cor 3:5-6). If it is being "in Christ" that preoccupies Paul, he is aware that there is a being "in God the Father" (1 Thes 1:1; 2 Thes 1:1). The relation to God was established at the moment of conversion (1 Thes 1:9): it is "through Christ that we possess such great confidence towards God" (2 Cor 3:4).

It is an important theorem of Pauline theology that "man is justified by faith apart from works of the Law" (Rom 3:28). His whole Christian existence is a life lived "by faith in the Son of God, who loved me and handed himself over for me" (Gal 2:20). Yet by this he means "faith operative through love" (Gal 5:6), since he has grasped Jesus' teaching that "the whole Law has been fulfilled in one saying, 'Thou shalt love thy neighbor as thyself' " (Gal 5:14; Rom 13:8-9; 1 Thes 4:9). For the reception of the gospel, viewed as an inner dynamic, "God's power [leading] to salvation" (Rom 1:16), it is not merely faith, but also love and hope which are necessary (1 Thes 1:3; Col 1:4-5). Paul is rightly regarded as the theologian of hope, since he has reflected upon its vital function in Christian living more thoroughly than any other New Testament writer (Rom 5:2-5; 8:23-25; Col 1:5; Phil 3:20-21). It is significant that he customarily relates hope to the Christ of the second coming (2 Thes 2:16; Col 1:27). In fact he has transposed the eschatological expectation of the Old Testament prophets in "the day of Yahweh" (Amos 5:18; Joel 4:14; Is 2:12) into "the day of the Lord" (1 Thes 5:2), "the day of Christ" (Phil 1:10). Paul's anticipation of standing "in the presence of our Lord Jesus Christ at his coming" (1 Thes 2:19), of "appearing before the judgment-seat of Christ" (2 Cor 5:10), seems to have outstripped his interest in God's judging of the world (Rom 2:16; 3:6; 14:10), which he mentions far less frequently. Paul consistently regards salvation as an eschatological reality, related to the glorious resurrection of the just (Rom 8:23). Here again he depicts the consummation in terms of the agency of "Lord Jesus Christ as Saviour" (Phil 3:20-21). Indeed, it is inextricably linked with the final vindication of the lordship of the risen Christ (1 Cor 15:24-28).

At the same time Paul is aware that "the end of the ages" has truly become a contemporary reality through the death and resurrection of Christ (1 Cor 7:31; 10:11). Mankind has attained its majority (Gal 4:1-4) by God's "sending forth his Son". The presence of the Spirit (Gal 4:6) in the Christian community (1 Cor 3:16; 6:19) and in the individual believer (Rom 8:9, 11) attests that in a very real sense "the old order of things has passed away, lo! it has become new" (2 Cor 5:17). The presence of the Church in history as "Christ's body" (1 Cor 12:27; Col 1:24) and as the earthly realization of his "Kingdom" (Col 1:13; 1 Cor 15:25) is also a sign of the end-time. So too is the Christian's summons "to the freedom by which Christ has set us free" (Gal 5:1)—from sin (Rom 6:18), from the Law (Rom 8:2), and from death (Rom 5:21).

From this very rapid survey one might, not altogether unfairly, characterize Pauline theology as a theology of discontinuity. To be sure, this is only a question of emphasis, since there are to be found in Paul's letters certain themes where continuity is a crucial element: the consistency of God's dealings with man in the Old and the New Testaments, as illustrated by the justification of Abraham and the Christian (Rom 4:23-25); the need of dependence upon the evangelical traditions; the solidarity of sinful man with the first Adam (Rom 5:12-21), of redeemed humanity with "the last Adam" (1 Cor 15:45). Yet Paul's highlighting of the discontinuous character of the events involved in the Christian mystery stands out by contrast with the emphasis upon continuity by the theologians of the Johannine school.[4] It is only Paul who speaks of the "old testament" (2 Cor 3:14) as the antithesis of "the new testa-

---

[4] I have compared and contrasted Pauline theology with that of the school of John in "Lo! I make all things new" *The Way* 9 (1969), 278-291; see also P. Benoit, "Paulinisme et Johannisme", *New Testament Studies* 9 (1962-63), 193-207.

ment" (2 Cor 3:6). An indication here of his attitude is his
use of the Greek term for "old' which means "outmoded"
(*palaios*). Similarly, he speaks of the "old man" crucified with
Christ (Rom 6:6) as the negation of that "newness of life"
(Rom 6:4) [5] characterizing Christian existence. Rom 7:6 refers to the opposition between "newness of spirit" and "the
outmoded way of the letter" (cf. 2 Cor 3:6). While the preferred Johannine image of "new birth", or "rebirth" (Jn 3:5;
cf. Jn 12:24; 16:21; 1 Jn 2:29) suggests that account be taken
of the antecedents of Christian life,[6] Paul chooses to call it "a
new creation" (Gal 6:15; 2 Cor 5:17), an absolute beginning.

It is the cross, which acts as the fulcrum in the equilibrium
of Paul's thought, that dramatizes the discontinuity between
Jesus' earthly life and his glorified existence. His death was
"a death once for all to sin" (Rom 6:10). "Christ redeemed
us from the curse of the Law by becoming on our behalf a curse"
(Gal 3:13). "He was handed over for our sins: he was raised
for our justifying" (Rom 4:25). "Truly he was crucified out of
weakness, but he is alive by the power of God" (2 Cor 13:4).
It was the logical conclusion of that "emptying himself" (Phil
2:7), of his coming "in the likeness of sinful flesh" (Rom 8:3),
of his "being made into Sin" (2 Cor 5:21). "For you know
the graciousness of our Lord Jesus Christ, how being rich, he
became poor for your sake, in order that you by his poverty
might be made rich" (2 Cor 8:9).

The realism with which Paul views the incarnation of the
Son of God leads him to admit a certain element, mysterious
yet utterly real, of alienation from the Father on the part of
him who thus joined the sinful solidarity of rebellious man,
and accepted the penalty of death in Adam. Through death,
the event that marks discontinuity most perfectly, Christ broke
the ties binding him to the old, sinful family of the first Adam,
and by his resurrection created the new family of grace. In-

[5] The Greek word which Paul uses for "new" (*kainos*) in most of
these texts signifies "unprecedented", that is, inexplicable except in terms
of the divine intervention.

[6] The author of the Fourth Gospel takes a more positive view of the
Law and the Mosaic dispensation: it was a "gift" from God (Jn 1:17);
it gives testimony to Jesus (Jn 5:39, 46).

deed, by resurrection Christ "was constituted Son of God in power" (Rom 1:4). Perhaps nothing in Paul's writing surpasses the boldness of this conception. Although Paul is fully aware of the pre-existence of Christ as unique Son of God (Gal 4:4; Rom 8:3; Col 1:16-17), he can nonetheless assert that, by "being raised by the glory of the Father" (Rom 6:4), his unique relationship to God as Son was somehow deepened and enhanced. For Paul the earthly life of Jesus has meaning only insofar as what he then said can be regarded as "sayings of the Lord" (1 Thes 4:2). His actions during his mortal life are of moment as actions "of the Lord Jesus" (1 Cor 11:23). It is as "the death of the Lord" (1 Cor 11:26) that the last act of "the days of his flesh" (Heb 5:7) is significant in Pauline soteriology.

For Paul the ongoing process of history is not governed by any law of evolution: it proceeds by crisis, a pattern imposed upon human existence in this world by the death and resurrection of Jesus (Phil 3:10; 1 Cor 15:31; 2 Cor 4:10). This dialectic can be seen at work in the history of the chosen people: "Indeed, if their rejection [signifies] the reconciliation of the world, what will their admission [mean] but life from the dead?" (Rom 11:15). So also in Israel's sacred history, the regime of the Mosaic Law was intercalated as a kind of *bloc erratique* interrupting the continuity between the promise to Abraham and its fulfilment in Christ. "It was added with a view to transgressions" (Gal 3:19). In Paul's own past life the confrontation with the risen Lord on the Damascus road had introduced the factor of discontinuity (Phil 3:7), and he discerns a certain repetition of the pattern in his own practice of the Christian life (Phil 3:13).

If we are correct in isolating the mystery of the risen Christ as the dynamic element in Paul's theological reflection that has imposed its stamp upon the structure of his theology, we may expect to perceive certain resonances between it and the quality of Pauline prayer uncovered by our inquiry. In order to make the comparison of the two as specific as possible, we have selected passages from Paul which appear to stand midway between theology and prayer. The procedure also possesses the advantage of broadening the basis for our investigation into the phenomenon of Pauline prayer.

II
PRAYER TRANSPOSED INTO
THEOLOGICAL DISCOURSE

There are certain theological statements in Paul's letters which appear to be unrelated to his prayer. Such for instance is the parallel-contrast between the redemptive work of Christ and the evil introduced into history by Adam (Rom 5:12-21). The argument for the resurrection of the faithful (1 Cor 15:12-34) and especially the development on the nature of the risen body (1 Cor 15:35-49) appears similarly devoid of any such relationship, unless it be regarded as a prolegomenon to the doxology of v.57. Certainly the theological presentation of Christ's death in function of "the justice of God" (Rom 3:21-26) has no discernible relation to prayer.

A paragraph in Philippians however (Phil 1:18b-26) provides an example of prayer that has been transposed into a description in Christological terms of the present and future life of the Christian. The historical setting of the original prayer was Paul's imprisonment, where he faced the real possibility of death (v.20). He appears to have presented Christ (there is no mention of God) with his dilemma: his desire to die in testimony of his Christian belief (v.23) and the need of his support by a young church like that at Philippi (v.24). There is a real change in Paul's attitude in vv.25-26, where he suddenly voices his conviction that he will be spared. How is this change of perspective to be explained? The comment by Pierre Bonnard is worth citing. "The simplest is to represent to ourselves the Apostle meditating as he writes, and arriving, at this point in his letter, at a firm conviction." [7]

18b "Moreover, I will continue to rejoice, 19 for I know this will eventuate in my deliverance through your prayers and the

[7] Pierre Bonnard, *L'Épitre de Saint Paul aux Philippiens* (*Commentaire du Nouveau Testament* X) (Neuchatel: Paris, 1950), p. 31.

assistance of the Spirit of Jesus. 20 As I passionately hope, I shall do nothing to be ashamed of. Now as always I shall speak out boldly, so that Christ will be glorified in my person whether in life or through death. 21 For me living is Christ, while to die is an asset. 22 Yet if to continue living on in this present existence is of advantage to my work, what am I to choose? I do not know! 23 I am caught on the horns of a dilemma. On the one hand, I am possessed by the desire to die and to be with Christ—by far the better thing! 24 And yet, on the other hand, to continue in this present life is more necessary where you are concerned. 25 Indeed, this I know for certain: I shall remain on, and will stand by all of you for your progress and joy in the faith. 26 Thus I shall be a fresh cause of your untrammelled boasting in Christ Jesus through my presence among you once again."

There are a number of indications of those elements we discovered earlier to be characteristic of Paul's prayer-style. The triad joy (v.18b), thanksgiving ("boasting", v.26), petition (implied in vv.23-24), is present. Paul's petition is answered in v.25. He expresses faith in Christ (vv.20-21), in the Spirit (v.19), love of Christ (v.23), of the Philippians (v.25), and hope for "deliverance" (v.19), for a martyr's testimony (v.20), for eternal life with Christ (v.23). The language of the Psalter is discernible: "I shall do nothing to *be ashamed* of" (Ps 25:3; 119:6); "Christ will *be glorified*" (Ps 34:3; 35:27; 70:4).

The passage demonstrates in a striking way the central and dynamic role which the risen Christ plays in Paul's prayer and in his theological reflection. The statement in v.21 is paralleled by Gal 2:20, but there the relationship to prayer is not so palpable.

III
THEOLOGY OF APOSTLESHIP AND APOSTOLIC PRAYER

There are several passages where Paul presents his view of his career as an apostle, when admonishing the Corinthians (1 Cor 4:9-13), or exhorting them to a change of heart (2

Cor 6:1-10), or in a polemical section (2 Cor 11:23-33). However, the paragraph which perhaps best represents his theology of Christian apostleship is one which also reflects the essentially apostolic character of his prayer (2 Cor 4:7-15), which may be perceived behind this theological statement. The new life with which he was endowed by God's creative action through Christ near Damascus (2 Cor 4:6) is manifest in his person in two ways: through his preservation by God's providence in the midst of perils (vv.8-9) and through the communication of "the life of Jesus" to his converts (v.12).

Certain characteristics of the Pauline prayer-form can be easily detected. There is the antithesis between Paul's weakness and "God's transcendent power" (v.7); the awareness of the dialectic death-resurrection governing his apostolic life (vv.10-11); the reference to Ps 116:10; and the eschatological orientation of the implied petition in v.14. Faith and hope are prominent, with love implied in v.15. Paul's prayer is directed to the Father "who raised the Lord Jesus" (v.14). Once again the risen Christ is prominent in the life he communicates to Paul (v.11) and his converts (v.12). There is a veiled reference to the Spirit in the phrase "grace already abounding" (v.15). Joy is suggested by the psalm-citation (v.13); thanksgiving is mentioned with praise of God (v.15); petition underlies the hope expressed (v.14).

7 "But we carry this treasure in what is no stronger than earthenware jars—which shows that such transcendent power is God's and does not come from us. 8 Hard pressed on every side, I am never cut off; though perplexed, I am not driven to despair; 9 when hunted down, I am not abandoned to my fate. I am struck to the ground, yet I am not utterly destroyed. 10 Continually I carry about in my person the dying of Jesus, in order that Jesus' life may in turn be manifested in my person. 11 For as long as I live, I am being handed over to death for Jesus' sake, in order that the life of Jesus may be manifested in my mortal flesh. 12 Hence death is at work in us, but life in you.

13 Yet I have the same spirit of faith as the man who wrote, 'I have believed, hence I spoke out.' I too have faith, and that is why I in turn speak out, 14 knowing that he who

raised the Lord Jesus will raise us also with Jesus and will place us with you in his presence. 15 All this has been done with you in mind, that grace already abounding might swell the chorus of thanksgiving, as more and more men share it, that ascends to the glory of God."

This vivacious picture of Paul's apostolic experiences is at once a profound theological statement and a precious souvenir of the apostolic prayer that inspired it.

IV
PROLEGOMENON TO PAUL'S SELF-OBLATION TO DIVINE LOVE

The concluding paragraph of the extended theological development on the relation between justification and final salvation (Rom 5:1—8:30) is one of the most moving statements in all Paul's letters. It might be called a "Contemplation to attain the love of God", similar to that which Saint Ignatius has appended to his *Spiritual Exercises*.[8]

31 "What response shall we make then to all this? If God be on our side, who can be against us? 32 If he did not even spare his own Son, but handed him over on behalf of us all, how can he fail, when he has given him to us, to give us graciously all he has? 33 Who can bring an accusation against God's chosen people? It is God who pronounces them upright! 34 Who can condemn? Christ Jesus is the one who died,—or rather, the one that has been raised, who is moreover at God's right hand, who even intercedes on our behalf!

35 Who then can separate us from the love of Christ? Can tribulation or hardship, persecution, hunger, or nakedness, or the danger of the sword? 36 'For your sake we are being done to death all the day long', as Scripture has it; 'We count no more than sheep destined for slaughter.' 37 Still, in all this we are winning the victory decisively through him who has loved us!

38 I have been in fact persuaded that not even death nor life, no angel, not any power, neither the world as it is, nor the

---

[8] *The Spiritual Exercises of St. Ignatius,* edited by Louis J. Puhl (Chicago, 1951), pp. 101-103, ##230-237.

world to come, not even forces 39 on high or in the depths—
No! not anything in all creation, can separate us from the love
of God in Christ Jesus our Lord!"

In the verses immediately preceding this section Paul has
described the divine plan of salvation in terms of adoption into
God's own family (vv.28-30), where the glorified Christ figured
as "the eldest of a large family of brothers". This indicates that
the response awaited to the manifestation of God's love in the
gift of "his own Son" is that prayer of adoptive sonship, described in vv.14-16, where the Spirit plays a leading part.
Paul's allusion to the sacrifice of Isaac (Gen 22:1ff.) gives a
particular poignancy to the traditional statement (1 Cor 15:3)
of faith in Christ's redemptive death. In the gift of his Son God
has lavished "all he has"—especially the favor of adoption.

The questions with which vv.31-35 are interspersed are
surely not rhetorical; they are real questions which Paul puts to
himself as he contemplates the wonder of the love of Christ
and the love of the Father. These questions elicit a response of
faith in God, who is "on our side" (v.31), "who pronounces us
upright" (v.33), a response of love for God, who has given us
"all he has" in the Son "he handed over on behalf of us all"
(v.32), and a response of hope in the graciousness of God, who
cannot "fail to give us graciously all he has" (v.32). In addition, there is required a reply of love for Christ, "the one who
died", as in 2 Cor 5:14, of faith in "the one that has been
raised", and of hope, because of his exaltation and intercession "on our behalf" (v.34). Paul's reference to Christ's heavenly intercession (unique in his letters) recalls that of the Holy
Spirit (vv.26-27) before God. One senses also in these questions,
as a kind of counterpoint, the unvocalized accompaniment of
joy, petition, and thanksgiving.

Paul returns, in vv.35-37, to contemplate in more leisurely
fashion the love of Christ as it continues to be manifested to
him in his journey through this world. He had discussed this
love in the language of theological discourse earlier in this letter
(Rom 5:6-7), where he also developed the theology of the love
of God (Rom 5:5, 8-10). Here his expression approximates the
language of prayer, as is indicated by the citation from Ps
44:22—noteworthy as the single scriptural quotation in this

entire chapter. Paul voices his exultant joy and thanks by his use (v.37) of a verb found nowhere else in the New Testament, which means "to win a brilliant victory". Here Christ is the predominant figure as the one "who has loved us" by his act of dying for us.

The passage terminates with a cry of wonder and grateful joy as Paul finally considers "the love of God" (vv.38-39). His avowal, "I have been in fact persuaded", articulates his faith and love, as well as his hope in the loving goodness of God. He endeavors to do justice to the expression of his response by reaching outside human experience to think of possible obstacles to the divine love of the Father, but he can find none— "not anything in all creation". Before ending this magnificent tribute to "the love of God" however, Paul cannot help referring once again to him who is the embodiment of that love, "Christ Jesus our Lord".

This beautiful declaration of Paul's deepest Christian convictions is not prayer in the formal sense, in which the "confession" of 2 Cor 1:3-11 may be called prayer. Yet the language and the style are far removed from the sober and reasoned expression of Pauline theological discourse, exemplified at the beginning of this chapter in the description of Christian existence as "the law of the Spirit of life in Christ Jesus" (8:1-13). It is also substantially different in tone and quality, from the theological discussion of Christian prayer (vv.14-30), Paul's most complete and detailed instruction on that topic. There is perhaps no passage in Paul's letters that attests the depth and the texture of his prayer so impressively as this invitation to himself to offer everything he has and is "through him who has loved us" to the Father, who has, "in Christ Jesus our Lord", given "us graciously all he has".

V

THE PHENOMENON OF PAULINE PRAYER

We have reached the end of our inquiry into prayer in Saint Paul. It can aptly be described as a phenomenon, since it is discernible only through his letters, that is, chiefly through what he himself chose to reveal concerning it. For this reason we have passed under close scrutiny everything that might possibly throw light upon it. We examined all those experiences (and in the first place Paul's momentous meeting with the risen Christ near Damascus) which might be judged to have a formative influence on his prayer; or more accurately, we attempted to grasp the construction which he himself put on such experiences. We culled from his letters whatever might be judged authentic prayers, probed his instructions on prayer, audited carefully those accounts of his prayer, the formal thanksgivings, and finally, tested certain passages, which the style and a peculiar religious tonality appeared to differentiate both from the language of prayer and the manner of theological discourse. It has been by reflection upon these varying data that we have attempted to draw our conclusions as to the quality and character of a reality that always remains for the better part hidden from us. We have become keenly aware that we have been dealing with *phenomena,* with what Paul's prayer appears to have been.

At this point it seems not inappropriate to sum up our findings by presenting them as *seven lessons in Christian prayer.*

Prayer remains for Paul above all a mystery. His reticence about his own prayer-life was not simply the result of modesty or innate reserve. The essence of prayer springs from what Paul so often refers to as "the Mystery" (Col 1:26-27), God's saving design communicated, yet never wholly disclosed, through the revelation of his Son. The mystery of Jesus Christ has been seen to be the focal point of Paul's prayer as of his theology: *who Christ truly is* remained, to the end of Paul's life, a continuing quest. Paul perceived with utter clarity that if "Jesus is Lord", his lordship remains to the end of history a piece of unfinished business (1 Cor 15:25-26). Moreover, prayer with its characteristic emphasis upon continual thanksgiving bears a relation to the mystery that occupies the center of Christian cultus, the Eucharist. In his prayer as in his apostolate Paul is conscious of being a "steward of the mysteries of God" (1 Cor 4:1).

Prayer is also inextricably bound up with the mystery that is

man, which brings us to the second lesson. Prayer is the result-
ant of the meeting of God's power with human weakness (2
Cor 12:7-10). It is a personal experience of the "graciousness
of God" in Christ. Paul shows that he has known the agony of
prayer (Rom 8:26-28), and it is perhaps for this reason more
than any other that he attaches such great significance to Jesus'
earthly life, of which the cross is the diagnostic sign. Paul's
conversion gave him a deep sense of sin, of the discontinuity
that marks man's existence in this world. Prayer, as man's
response to the divine graciousness, must retain its essentially
petitionary character with recurring sentiments of joy and
thanksgiving. Since this duty of responding to God in Christ is
an ongoing one, the quest and request must continue "always", "without ceasing", "in every eventuality" (1 Thes
5:16). For part of the mystery of God's power is that man's
weakness is never removed by its dynamic; and so prayer must
be operative "day and night", and "beyond all measure" (1
Thes 3:10).

Accordingly, prayer is to be seen, in the third place, as a
species of dialogue in which there is perceptible a drive towards
greater understanding. This momentum is imparted to it by
"the Spirit who comes from God, in order that we may know
those things God has graciously given to us" (1 Cor 2:12).
Hence Paul insists, "I shall pray with my spirit, but I shall also
pray with my mind" (1 Cor 14:15). The Spirit has been given
that the Christian may recognize his own self-identity as an
adoptive son of God and heir with Christ (Gal 4:6-7). Thus
it is essential that the dialogue be conducted by crying "Abba,
dear Father" (Rom 8:15) with the aid of "the Spirit of his Son"
(Gal 4:6). Pauline prayer always retains its filial quality, its
desire to deepen the sense of family —*familiaritas cum Deo.*

The fourth lesson is that Christian prayer is Trinitarian in its
dynamic and in its orientation. It centers in the Son of God "revealed in me" (Gal 1:15), "who loved me and handed himself over for me" (Gal 2:20). He is "Christ Jesus, the one who
died,—or rather, the one that has been raised, who is moreover at God's right hand, who even intercedes on our behalf!"
(Rom 8:33). Since the Spirit "comes to the aid of our weak-

ness" and "is interceding through our inarticulate groaning" (Rom 8:26), Christian prayer is "in the Spirit" (Eph 6:18). Paul, as we have seen, prayed to the risen Christ. In fact, there is sufficient evidence that he prayed frequently to Christ, without however allowing his prayer to terminate with him. For it was always through the risen Jesus that Paul addressed the Father (2 Cor 1:20). If Paul belonged to those "who invoke the name of our Lord Jesus Christ" (1 Cor 1:2), he was aware he was also of those "who worship God by his Spirit and found our boast in Christ Jesus" (Phil 3:3). He describes "our spiritual worship" as "to present our persons as a living sacrifice, holy, and pleasing to God" (Rom 12:1). It is to "God our Father" that Paul's praise and thanksgiving are invariably addressed.

In the fifth place we learn from Paul that the dialectic of prayer is governed by faith, love, and hope—"the three that remain" (1 Cor 13:13). It is faith that carried him "into Christ Jesus" (Gal 2:16), and his life here below was "a life of faith in the Son of God, who loved me" (Gal 2:20). In prayer Paul never wearied of responding with love to that love of Christ, which "continually constrains us" (2 Cor 5:14), and to the love of God "poured forth in our hearts" by God's gift of the Spirit (Rom 5:5). Through hope prayer flies off to infinity, yet its constant companion, "endurance", guarantees that it is in no sense a technique of escapism from the realities of life. Indeed, the prayer of the Christian is in a very special sense a prolonged exercise in hope, because of the unfulfilled nature of his adoptive sonship (Rom 8:18-25).

The sixth lesson is that Christian prayer is apostolic. Its immediate preoccupation is the contemporary situation in which the believer finds himself. In presenting its needs it makes no distinction between "temporal" and "spiritual" (2 Cor 1:10-11). Always it is "prayer for others", and it relies in turn upon the prayers of others. At the same time, its involvement in the actual train of events is founded upon the past, on what God has in Christ done for man; and it reaches out in hope and anticipation to the future beyond history.

And this brings us to the seventh and final lesson. Prayer is by its whole dynamism eschatological. It is made always under the sign of the parousia, seeking to know Christ "and the power of his resurrection" (Phil 3:10). It never allows the Christian to forget that his vocation is a "call heavenwards by God in Christ Jesus" (Phil 3:14). The structure of the formal thanksgiving shows that Paul's prayer inevitably moved towards "heaven, whence we await also as Saviour the Lord Jesus Christ, who will transform this humble body of ours, remolding it in the likeness of his own glorious body through the dynamic power, by which he is able also to subject all things to himself" (Phil 3:20-21). This eschatological character of Christian salvation remains a constant in Pauline theological thought, and for the theologian of hope, the believer is in tension towards the parousia. Like the supreme act of Christian thanksgiving, the Eucharist, which is a proclamation "of the death of the Lord until he comes" (1 Cor 11:26), so Christian prayer lifts its face in expectation of the Christ of the parousia, since it is "through him that we have access in one Spirit to the Father" (Eph 2:18).

Index of Authors

Allo, E.-B., 114
Aquinas, St. Thomas, 29
Arndt, W. F., 54

Benoit, Pierre, 90, 153, 162, 171
Blank, Josef, 13, 23
Bonnard, Pierre, 84, 174
Bonsirven, Joseph, 45
Bornkamm, Günther, 13, 34
Bromiley, Geoffrey W., 47
Brown, Raymond E., 51
Bultmann, Rudolf, 47

Celsus, 54
Cerfaux, L., 1, 2, 18, 35, 53, 62
Charles, R. H., 49
Chrysostom, St. John, 114
Conzelmann, Hans, 79

Davies, W. D., 63
Dupont, Jacques, 14

Eschlimann, J., 2

Feuillet, A., 108
Fitzmyer, Joseph, 89

Gingrich, F. W., 54
Gnilka, Joachim, 19

González, Ángel, 2
Guillet, Jacques, 121

Haenchen, Ernst, 26
Hamman, A., 2
Harder, Günther, 2
Heiler, Friedrich, 3
Huby, Joseph, 1, 50

Ignatius of Antioch, 104

Jeremias, Joachim, 13
Juncker, Alfred, 2

Käsemann, Ernst, 154
Ketter, Peter, 2
Kittel, G., 47
Koch, Ludwig, 2
Koester, Helmut, 16

Léon-Dufour, X., 167
Lietzmann, Hans, 92
Lightfoot, J. B., 107
Lohfink, Gerhard, 40
Lohmeyer, Ernst, 90
Loyola, St. Ignatius, 177
Lyonnet, Stanislas, 110

Malatesta, Edward, 131
McComb, Samuel, 3
Menoud, Philippe-Henri, 12

Moule, C. F. D., 155, 157, 158

Origen, 54
Orphal, Ernst, 2

Pfitzner, Victor C., 18, 111
Philo, 111
Prat, Fernand, 1
Puhl, Louis J., 177

Quinn, Jerome D., 2, 106

Richards, Sr. Innocentia, 131
Rigaux, Béda, 14, 81, 88, 105, 135

Schlier, Heinrich, 93, 102, 103

Schneider, Carl, 36
Schubert, Paul, 138, 145
Schweitzer, A., 52
Sheets, John R., 1
Smith, C. W. F., 2
Stanley, D., 26, 32, 85, 86, 158
Sylvia, Mary, Sr., 1

Travers Herford, R., 44

Vawter, Bruce, 153, 154, 162
Von der Goltz, Eduard Freiherr, 35

Whiteley, D. E. F., 63
Wikenhauser, Alfred, 2, 49
Wood, H. G., 14

Zerwick, Maximilian, 84

Index of Pauline
Passages Explained

1 Thes

1:3-5; 2:13; 3:9-13, 148-150
3:11-13, 81-82
5:16-22, 100-106
5:23-24, 82

2 Thes

1:12, 108-109
2:16-17, 83
3:5, 83-84
3:16, 84

Phil

1:3-11, 140-144
1:18b-26, 174-175
3:7-15, 15-21
4:4-7, 106-107
4:20-21, 76-77

1 Cor

12:10, 131
15:8, 21-25
15:57, 79

2 Cor

1:3-11, 93-96
1:8-11, 69-72
2:14, 79-80
4:6, 31-33
4:7-15, 176-177
9:15, 79
11:31, 76
12:1-6, 44-52
12:7-10, 52-59
13:7-9, 80-81
13:13, 91-92

Gal

1:3-5, 77-78
1:15-16, 33-40
2:15-21, 60-69
4:4-7, 117-122
6:16-18, 84-85

Rom

1:25, 75-76
7:24-25, 79
8:14-29, 122-129
8:31-39, 177-179
9:5, 76

15:13, 86
15:30-32, 111-112

Col

1:3-20, 153-164
1:28—2:1, 112-113
3:16-18, 109

Phlmn

4-7, 138-139

Eph

1:3-14, 96-98
5:18-20, 109-110

Topical Index

Abba, 120, 121, 124, 181

Adam, 171, 172; 'Last Adam,' 32, 96, 171

'abnormal birth,' 22-23

Abraham, 117, 173

adoption, 39, 98, 115-130, 178; in O.T., 119; rel. to Holy Spirit, 119, to redemption, 118; inchoative nature, 125, 129

aiteisthai, 6

aitēma, 6

Amen, 75

Antioch, 60-62

apostleship, 22, 38; Luke's view of, 25, 26

apostolic prayer, 22, 80, 81, 110-113, 139, 176, 182

athletic metaphors, 18-20, 110-112

baptism, 17, 94, 118, 125, 169

bārûk, 7

benediction, 73, 93-98

boasting, 16, 20, 46-49, 85

charis, 87

Christ, pre-existent, 162, 173; earthly life of, 26, 29, 30, 118; as judge, 143; identity of, 17, 20, 68, 109, 110, 180; divine filiation of, 39, 173; cosmic, 83, 153; indwelling of, 38, 67; incomplete lordship of, 171; image of God, 32, 162; mediation of, 109

Christian as son of God, 35, 39, 117, 122, 126

Church, body of Christ, 161; 'building up' of, 113-115; rel. to Paul's conversion, 40-41

confession, 93, 166

conscience, 130-131

consolation, 95

contemplation, and action, 80, 159

conversion, of Jew and pagan, 64, 66; of Paul: effects, 11, 19, 20; contemporary views of, 12-15; change of religion, 66, 76; revelation of God as Father, 116, of Trinity, 98; source of apostleship of Paul, 22

covenant, 58

creation imagery, 31, 32, 85, 172

cross, 84, 168, 172

cultus, 16, 44, 90, 94, 167

death, 69, 70, 71, 123; of Christ, 14, 78; Christian, 94; of Paul, 69-71

deēsis, 6, 9

deisthai, 6, 8

dialectic of sacred history, 173

discernment, 67, 68, 130-133, 142

discontinuity, theology of, 171-173, 181

doxa, 7

doxology, 74-78

election of Israel, 97

Elijah, intercession of, 7

endurance, 83

enthusiasm, 13, 124, 160

entynchanein, 7

Ephesian captivity (Paul), 9-10

epikaleisthai, 7

erōtan, 7

eucharistein, 7

eucharistia, 8, 104

euchē, 6

euchesthai, 6

eulogētos, 7

exhomologeisthai, 7

existēmi, 46

existence, Christian, 16, 123, 125, 169; ambivalence of, 132

faith, 20, 33, 64, 81, 86, 116,

118, 125, 133, 176, 182; of Israel, 27; 'into Christ,' 66; prayer of, 69

familiaritas cum Deo, 181; see also 157

Father, God as, 35-39, 116, 157, 168

'for the sake of our sins,' 78

formal thanksgiving, 134, 146; Paul's creativeness in, 135, 136; rel. to Eucharist, 135, 136; content, 136, 137; epistolary function of, 138-140; personal element in, 145, 158

'fulness' (*plērōma*), 163

'fulness of time,' 118

Gethsemane, 97-99

glorify, 108

glory, 20, 74, 77, 143

glosses (Col. hymn), 265

God, Pauline notion of, 35-37, 170; source of Christian call, 18, 20, 116, 143, of Christian holiness, 101; goal of Christian life, 116, 170; initiative of, 33, 143, 170; fidelity of, 85, 116

'God of peace', 82, 114

gospel, 34, 63, 65, 157, 160, 167

grace, 13, 87-88; and peace (O.T.), 89; of God, 91; of Christ, 91

graciousness of God, 13, 23-25, 33, 69, 85, 88, 104,

170, 180; of Christ, 57, 88
gratitude, 8, 105, 106, 150

heir, 117, 125
historical Jesus, 30
holiness, 100
Holy Spirit, 30, 39, 119, 120, 133; gift of, 159; intercession of, 127, 128; pledge of inheritance, 97; rel. to Christ, 120, 123, 168, to Christian affectivity, 124, to hope, 86, 148, 182, to joy, 102, 151, to prayer, 92, 103, 142, to sonship, 124, to understanding, 98
'holy war,' 102
hope, 21, 72, 79, 86, 125, 128, 129, 144, 157, 158; at prayer, 128, 148; rel. to discernment, 132, to endurance, 158, 160
humanness of Paul, 96
hymn in Col., non-Pauline character of, 153, 154, 161-163

identity of Christian, 119, 120, 122, 181
imitation, 86
'in Christ,' 39, 48, 50, 67-69
'in the name of,' 107
Incarnation, 118, 172
infallibility of prayer, 53, 106, 107
inheritance, 117, 123

intercession, 182; of Spirit, 7, 127, 128, of Christ, 7, 178
'it is necessary', 48, 128

Jesus' earthly history, 25-29, 44, 59, 118, 158, 164, 180; Gethsemane, 58-60
Johannine theology, 123, 136, 154, 162
joy, 101, 102, 136, 142, 150
judge, Christ as, 143, 170; God as, 37, 82, 150, 170
juridical terminology, 123
justification by faith, 17, 19, 63, 115, 117, 157, 169, 170

knowledge, 17, 21, 30, 69, 142, 159

learning, 158
letters of Paul, 4-5, 9-10, 120, 127, 166
liturgy, 16, 44, 90, 94, 109, 135, 136, 152, 162
Lord, 13, 14, 173; 'Jesus is Lord,' 180
love, 81, 99, 129, 182; of Christ, 178; of God, 120, 178; for Christ, 21, 115; basis of discernment, 132
Luke, 40-42

'magnanimity,' 106
'Marana tha,' 91, 106
material creation, 125
mediation by Christ (prayer),

101, 104, 109, 137, 142, 144

merit, 65

methodology, 2-5

Mosaic Law, 16, 67, 85, 123, 173

'my God,' 76, 138, 139

mystery, 51, 96, 98, 120, 173

mysticism, 1-2, 45, 48-53

name, 107

nearness, of Christ, 38, 106, 151; of God, 39, 67, 151, 157

needs, 182

'Our Father,' (Lord's prayer), 77, 78, 82, 121

'our Father,' (Paul), 77, 82

parakalein, 6, 56

parables, 158

participation, 92

peace, 82, 84, 89, 162; 'Lord of peace,' 84, 89; 'God of peace,' 89; of God, 107

petition, 53, 56, 57, 106, 107, 141, 181

post-resurrection appearances, 28, 90

power, 57

praise, 7, 74, 99, 159

prayer, 41, 102, 103, 120; apostolic, 22, 81, 110, 147, 150, 151, 182; continuous, 69, 103, 105, 122, 181; dialogue, 148, 152,

181; eschatological, 21, 40, 82, 126, 183; filial, 150; for others, 182; growth in self-awareness, 126; infallible, 128; 'in the Spirit,' 102, 103, 181; mystery of, 4, 52, 180; rel. to Eucharist, 136, 183, to suffering, 128, to understanding, 114, 168, to work, 147; terminology of, 11-17; to Christ, 52, 81, 104, 109, 110; to God, 52, 53, 82; Trinitarian orientation of, 143, 151

presence, of Christ, 38; of God, 39, 80, 149, 150

proseuchē, 6

proseuchesthai, 6

Psalter, influence of, 36, 44, 76, 106, 175, 176, 178

redemption, 77, 78, 96, 116, 122, 126, 157, 161, 169; of material creation, 125

reign of Christ, 171

'remain wakeful,' 105

repentance, 23

resurrection (of Christ), 59, 83, 87, 161, 171

reticence (Paul), 44, 52, 70, 151

'revelation of Jesus Christ,' 30, 38

salvation, 17, 171

sanctifying, 101

Satan, 54, 55

second coming, 170; rel. to prayer, 83, 106, 183

segŭllāh, 97

sense of sin, 181

Septuagint, 7, 36

shālôm, 87, 96

speaking with a tongue, 113-115

'spiritual,' 96, 124

'spiritual man,' 131

Spiritual Exercises, 177

'stigmata of Jesus,' 84

struggle, 110-113

suffering, 83, 84, 94, 111-113

terminology of prayer, 5-9

thanksgiving, 83, 104, 109, 180; and doxology, 75, 78; to God, 141, not to men, 141; spontaneous acts of, 78-80

theology (Pauline), 166-174

theophany, 94

'thorn for the flesh,' 54, 55, 127

tradition, 29-30, 158

tribulation, 71, 72, 94, 102

triadic formula, 91, 92

Trinitarian orientation (prayer), 16, 92, 97, 98, 144, 151, 181

Twelve, the, 25-29

understanding, and prayer, 114, 168, 181

weakness (and power), 57, 127, 128, 181

will of God, 100, 101; and discernment, 132; knowledge of, 128

wish (prayer), 80-93; introductory, 87-89; final, 89-93

'works of the Law,' 63, 65